ISLAM
IN
ASIA

ISLAM IN ASIA

CHANGING POLITICAL REALITIES

JASON F. ISAACSON AND COLIN RUBENSTEIN
EDITORS

Transaction Publishers
New Brunswick (U.S.A.) and London (U.K.)

Library of Congress Catalog Number: 2001041594
ISBN:0-7658-0061-6 (cloth); 0-7658-0769-6 (paper)
Printed in Canada

Library of Congress Cataloging-in-Publication Data

Islam in Asia : changing political realities / Jason F. Isaacson and Colin Rubenstein, editors.
    p. cm.
    Includes bibliographical references and index.
    ISBN 0-7658-0061-6 (cloth : alk. paper) — ISBN 0-7658-0769-6 (pbk. : alk. paper)
    1. Islam—Asia, Southwestern 2. Islam and politics—Asia, Southeastern. 3. Islamic fundamentalism—Asia, Southeastern. 4. Asia, Southeastern—politics and government. I. Isaacson, Jason F., 1953- II. Rubenstein, Colin Lewis, 1943-

BP63.A38 I85 2001
959'.0088'2971—dc21
                                                             2001041594

Contents

Introduction   *Colin Rubenstein*   i

1. Islam and Politics in the
   New Indonesia   *Greg Barton*   1

2. Islam, Society, Politics, and
   Change in Malaysia   *Greg Barton*   91

3. Militant Islamic Separatism
   in Southern Thailand   *Peter Chalk*   165

4. Militant Islamic Extremism
   in the Southern Philippines   *Peter Chalk*   187

Conclusion   *Jason F. Isaacson*   223

Index   233

Contributors   242

Introduction

Political Islam in Southeast Asia

The political centrality of Islam, sometimes of the more radical brand prominent in parts of the Middle East and Central Asia, has been observed as a growing phenomenon in Asia in recent years. Since the end of the Cold War, an Islamic revival has gained a foothold in a number of Central Asian countries - most notably in Afghanistan. The renewed and often politicized interest in Islamic identity and values has woven its way eastwards, as far afield as Southeast Asia.

While the collapse of the Soviet Union and the Eastern bloc has contributed to the decline of communism as a revolutionary political force, religious, and ethnic issues have now assumed renewed and increased significance in Southeast Asia. Religious divisions based on Islam have exacerbated ethnic differences in some countries and pose a potentially serious long-term threat to stability in Southeast Asia, as some religiously oriented groups tend to engage in violent and extreme acts.

Islam in Southeast Asia is hardly new. Arab-Muslim traders first visited the shores of Southeast Asia as early as the seventh and eighth centuries. Commercial linkages were established several centuries later as well as scholarly exchanges and pilgrimages. There was little settlement until the late thirteenth century when a Muslim town was established in the Pasai region of north Sumatra. Trade and commerce, however, overrode questions of identity and religion. Over the centuries, Sunni Islam flourished in Asia to become the established religion that it is today.

Since the Islamic resurgence of the early 1980s and 1990s, elements of a more radical political Islam have migrated from the Middle East to Asia. Although traces of these radical elements in Asia currently appear only at the margins, if left unchecked, they could aggravate a number of security and political crises in countries weakened by the consequences of the devastating Asian financial crisis, which has delivered new governments in Indonesia, Thailand, the Philippines, and South Korea. The emergence of new leaders and political administrations in almost all of the Southeast Asian "tiger" economies during 1997-98 has ramifications as to whether radical Islam will be capable of growing in Asia. However, as the independence vote cast by the East Timorese in September 1999, its bloody sequel and the surge of chauvinism in Indonesia at that time reveals, a rallying within internal politics to reflexive anti-Western slogans and influences is always a possibility where economic and political dislocation is apparent.

The purpose of this volume is to examine the advance and contours of "Islamism" and to analyse the potential consequences that such activity poses for the region and beyond. Additionally, the study tracks the activities in the region of external countries such as Iran, Libya, Pakistan, and Saudi Arabia. The key role these countries play in Southeast Asian economics, politics, religion, and weapons procurement, and their contribution to the growth of radical Islamism in the region is also highlighted.

Islamism

For the purposes of this study the definition of radical Islam, also known as "Islamism," used is the perception of Islam more as a political ideology than as a mere religion. Traditional Islamic fundamentalism, however, can be defined as the will to have the Sharia and only the Sharia as the law. Some experts observe that fundamentalism presupposes the existence of a single sacred text or a set of texts in hierarchical relation with each other; direct access for the believer to the text or texts; and authority within the religion for using the state to enforce religious identity. For Islamists, the Sharia is just part of the agenda. They address society in its entirety, in politics, economics, culture and law; they claim to reshape society along purely Islamic lines, returning to an idealized "golden age" society in line with divine intention.

This study should not be misconstrued as being anti-Islam. There are many in the Muslim community, if not the overwhelming majority, who are vigorously opposed to "fundamentalism" and radical

Islamism. Nor is a "fundamentalist" version of Islam necessarily dangerous, providing those believing in such a pure Islamic society seek it through peaceful means. Rather, it is hoped to provide here an analysis of radical Islam in so far as it affects issues including sovereignty, terrorism, separatism, security, anti-Western sentiment, and anti-Semitism.

The popular perception of Islam being intrinsically militant and synonymous with violence and terrorism is far from accurate. Islam is neither a single, unified religion, nor is it necessarily fundamental in nature. Furthermore, just because one is an Islamic fundamentalist does not inevitably mean that one is also a holy warrior and prepared to die to further a religious vision.

At the risk of gross over simplification, Islamic practice can be found in one of two forms: either moderate or radical. More moderate, accommodationist versions do not seek the total rejection of modernization and development, but rather seek to transform these influences to make them more compatible with traditional Muslim values and beliefs. The more radical approach, however, views modernization as a force responsible for the wholesale and systematic corruption of the Islamic ideal. For those committed to the radical approach, the only way to achieve true moral virtue and enlightenment is the revolutionary transformation of society through a return to the traditional Islamic community.

Islamic extremism is associated with this second, anti-accommodative branch of the Muslim religion, which advocates a *jihad* (literally meaning "striving in the path of God") against the corrupt Muslim establishment. The main purpose of the *jihad* is to achieve the cleansing and purification of the Islamic religion. However, whilst it would be correct to state that virtually all Islamic fundamentalists are pre-occupied with the *jihad*, it would be incorrect to argue that this necessarily means that they also have a penchant for violence and "holy war."

There are a number of ways in which Islamic extremists have pursued the jihad through peaceful means. These include:

- The *jihad al-lisan* (literally "striving of the tongue").

- The *jihad al-qalam* (literally "striving with the pen").

- The *jihad al-daíwa* (literally "striving by propagating the faith").

These peaceful ways of pursuing the jihad are distinguished from the *jihad al-saghir*, regarded as the lesser *jihad*, which advocates legitimate forms of striving with other human beings through war and violence. It is thus only possible to equate radical Islamism with a form of religious teaching that rationalises the use of violence as a legitimate and sacred means to an end within the context of the second, more narrow interpretation of the *jihad al-saghir* (hereafter simply referred to as jihad). It is the latter category, which is the focus of this study.

An Islamic Resurgence in Asia?

Southeast Asia is home to the most populous Muslim country in the world. Indonesia's aggregate Muslim population is greater than that of the Arab Middle East. The ties that link the Middle East to East Asia have become more binding in recent years, with a concomitant rise in radical Islamic activity in the region. Yet, in simple geographic terms insular Southeast Asia lies far from the Middle Eastern terrains conventionally associated in Westerners' minds with Islam. Many Middle Eastern Muslims are unfamiliar with Southeast Asia or uncertain as to the precise contours of their fellow believers' faith.

In this study, analysis focuses on four locations in Southeast Asia, namely Indonesia, Malaysia, the southern Philippines, and southern Thailand. In the former two countries Islam is the dominant religion and has emerged as a growing dimension of mainstream political life. The latter two countries have minority Islamic populations but are more prone to terror and separatist insurgency.

In this context it is worth noting that in the province of Xinjiang, in China's northwest, militant Muslim Uighurs have resorted to bombings and armed hostility in an attempt to effect a split from mainland China. Even the Sultan of Brunei, not previously noted for Islamic practices, has recently become "increasingly devout" and defined his regime as a "Malay Muslim Monarchy." In 1998, the Sultan's profligate brother, Prince Jefri Bolkiah, was banished from the Sultanate and stripped of control of the family's businesses. Prince Jefri claimed in exile that Brunei had become subservient to "conservative Muslims backed by shadowy advisers" from Iran and Libya.

In an increasingly globalized world, it is not only the exchange of tangible goods across borders that is transmitted with multiplying efficiency and speed. Ideas are also exchanged across seamless borders, assisted by ever-improving communications technology such as the Internet and electronic mail. Paradoxically, globalization both creates social change that can spark a backlash in the form of Islamic radicalism, and can provide improved means for the spread of the Islamic ideal.

Asia's Islamic revival has benefited from these new technologies as well as the ease of travel between the Middle East and Asia. Terrorist organizations, such as the Moro Islamic Liberation Front (MILF) based in the Philippines, have a web site where supporters can send monetary contributions by submitting credit card details. Malaysia's International Movement for a Just World Trust is an Islamic think-tank, which is run by Professor Chandra Muzaffar. Their web site (www.jaring.my/just/) sets out to "create public awareness about injustices within the existing global system" but it also contains materials notoriously anti-Western and anti-Semitic in outlook.

The purpose of this study is to assess the factors which have produced Islamic radicalization, as well as those which have militated against it; to evaluate what variables in the four polities under review have made for greater or lesser stability and for the interplay of militant Islam in local politics. It will also be the purpose of this study to examine the nature and diversity of external influences, which have played a role in the emergence of militant Islamism.

Indonesia

Indonesia is home to the world's largest Muslim population of approximately 190 million people. Previously suppressed by former President Soeharto, Political Islam is now firmly entrenched as part of the nation's ideology. Soeharto's successor, former President BJ Habibie, a devout Muslim, facilitated the swing towards political Islam. While he was a minister, Habibie played a major role in the emergence of political Islam by founding the Association of Indonesian Muslim Intellectuals (ICMI) in 1990. Many of its members declared openly that the organization's primary purpose was to promote the Islamization of the Indonesian state and society.

There are clear indications that under such influences Indonesian political life started to be conducted in a more Islamic vernacular. The country's first "democratic" elections were held in June 1999, and at least ten new Muslim political parties participated in the contest for the People's Consultative Assembly (MPR). Most commentators had expected the elections to include a tussle between traditionalist and modernist Islam, essentially a contest between the two rival Islamic organizations Nahdlatul Ulama and Muhammadiyah, represented by the National Awakening Party (PKB) and National Mandate Party (PAN), respectively. Political competition and alliances were played out between secular and Islamic parties.

The Indonesian presidential elections in October 1999 also pitted Islamic contenders against more secular-oriented candidates. Dr. Amien Rais, now chairman of the Consultative Assembly, certainly has a solid record as a reforming democrat and a leader who accepted East Timor's secession yet, there is also in his profile, dormant over the last year and hopefully diminished, a record of sectarian, anti-Western and anti-Semitic sentiments. The upheaval over East Timor in 1999 and the positioning of an Australian-led peacekeeping force following the bloodshed inflicted on East Timorese by pro-integrationist militias did not produce any fresh outbursts during its period of operation until March 2000. However, it initially witnessed an increasing stridency in the tone and content of general anti-Western sentiment and, particularly, hostility towards Australia.

In the past, Rais courted extremist organizations inimical to Western interests. He has appeared at World Muslim Committee for Solidarity (KISDI) rallies, stirring crowds of more than 10,000 against Israel. KISDI was formed at the start of the Palestinian *intifada* in order to show solidarity with Palestinians and also emerged as an anti-Chinese, sectarian organization. Another organization courted by Rais in the past is Libya's Islamic Call Society, an educational, religious and ideological institution funded by Colonel Gaddafi's Jihad Fund. Its web site is peppered with affirmations of support for Libya and pledges from its global membership to resist and challenge the "Western Crusade" campaign led by America.

Despite the obvious turbulence and volatility in Indonesian politics, the October presidential and vice presidential elections resulted in the success of Abdurrahman Wahid and Megawati Sukarnoputri respectively, thereby witnessing the emergence and triumph of far more pragmatic and moderate elements to the nation's leadership. At this stage, the Indonesian government has strongly reaffirmed tolerant and inclusive forms of Islam, epitomized by its traditionalist but inclusive leader Abdurrahman Wahid, formerly head of the 35-

million strong Nahdlatul Ulama organization. Wahid, an ardent supporter of secular democracy, claimed in 1996 that the riots that had by then broken out were in part the result of increasing encounters with radical Middle East-style Islam. Former President Habibie and Amien Rais were habitually asked by Western journalists whether Indonesia would become an Islamic state and they consistently responded that Indonesia would retain its secular tradition in line with the secular-nationalist Pancasila constitution of 1945.

Located on the northern tip of Sumatra, Aceh is a staunchly Muslim province that has been a hotbed of separatist activity since Dutch colonial times. In 1976, Hasan di Tiro formed a separatist organization known as Aceh Merdeka (The Free Aceh Movement) to give violent expression to the Acehnese claim of achieving full independence from Indonesian rule in northern Sumatra. A more radical manifestation of Aceh Merdeka emerged in mid-1990 calling itself the National Liberation Front Aceh Sumatra (GPK-Aceh), formed with the aim of setting up an independent Islamic state in the region.

Indonesia has been beset by a number of ethnic clashes over the last three years, the victims most often being ethnic Chinese. More than 400 churches, Buddhist monasteries and temples have been ransacked or razed to the ground in the last three years. The island of Ambon has been the site of what has essentially been a pitched war between Muslim and Christian communities, leaving hundreds dead.

In the lead-up to the general elections of June 1999 and presidential elections in October, more than ten Islamic parties were formed. The pre-existing Partai Persatuan Pembangunan (PPP) has been "Islamized." Its flag now includes the Ka'bah which Muslims face during prayer, and its executive board decided to alter its party principle from Pancasila to Islam. Meanwhile, the recently formed Islamic party, Crescent and Star, has an agenda which includes including redistributing wealth away from the ethnic Chinese to the Muslims (90 percent of Indonesia) and strict religious incorporation.

In the event, Wahid won a surprise victory in the presidential elections, given that Megawati Sukarnoputri had been the favorite. As head of Indonesia's largest group of Muslims, Nahdlatul Ulama, he consistently blamed Islamic activists such as Adi Sasono, who was in Habibie's cabinet, for fuelling the swing towards Islamic parties that feed on the instability and turmoil they create, such as the radical Crescent and Star Party.

Wahid himself has been a force for moderation and mutual respect between diverse ethnic and religious groups. He has demonstrated his belief in reconciliation and tolerance across the political spectrum, from dealing respectfully with Indonesia's Chinese community to East Timor, where he travelled in March 2000 on a mission to apologise and seek reconciliation with the East Timorese.

Clearly not all Islamic parties are the same. Wahid's Partai Kebangkitan Bangsa (PKB) has a democratic and secular bent. However, Yusril Mahendra's Crescent and Star Party (Partai Batan Bintang —PBB) has a radically Islamic agenda, with non-Muslim minorities such as the Chinese and Christians being likely targets for a redistribution of wealth and diminution of influence.

Pancasila—a national ideology of pluralism and secularism, under which theocracy is anathema - is enshrined in the Indonesian constitution. Yet Pancasila as a dominant force is no longer a germane ideology. Islamic political parties, once banned under the Pancasila provisions by Suharto, resurfaced under Habibie's leadership.

Greg Barton, in his chapter on Indonesia, explains the agenda of radical movements such as The Crescent and Star Party, KISDI and Dewan Dakwa and documents the dangers Indonesia and its neighbors face if such organizations were to align themselves with mainstream Muslim parties. Barton notes that Indonesia will proceed politically in one of two ways: either on democratic-pluralist lines, or the way of Pakistan, subject to hard-line Islamic agendas and more violence. The latter scenario has devastating implications for Australia's security. The results of the parliamentary and presidential elections are a heartening indication that the more moderate path may yet prevail.

Student protesters, who in their clamor for REFORMASI and in their participation in the student riots of May 1998, brought on the demise of President Suharto, regularly wave posters of radical Iranian leaders such as Ayatollah Khomeini and speak glowingly of Taliban generals. At this stage, they are accepted in the broader Indonesia community as simply hot-headed students who crave reform rather than as marshals for radical Islam. Barton points out that Indonesia's Muslims are not politically united and are currently more factionalized than ever before.

There are, as Barton, argues, a number of pressing issues, structural, political and cultural, which need to be attended to by the new Indonesian leaders. With the election of a moderate and inclusive fourth president, a highly popular secular and female vice-president, progressive ministers like Foreign Minister Alwi Shihab and reforming Attorney General Marzuki Darusman, as well as a government produced by democratic processes, there is now good reason to entertain an optimistic scenario of Indonesia's future, in which the recent inter-communal breakdown and violence will subside. However, the speedy emergence of untrammelled and untroubled democracy in the near future appears less likely, as he explains, despite the good auguries.

Malaysia

In terms of political Islam, Malaysia has experienced a more active record and has been subject also to the growth of overtly radical elements for the last two decades. In the wake of the Asian financial crisis and the trial of former deputy Prime Minister Anwar Ibrahim, a major challenge today to the ruling UMNO (United Malays National Organization) is the radical agenda of the opposition party, Partai Islam se Malaysia (PAS). Since the Anwar trial and despite Dr Mahathir's closure of Malaysia's economy to insulate it from what he calls "Jewish speculators," PAS has still been able to attract thousands of UMNO members. PAS has a radical platform, the most basic of which is the creation of an Islamic state. This would include the introduction of traditional Islamic laws and punishments such as chopping off a thief's hand or stoning an adulterer.

In the national election of late November 1999, Dr. Mahathir secured his stated aim of a two-thirds majority but lost ground where it hurts most—in his own Malay heartland in the north. PAS won state-level control of both Kelantan and, for the first time, Terengganu, where it won all eight parliamentary seats; while significant gains were made in Perlis, a heavily Malay state, and Kedah, the home state of Dr. Mahathir himself. Moreover, the election saw PAS emerge as the clear opposition frontrunner, well ahead of its election allies in the Democratic Action Party and the National Justice Party.

Circulation of PAS' twice-weekly newspaper *Harakah* had soared from 65,000 copies before Anwar Ibrahim's arrest to some 300,000 by election time. This is notwithstanding the record number of Malaysians who have accessed the Internet to obtain the latest information on the Anwar trial. More than thirty web sites have been set up devoted to providing information about Anwar. These sites are regularly accessed by those citizens dissatisfied with the state-sponsored coverage offered in the local media.

Prime Minister Mahathir Mohammed's personal crusade against colonialists, speculators, and Jews, has been well publicized. His book, the *Malay Dilemma*, succinctly states the basis of his mindset as: "The Jews for example are not merely hook-nosed, but understand money instinctively. The Europeans are not only fair-skinned; they have an insatiable curiosity. And the Chinese are not just almond-eyed people, but they are also inherently good businessmen." He has portrayed Israelis as Nazis, railed against the material corruption of the West and most recently sheeted the blame for Malaysia's financial turmoil to "Jewish" speculators such as George Soros. During 1999, however, he appeared to have toned down his rhetoric in the face of significant challenges to his political future resulting from the decline in the Malaysian economy and the trial of Anwar Ibrahim. His reference to the evils of the Holocaust in claiming the lives of six million Jews in his address to the United Nations General Assembly in October 1999 was perhaps a significant gesture towards possible reconciliation with the Jewish world, even though his anti-Western rhetoric and hostility to free-market capitalism was still in full flight.

As stridently anti-Western and anti-Semitic as Prime Minister Mahathir's record has been, his UMNO party faces greater opposition than before from the conservative PAS, which controls the states of Kelantan and Terengganu. PAS leaped to support Anwar Ibrahim's cause and has brought non-Muslims into its fold in seeking to expand its membership. After it won the state of Kelantan in 1990, laws in that state were changed so that men and women queue separately in supermarkets, women are obliged to wear headscarves and public singing and dancing have been banned.

Anwar Ibrahim is not universally viewed as a beacon of hope. His critics view him as having tried to import an Iranian-style Islamic revolution when he first came to prominence in the 1970s. In the early 1980s he travelled to Teheran to meet with Iran's newly installed leader, Ayatollah Khomeini. He set about forging links with Islamic movements in Indonesia, Pakistan and Bangladesh. His choice of Kuala Lumpur's mosques as a venue from which to launch his "reformasi" campaign was not coincidental.

In his report, Greg Barton maintains that Malaysia's future is less precarious than Indonesia's, despite the weakness of its civil society and the existence of a press that has little freedom. Prime Minister Mahathir has been a consistent and forthright opponent of Islamism, which he has succeeded in marginalising in his country. Radical Islamic movements such as Al-Arqam have been sidelined and Mahathir will continue to sideline those who align themselves too closely with his former deputy, Anwar Ibrahim. There is the danger that a more conservative UMNO will use Islam for partisan purposes and pick up on the prevailing Islamist sentiment, but if anything, UMNO has been weakened dramatically by the Anwar episode as has Malaysia by the financial crisis, although on the latter score a recovery of sorts has been unfolding.

The Islamic revivalist movement, popularly known as the Dakwah (literally, "to summon or call") movement emerged in Malaysia in the 1970s. One consequence of the Dakwah movement was that Islam came to be highlighted as the pillar of Malay identity. The state was forced to respond to this revivalist movement by increasing attention to Islam and the subsequent adoption of an Islamization strategy of its own.

The pivotal moment in the institutionalization of the revivalist movement occurred in 1969 at the University of Malaya when the National Association of Muslim Students established a Muslim youth organization named Angkatan Belia Islam Malaysia (ABIM), or the Malaysian Muslim Youth Movement. ABIM grew to a position of strength in the mid-1970s under the stewardship of a student activist named Anwar Ibrahim.

In the late 1970s, a new Dakwah group known on campus as the IRC (Islamic Representative Council) attracted undergraduates from science faculties who established secret cells to spread their Islamic message and infiltrated existing organizations to try to initiate change from within. Compared to ABIM, the IRC adopted a black and white approach to Islam. In their view, one either practices Islam completely or is an infidel, one either fights for Islam or is irreligious. The Dakwah movement in Malaysia had become "pluralized and radicalized."

The Dakwah movement had not only achieved a formidable position in the political sphere but also had transformed Malay thinking and culture. The government felt threatened by the opposition PAS and the student-based Dakwah movement. It decided to approach any Islamic issue in a positive manner, politically and economically. Dakwah groups were co-opted and the government embarked on projects such as subsidising pilgrimages to Mecca and helping to set up the Bank Islam Malaysia Bhd, the International Islamic University and a think-tank called the Institute of Islamic Thought to combat misinterpretations of Islam.

Other Islamic-oriented programs were introduced after Anwar Ibrahim joined UMNO in 1982, including the establishment of the Islamic Medical Centre and the upgrading of the Islamic Centre as the nerve centre of the government's Islamic bureaucracy. By the end of the 1980s more and more of the government's policies became "ABIMized." In general however, university campuses resisted government mainstreaming and remained bastions of non-governmental Dakwah.

In August 1994, Mahathir moved decisively to ban Al-Arqam, a Sufi sect based on radical Islamic principles, which was founded in Malaysia in 1968. So great was the Association of Southeast Asian Nations' (ASEAN) fear of the sect that the religious affairs ministers of the six ASEAN states at the time met on the Malaysian resort island of Langkawi to discuss measures to be taken against it. The day after the ASEAN meeting, Malaysia's National Fatwa Council issued a decree forbidding the sect from spreading its teachings or running its substantial businesses in Malaysia.

Chief among Malaysian authorities' concerns about the sect, which was funded by its own businesses and members' contributions, was that it had trained and armed a 313-man "death squad" in Thailand. Its leader, Ashaari Mohammed, was taken into custody in 1994 and emerged later after undergoing a "faith rehabilitation course."

The Dakwah ethos has permeated most levels of society, and the current radical Islamic ideology has settled alongside a multi-ethnic Malaysia. It is alleged that Al-Arqam is in the early stages of an underground revival. At the international level, there has been a manifold increase in Malaysia's trade relations with oil-rich Islamic nations in the Middle East and even Central Asia. Before the Asian financial crisis, Malaysia was perceived by the Muslim Bloc as being one of the most successful Islamic nations, firstly because of its Dakwah tradition and secondly because of its meteoric economic successes. The challenge after both the financial crisis and the Anwar trial will be the containment of radical Dakwah movements such as Darul Arqam and UMNO's ability to head off a groundswell of support for the socially conservative PAS.

Southern Philippines

In the predominantly Catholic Philippines, large chunks of the southern island of Mindanao are under the control of Muslim insurgent armies. The Moro Islamic Liberation Front (MILF) and the Abu Sayyaf Group (ASG) remain locked in a bitter religious-separatist struggle. Although a peace agreement with Nur Misuari, leader of the Moro National Liberation Front (MNLF) was signed in September 1996, it has been categorically rejected by the MILF and ASG. Both organizations have benefited from the huge flow of arms that have come out of Afghanistan as well as training in weapon handling, explosives and methods of unconventional warfare.

The Philippine government recognises the MNLF as representing the Bangsamoro Muslims of Mindanao. Only the MNLF is given recognition by the OIC (Organization of Islamic Conference). The MILF has countered this by arguing that on December 3 1997, over one million Bangsamoro people assembled in Maguindanao's Da'wah Centre and collectively voiced their longing for independence, a desire which was expressed through a resolution.

The MILF views its cause as a *jihad*, or holy war, to usher in a system of government based on the Koran. The MILF also declared a jihad against the United States for leading air strikes against Iraq. Clashes between government forces and MILF cadres of Mindanao occur almost daily. The organization has grown from 10,855 armed regulars in 1997 to 12,458 members as at the end of 1998 and, thus far, has not compromised on its demands for a fully independent Islamic state. The MILF has placed its strength at about 150,000 regular combatants. While this figure may be somewhat exaggerated, the number of skirmishes and kidnappings during the past year is on the increase.

Linked to international extremist organizations, Abu Sayyaf is the most radical of the Philippines' Muslim terrorist groups and has committed a series of deadly bombings, kidnappings and hijackings. The small but violent ASG, whose size is estimated at between 100 to 300 men, has been placed on the US State Department list as one of the world's most dangerous terrorist organizations. The slaying in 1999 of their Libyan-trained leader, Abubakar Abdurajak Janjalani, in a skirmish with Philippines police was followed by a wave of destructive bombings throughout the island which confirms that the small band has not yet languished away as was earlier predicted by Philippines authorities.

Peter Chalk outlines in detail the workings of the MILF and ASG, highlighting the established linkages that exist between Moro guerrillas in terms of financial assistance from the Middle East and external backing in the form of religious instruction and military training. Both organizations have benefited from the huge flow of arms from Afghanistan as well as training in weapons handling, explosives and methods of unconventional warfare.

Thomas McKenna, an anthropologist who has spent considerable time in Mindanao, has detailed the increasing availability of external funding sources for religious purposes. External funds arrived first in the form of scholarships from the government of Egypt in the 1950s, and expanded rapidly in the 1970s and 1980s. Libya, the Organization of Islamic Conference Foreign Ministers, and Saudi Arabia have provided financial support for various religious projects and Egypt continues to send missionaries for one- or two-year assignments in Cotabato. The governments of Libya and Saudi Arabia support a small percentage of local Islamic teachers as long-term missionaries.

Significant further funding has reportedly been made available from private institutions and individuals in the Middle East as the result of contacts developed by the MILF and local ulama. The MILF recently admitted that it is receiving financial aid from "unspecified" Arab countries, as well as Germany and Australia. It is possible that another source of funding for the separatists is the Saudi-based Islamic Development Bank, which has committed itself to spending US$61 million on new health and education facilities. The IDB also sponsored an investment conference in the region in December 1998. One of the chief financial backers of the ASG is Osama Bin Laden. The sophisticated support network also employs subversive techniques in recruiting Moro guerrillas for field training in Afghanistan.

Chalk concludes that the outlook for peace and stability in the southern Philippines remains bleak so long as the MILF and ASG exhibit a radical Islamic identity devoid of any willingness to compromise on its basic beliefs and demands. The international support network fuelling terrorism and ideological battles hinders prospects of accommodation and compromise. If, as he contends, the notion of granting independence to the south is completely out of the question, any permanent negotiated settlement will necessitate compromise on the part of the MILF and ASG.

Radical Islam in the Philippines has implications for economic growth and social stability. Intelligence sources in the Philippines have reported how, in the guise of missionaries and clergy from countries such as Iran and Pakistan, terrorists have infiltrated the southern Philippines since at least 1993. Ramzi Ahmed Yousef, who was convicted in the 1993 World Trade Center bombing, was able to move in and out of the Philippines undetected because of his ties to ASG. The Estrada government recognized the festering secessionist problem in Mindanao by initiating talks with the MILF, but its refusal to accept the MILF's key demand for an independent Islamic state has been backed up by a willingness to tackle the rebels with force if no peaceful solution can be found. A devastating raid on a key MILF base in February 2000 claimed the lives of up to 300 rebels and was the bloodiest clash since Estrada assumed the presidency.

Thailand

Until the beginning of 1998, Thailand suffered an ongoing separatist campaign in its south with Muslim rebels of groups such as the Pattani United Liberation Organization (PULO), New PULO, Barisan Revolusi Nationale (BRN), Mujahadeen, Pattani National Liberation Front (PNLF) and the Socialist National Front (BSN). Though it has received little publicity, PULO once claimed to have more than 4,000 armed fighters in southern Thailand.

Peter Chalk, in his chapter on Thailand, is optimistic about prospects for a permanent peace in southern Thailand. He predicates this conclusion upon Malaysia's co-operation in desisting from offering safe havens in northern Malaysia. The southern Thailand experience highlights the role of economic development and education in quelling separatist violence.

Relations between Iran and Thailand have been expanding with the help of high-level trade missions and government delegations. Thailand's Foreign Minister, Surin Pitsuwan, travelled to Teheran in November 1998 to meet with the Iranian President, Foreign Minister and Parliamentary Speaker. Religion was on the agenda when Surin, born Abdul Halim to a devout Muslim family in southern Thailand, called for expanding bilateral relations in the area of religion, politics and commerce.

Bilateral relations suffered a setback when an Iranian man was sentenced to death for the attempted bombing of the Israeli embassy in Bangkok in 1994. The sentenced man, who was arrested in southern Thailand, was acquitted in 1998 when the Thai Supreme Court ruled on appeal that there was insufficient evidence. Thai authorities have been on alert since the attempted bombing, and in 1998 deported a number of Pakistani men suspected of terrorist activities although they were only charged with overstaying their visas.

Recent evidence of Thailand's involvement in external ideological disputes surfaced when the Sri Lankan government expressed concern that Tamil Tiger separatist rebels were using Thai territory to receive arms supplies. The basis of Sri Lanka's complaint was that Tamil Tigers have been using Phuket and surrounding coastal areas as bases to funnel weapons and ammunition to their comrades in the northern part of Sri Lanka. A Sri Lankan army spokesman even accused Thai army officials of having collaborated with the militant group in arranging the procurement and transfer of the weapons from Thailand.

Iran has sought out Thailand as a gateway to Southeast Asia. A disturbing anti-Western stance has emerged in some Thai newspapers, particularly in response to U.S. actions against Iraq. While Thailand was the first to suffer from the Asian financial crisis, the government of Chuan Leekpai was praised by the U.S. and IMF for making the required structural changes to its economy. The challenge has been for countries such as America and Australia to show that they are not just fair-weather friends in order to preserve the strategic balance currently in place, challenges both countries have largely tackled positively.

Over the past year, the news from Thailand has been positive. Thailand's decision to dispatch troops to the U.N. force in East Timor in late 1999, its efforts to end crony capitalism, the adoption of a new constitution and its willingness to address regional issues normally left unspoken by many of its neighbors, has had a beneficial effect both within Thailand and on the region generally, and has greatly enhanced Thailand's international profile.

China and Xinjiang

China has not been the subject of detailed attention in this study. It is useful, however, to note briefly some of features of the situation in China's Xinjiang province as they relate to phenomena encountered in other areas examined.

China's north-western province of Xinjiang, which covers one-sixth of China's landmass, has been dogged by separatist violence. The protagonists are Sunni Muslim Uighurs (pronounced WEE-gurs) and comprise more than 7 million of Xinjiang's 17.5 million population. The contest for the strategically important western province of Xinjiang proceeds largely unnoticed outside China, except in the Islamic world.

Xinjiang's borders some of the most volatile countries in the world: Afghanistan, Pakistan, India, Russia, Tajikistan, Kazakhstan, and Kirgizstan. The Uighurs are Xinjiang's largest ethnic nationality and are more aligned to the Turkic countries west of the province than to the Beijing administration. Their quest for independence was reawakened with the Soviet invasion of Afghanistan in 1979.

The Soviet defeat and subsequent implosion of the Soviet Union had a radicalising effect on young Uighurs. Some had fought in Afghanistan alongside the Mujahadeen. As the Islamic revival swept across Central Asia, its reverberations also surged through Xinjiang.

Reliable information of the extent of violence in Xinjiang is hard to obtain. The official Chinese press downplays reports of terrorist outbreaks, while Uighur sympathisers give a different spin to the separatist position. What is known is that in April 1990, as many as sixty Uighurs were killed by local authorities near Kashgar in western Xinjiang while protesting at the banning of the construction of a mosque. Authorities responded to Uighur nationalism by cracking down on unregistered places of worship, screening imams for their political views and outlawing so-called illegal religious activities.

In 1996, Chinese security forces clashed with Uighurs armed with light weapons acquired from Afghan and Central Asian supporters in the town of Aksu. Several People's Liberation Army (PLA) battalions were despatched. Riots also followed in February 1997 in the northern city of Yining. Between ten and ninety Uighurs and Chinese died in the violence. Three bus bombings followed three weeks later, coinciding with the death of Deng Xiaoping. A bomb blast occurred shortly after in Beijing itself, indicating the potential for violence to spread to the heartland of the national capital.

Support for the Uighur cause, including financial support, comes not only from bordering countries such as Kazakhstan and Kirgizstan, but also from more distant Muslim states like Saudi Arabia and Iran. In August 1998, Xinjiang's Communist Party secretary, Wang Lequan, admitted at a press conference in Hong Kong that terrorist or "splittist" activity was flourishing in Xinjiang. The announcement was the first public acknowledgement that there was problem in Xinjiang.

China and its Central Asian neighbors are moving rapidly to establish new security mechanisms to counter new threats. The "Shanghai Five"—China, Russia, Kirgizstan, Kazakhstan and Tajikistan—now meet annually to discuss regional security in the face of destabilising activity, carried out largely by Islamic fundamentalists. While maintaining an iron grip across the province over the past year, Beijing remains aware that Uighur minorities in both Kirgizstan and Kazakhstan are sympathetic to their cousins across the border. More than ever, Beijing needs close cooperation from its western neighbors in clamping down on illicit cross-border movements of people and weapons.

Beijing's most pressing concern is that Uighur rebels are sheltering in Afghanistan under the patronage of Osama bin Laden, maintaining a base in the northern city of Mazar-e-Sharif in the company of other radical Islamic fundamentalist groups. The groups' operations are almost entirely funded through the opium trade. Chinese officials held talks with the Taliban in February 1999 in an effort to stem the flow of heroin into Xingiang, although Beijing was equally concerned with the trade's role in funding the separatist groups. The Taliban denies Chinese accusations that it is harboring any Uighur rebels. With the US having placed economic sanctions on the Taliban for harboring Osama bin Laden and not extraditing him for trial, the Taliban's disruptive role in aiding and abetting terrorism is likely to diminish.

Links to Middle Eastern Islam

How do countries like Iran, Libya, Pakistan and Saudi Arabia benefit from linkages with Asia? In a geopolitical framework increasingly divided between the west and the rest, it seems as if the above-mentioned countries have realized the importance of Asian support, in particular Asian Islamic support, for both economic and ideological purposes. The demand for oil in Asia is critical to sustainable oil prices.

The Middle East has looked to the dynamic economies of Malaysia and Indonesia and wondered whether Southeast Asian Islam might provide clues on how to manage market economies and cultural pluralism.

This is when Middle Eastern influences come into play. Libya has offered to pay ransom money to cash-strapped Muslim kidnappers. Saudi Arabia has recently given more than US$61 million to Mindanao through the Islamic Development Bank and sponsored an investment conference on the island.

Mosques have proliferated in towns and villages; religious schools and devotional programs have expanded; a vast market in Islamic books and magazines and newspapers has developed; the well-educated Muslim middle class has begun to question issues of gender, pluralism, economy and the relationship of religion to state. Influences in this religious resurgence stem from the Iranian revolution and the growth of Middle Eastern economic power since the 1970s.

Muslim students returning to Asia from study in Egypt and Saudi Arabia brought home with them the messages of the Iranian revolution which carried the negative associations given to the "Zionist entity." Anti-Semitic publications from the Middle East began to appear in Malaysia and Indonesia. Jewish conspiracy theories were given currency by leaders such as Dr Mahathir of Malaysia. In Indonesia, a monthly magazine entitled *Media Dakwah* regularly publishes anti-Semitic articles.

In some reformist Islamic circles in Malaysia and Indonesia, a demonization of the concepts "Jew" (*Yahudi*) and "Zionist" has taken root. Post-colonial complaints against modernization are directed against a "Jewish" minority known only as a theoretical construct. Jews appear to represent a disembodied, costless target for group hatred and ambivalence about the modernization process.

External Influences

Iran

Historically low oil prices and a deteriorating oil infrastructure has driven Iran to look beyond traditional oil markets in alleviating its fiscal malaise. The Iran Libya Sanctions Act of 1996 threatens penalties against any company in the world investing more than US$40 million annually in energy projects in Iran and US$20 million in Libya. The experience of the Malaysian state-owned oil company Petronas, which escaped penalty and has invested US$600 million in the Sirri oilfields, demonstrates the limitations of unilateral sanctions on a regime which has yet to prove that it has ceased sponsoring international terrorist organizations and consistently cracked down hard on dissidents. With Iranian financial backing, Sudan is believed to have developed a beachhead of militant Islamic radicalism in Africa. An estimated 5,000 volunteers pass through Iranian "military camps" every year, of whom about 500 are thought to be given extensive training in a wide range of terrorist skills.

Over the past three years, American security interests in Asia have deteriorated as Iran has forged strategic relations with China and India, involving trade, diplomatic support and military co-operation. In 1997, Iran publicly announced an "Asian tilt" in its foreign policy, primarily intent on breaking the U.S.-led containment policy and spreading anti-Western views into Asia. To some degree, Iran may claim modest success in its endeavors given the sharp criticism made by a number of Asian countries in response to the December 1998 U.S. and British air strikes against Iraq. Countries traditionally more sympathetic to Western ideals may have been swayed by Iranian rhetoric.

Malaysia and Indonesia showed a willingness to support Iran's foreign policy goals by joining the Iranian-sponsored D-8 organization of major Islamic states. The Philippines has fallen substantially into line with Iranian policy, denouncing U.S. sanctions against Iran and issuing guidelines to internal security forces to refrain from arresting Iranian and Pakistani citizens suspected of aiding the Abu Sayyaf Group. In November and December 1998, high level Iranian delegations embarked on a number of missions to East Asia. The Speaker of the Iranian parliament, Nateq Nouri, visited Thailand, Vietnam, and the Philippines while Iranian Foreign Minister Kamal Kharrazi visited Japan, the first visit by an Iranian foreign minister in eleven years. In addition, the Iranian deputy foreign minister visited Australia in 1999.

Nateq Nouri addressed the Muslim community in Manila, warning against cowardly efforts of enemies to deal a blow against Islam by trying to uproot it through sowing seeds of dissent. He fuelled the Islamic resurgence by saying "enemies of Islam are alarmed today to see that Muslims in countries such as Turkey and Algeria are on the move to revive their lost identity and propagate Islam for the perfection of mankind."

While Iran continues to pursue its "Look to the East" policy with enthusiasm, placing high priority on forging relationships with Asia and the ASEAN nations in particular, the growing influence of reformist elements within Iran may ultimately reduce its potency as both an ideological rallying point and a covert source of aid for Islamic fundamentalists in Asia.

Pakistan

The spread of an Islamic ideal and the invocation of Islamic solidarity are clearly among the not unimportant tools in the Iranian foreign policy arsenal. Since the Iranian agenda remains one fundamentally hostile to both democracy and human rights, as well as towards any western security role, the Iranian push into Southeast Asia using these tools pose a major danger to stability and security in the region.

A fulcrum around which questions of Islamic radicalism turn, Pakistan has already been the epicentre for three civil wars: in Afghanistan, Tajikistan, and Kashmir. Philippine authorities have referred to strong links between Afghanistan and the Muslims of the southern Philippines, with Pakistan as intermediary. All three conflicts involve fundamentalist elements, which have been clandestinely fuelled by Pakistan's religious parties and its military.

Factors such as the arrest of Ramzi Yousef in Islamabad in 1995, China's concern over Pakistani training bases for the Muslim Uighurs of Xinjiang and Pakistani support for the Taliban in Afghanistan all point to Pakistan as being relatively successful at exporting Islamic radicalism. Former Prime Minister Nawaz Sharif's introduction of a Sharia bill in parliament galvanized the extremists even more in a country beset by ongoing sectarian strife.

In the midst of a collapsing economy and a deteriorating law-and-order situation, the ruling Muslim Islamic League was politically energetic. Furthermore, there appears to be a rising sympathy for the Islamic extremists within the military. Of the extremist groups, Jamaat-e-Islaami, a powerful Muslim group, emerged as a real opposition to the deposed Sharif government. Because of Pakistan's growing reputation for exporting radicalism, further instability is likely to encourage extremists to continue to look to Asian hot spots such as Mindanao and Xinjiang in exporting its jihad. Bangkok has had a number of terrorist alerts and arrests of Pakistani individuals who have subsequently been deported on charges of overstaying their visas. The military coup in October 1999 which ousted Nawaz Sharif, while changing the constellation of power holding, has far from eroded the centrality of Islamic militancy.

Afghanistan

Muslim youths from the Philippines, Indonesia, Thailand, and Malaysia were sent to Afghanistan between 1979 and 1992 for training and Afghan Mujahadeen combat operations. These so-called Afghan veterans underwent rigorous paramilitary training and religious indoctrination while in Afghanistan.

With the successful entry of the Mujahadeen into Kabul in 1992, thousands of volunteer guerrilla fighters literally became "rebels without a cause." Lacking any effective outlet for their religious zeal and military enthusiasm, many left Afghanistan to take up the "cause" in places of Islamic unrest around the world. Many of the Philippines Mujahadeen guerrillas returned to Mindanao in 1993 to recruit Muslim youths for the fledgling ASG and Dutch intelligence sources have disclosed that Mujahadeen fighters were dispatched to Xinjiang to assist in the local jihad against China.

The involvement of Islamic radical states in the security situation in Southeast Asia is not confined to Iran. Saudi Arabia, Libya, and other states also sponsor particular Islamist movements, separatists and terrorist groups. The aforementioned "Shanghai Five" group is but one example of a regional security response that such developments have encouraged.

Policy Horizons

If economies falter, domestic political conflicts fester, and with desperate politicians seeking scapegoats and saviours, the dangers of violence remain real.

Ethnic conflict is linked in one way or another to economics. For example, in southern Thailand, the Malay-based ethnic separatist movement all but disintegrated as Thailand's economic growth accelerated in the 1980s. By contrast, the comparable Moro nationalist movement in the southern Philippines has persisted in part because of a wealthier national economy. Other factors are also at play including, for example, population density and religious links. Separatism is not merely a function of economic determinism.

This study, accordingly, highlights the range of variables—social, religious, economic and cultural—which stimulate or impede the development of militant Islamism in Southeast Asia. It offers, through the four central case studies, an insight into the workings of these factors in producing particular developments with regard to Islamism and suggests likely short- and medium-term prognoses for the future. It is obviously a matter of deep importance to Australia and the Western world more generally that its understanding of the Southeast Asian region and the phenomenon of militant Islamism is understood in a substantive, balanced way, so that our engagement with the region is both sophisticated and pertinent to the ever-changing political realities involved.

Postscript

Since the initial drafting of this volume, events in Asia have taken some significant turns.

Most momentous has been the untimely downfall of Abdurrahman Wahid in Indonesia. His removal as President of Indonesia on July 23 2001 does not diminish his contribution as a long-standing proponent of human rights, religious tolerance, and democracy. While he was often his own worst enemy as President and a poor executive administrator, one should not forget the genuine accomplishments of his tenure; in pursuing reconciliation with East Timor; in innovative approaches to separatist challenges in Aceh and West Papua based on dialogue; in his successful removal of the seemingly immovable General Wiranto and attempts to establish civilian control over the military; and in the pursuit of human rights abuses and corruption.

New President Megawati Sukarnoputri will confront a number of serious economic, ethnic, religious, and political problems, while trying to harness a stable coalition of supporters as parties compete for ministries, and particularly those with strong patronage opportunities. Her nationalistic approach may aggravate some of the separatist conflicts, while her growing relationship with former Suharto elites and the military may make genuine economic reform and effective human rights and corruption investigations problematic.

Similarly, the Philippines has seen a change of government in unusual circumstances. Since the ignominious downfall of Joseph Estrada, new President Gloria Arroyo has moved positively to restore the credibility of government and initiate renewed negotiations with the Moro Islamic Liberation Front in the south. The Abu Sayyaf Group remains a threat to the security and safety of all who venture near their stronghold in the small islands south of Mindanao. The series of highly publicized kidnappings embarked upon by the ASG during 2000-2001 were redolent more of extortion than any furthering of their political claims.

Developments in Malaysia and Thailand have not been nearly so dramatic. Malaysian Prime Minister Dr. Mahathir appears determined to hold on to the reins of power, despite the urging of younger members of his own party UMNO. The main opposition party remains the Islamist PAS, which has made inroads in by-elections and most significantly on the campuses. In Thailand, a low-level Islamic-separatist rebellion in the south has continued, with two of the rebel groups, the PULO and the BRN merging in April 2001 under the name Bersatu and immediately setting off two bombs to announce themselves. At this stage, new Prime Minister Thaksin Shinawatra is backing the military's hard line against the rebels, who remain a small but elusive target.

In the wider regional context, the role of Islamic fundamentalism in Asian political and economic instability is receiving greater attention from major players in the region. China and Russia have been drawn closer together by the common threat posed by Islamic insurgencies both within their own territories and in neighboring states, particularly in Central Asia. The United States, under the Bush Administration, has also taken a more active focus on the region, partly motivated by an emerging rivalry with China but also by a desire to buttress democratic and emerging democratic states in a period of continuing economic malaise. Recent political developments in Indonesia, and to some extent in Malaysia, give the clearest indication yet of how a more prominent strain of Islamic radicalism can create a profound impact on national political affairs.

1

Islam and Politics in the New Indonesia

Greg Barton

Introduction: Whither Indonesia?

Religious Violence in the Headlines

For some years now the headlines had been cropping up in the national media. Now and then, a violent incident would occur which appeared, on the surface at least, to represent ethnic and religious conflict. And the headlines had screamed the fact. But they didn't come that often, and when they did it was generally with good reason. The 1996 church burnings in Situbondo, East Java, for example, appeared to offer fairly dramatic evidence of inter-communal conflict. Similarly, rioting and violence in Tasikmalaya, West Java, or the 1997 fights between transmigrant Madurese and local Iban in West Kalimantan appeared to bear all the hallmarks of ethnic and religious conflict. Across the nation as a whole, however, these incidents were reasonably sporadic, and most journalists, accustomed to a reasonably harmonious and tolerant society in Indonesia were cautious in applying such labels as "religious and ethnic violence." By 1998 however, the apocalyptic headlines were common place and by year's end appeared to be reaching a crescendo. By then it was not only the international media that talked of Indonesia breaking up, collapsing under the weight of inter-communal tension and religious ethnic conflict, it was also the local Indonesian media. Indeed, commentators from the level of President Habibie down began to talk of Indonesian society being at a crossroads and of the real possibility of the nation descending into a relentless spiral of violence. Evidence for this view was seen to be the conflict between Ambonese Christians and Muslim migrants to Ambon that continued to fester throughout 1999. On the surface at least, this violence appeared to be markedly religious in nature and unlike most other outbreaks of violence the local communities appeared unable to quickly extinguish it.

Mercifully, however, often just as Indonesian society appeared to be slipping over into the abyss it would pull back. Time and time again across the archipelago, social tensions would erupt into violence and it looked as if whole communities would be swallowed up in anarchy but on most occasions within a day or two the tension would begin to dissolve and the community would pull back from the brink. Mercifully, although the nation seemed just like its drought ravaged forests, tinder dry and ready to burst into flame at the slightest spark, when it did burn the conflagrations remained more spot fires than wildfire, suggesting that Indonesian society was much less combustible than might have been feared. Moreover, there has been significant anecdotal evidence to suggest that many of the most serious eruptions of violence have been deliberately triggered.

Is Religious Fundamentalism a Threat?

So what is going on in Indonesia? On one hand, the nation appears to have all the ingredients for the emergence of virulent religious fundamentalism, along the lines of so many other nations where all hope of building a prosperous and stable future has dissolved in a sea of hatred, attack, reprisal, and counter-reprisal. Indonesia is not, of course, an Algeria or an Afghanistan, by any measure, nor even a Pakistan. But what is to stop it sliding in that direction? According to some analysts the combination of 215 million people struggling to survive in a very tough economic environment where the national currency has lost three-quarters of its value and where around half the population lives below a very meager poverty line, where an authoritarian, and at times dictatorial, military-backed government ruled for over thirty years, and where myriad human rights abuses have occurred wherever the military has enjoyed free reign, is a certain recipe for disaster. And where, in such a country, 87 percent of the population is Muslim, and much of that 87 percent is very poor, it is not surprising that some see the emergence of Islamic fundamentalism as almost inevitable. In recent years even respected moderate religious leaders such as Abdurrahman Wahid, previously leader of the 35-million-strong traditionalist Islamic organization Nahdlatul Ulama and now Indonesia's fourth President, have spoken of the possibility of an Algeria scenario. Such statements are intended as a "wake up" call rather than a literal prediction, but are worrying nevertheless.

And who can blame the Christians, especially the Chinese (and one term is often used as a euphemism for the other) for feeling vulnerable, even to the point of being somewhat paranoid? If the years of sporadic anti-Chinese rioting and attacks on shop houses was not enough, the awful violence of mid-May 1998, in which Chinese shops and residences were targeted in Jakarta and Solo, Chinese were burned to death as their shop houses were set on fire and Chinese women gang-raped, it is no surprise that members of this small and conspicuous community wonder about their future in Indonesia.[1] That the Habibie government has clearly been unwilling to investigate the rapes and other related acts of terror linked to ABRI only compounds the sense of vulnerability among Indonesian Chinese.

Grounds for Hope?

Are there grounds for hope in Indonesia? Is a slide into religious violence and the emergence of a pervasive fundamentalism inevitable? Or does Indonesia possess sufficient cultural resources, and lessons learned from historical experience to build something better?

Should we be pessimistic or optimistic about the future of Indonesia? And more specifically, should we be concerned about the prospect of religious conflict and the emergence of a fundamentalistic form of Islam? In my opinion, there are very good grounds for being cautiously optimistic. I believe that it is extremely unlikely that we are going to see the kind of Islamic fundamentalism recently seen in Afghanistan and Algeria, emerging on a large scale in Indonesia. One would be foolhardy, however, not to be concerned about current developments in Indonesia. Ongoing violence in which religion appears to play a major role now seems to be inevitable. The only question that remains is not: "will there be further 'ethnic and religious' violence?" but rather: "will this violence be contained or will it blaze out of control?"

The Place of Islam in Indonesian Society—
The Historical Background

Recognizing the Potential of Islam

Clearly one of the major factors in determining Indonesia's future is Islam. Perhaps a good place to start this discussion is with a quotation from Daniel Lev, the respected Indonesianist and scholar, who when in 1998 asked his opinion on the danger posed by Islam in Indonesia responded by saying that "There will be no reform in Indonesia over the long-term unless Islam is recognized as the powerful moral force it is." One of the points that Lev was making was that to see Islam as simply part of the problem is to profoundly misunderstand the whole situation. This is not to say that there may not be problems linked to certain expressions of Islam, indeed that will certainly be the case, but rather that Islam and the way in which it is used by all sides in politics needs to be understood in its context. In particular, we need to understand the potential for Islam in Indonesia to be a powerful, constructive moral force, as well as being simply exploited for narrow sectarian and partisan interests.

If we are to arrive at any useful and genuinely insightful conclusions about the role of Islam in Indonesian society, then we will need to take the time to learn something of the historical, cultural and social context of Islam in Indonesia, and to understand something of all of the forces at work.

The Central Role of Islam

The first point that needs to be made is that, contrary to popular perception in some quarters, Islam plays a central role in modern Indonesian life. For long it has been asserted that Indonesian society is not really Islamic and that Islam in Indonesia represents but a thin veneer over a Hindu-Buddhist core. To the extent that this view makes the point that Muslim society in Indonesia differs significantly from Muslim society in the Arab world it has some validity. Nevertheless, it is based on a serious misunderstanding of the role and nature of Islam in Indonesia.

For most of this century Islam in Indonesia has been dominated by two large mass organizations: Muhammadiyah and Nahdlatul Ulama. By most measures these two organizations are the largest

Islamic organizations in the world, Muhammadiyah claims a membership of 28 million, while Nahdlatul Ulama claims between 30 and 40 million members. And while neither organization is able to produce membership rolls to entirely substantiate these figures there is no doubting that between them they represent a substantial portion of Indonesia's 190 million Muslims. As is to be expected of such large organizations, each covers a diversity of opinion, political outlook, and religious convictions.

Consequently it is possible to find individuals in both organizations who are unambiguously liberal just as it is possible to find individuals with a reactionary and fundamentalistic frame of mind. Nevertheless, it is possible to speak of the general character of each organization. And in both cases these organizations, in their track records, in the stances of their leading figures, and in their historical approach to engagement in social issues, have shown themselves to be essentially moderate. Indeed an examination of both Muhammadiyah and Nahdlatul Ulama provides plenty of evidence for Daniel Lev's assertion that Islam in Indonesia needs to be understood as an important moral force. Moreover, in recent years, there has been good reason to believe that without the stabilizing effect of these two large mass organizations, with their extensive national networks and strong sense of community, the sporadic outbreaks of violence we have witnessed may well have raged out of control and burned without check.

Muhammadiyah and Islamic Modernism

Muhammadiyah was founded in 1912 as a direct outcome of the successful reception of Islamic Modernist ideas bought back to Indonesia by pilgrims and scholars returning from the Middle East. The early Modernists in Indonesia were very much inspired by the ideas of Egyptian reformist, Muhammad Abduh and also by his disciple Rashid Rida. The Modernist movement in Indonesia early in the twentieth century had four broad aims, firstly the encouragement of piety and a serious attitude to the carrying out of religious obligations, secondly the purification of Islamic belief, in practice this meant the rejection of so-called animist or Hindu Buddhist elements of Javanese culture, thirdly, the provision of the sort of social services to their community that the Dutch were unwilling to provide, and fourthly, the development of a modern and sophisticated expression of Islam able to respond to the challenges of modernity and benefit from modern technology and scientific advances. As far as Islamic thought was concerned the main innovation of the Modernists, whether in Indonesia or elsewhere in the Muslim world, was to argue in favor of *ijtihad*, rational, individual, interpretation of Scriptures and traditions, and against *taqlid*, or the uncritical acceptance of established interpretation as delineated by the four orthodox *mazhab* or schools of Islamic jurisprudence.

The practical out-workings of Modernist thought in Indonesia were to be seen in the modern network of schools established by Muhammadiyah, and by its philanthropic institutions such as orphanages and hospitals. Sociologically, Muhammadiyah drew its members from the midst of the lower middle classes of small and medium-sized towns and cities, from Muslim traders, and later increasingly from white-collar professionals, clerks and civil servants.

Nahdlatul Ulama and Islamic Traditionalism

The initial response to the Modernist movement by traditional *ulama* was reasonably positive. Nevertheless they did take issue with two aspects of the Modernist movement, namely the Modernists' rejection of traditional religious practices such as praying at the tomb sites of saints and the negative attitude of Modernists to classical Islamic scholarship. Their main concern was that the spread of Modernism would pose a threat to the traditional *pesantren*, or Islamic boarding school system that was the backbone of classical religious instruction. Not without reason, they feared that the *pesantren* network might wither and eventually disappear altogether. Consequently, in 1926, a group of leading *ulama* in East Java got together to form an organization to facilitate networking and co-operation among *ulama* and their *pesantren*. They called this organization Nahdlatul Ulama, an Arabic name meaning the awakening of the *ulama*, commonly shortened to NU. From the beginning NU enjoyed rapid growth and substantial consolidation but never achieved the organizational efficiency and sophistication of the more urban-based Muhammadiyah. Relations with the Modernists in Muhammadiyah were generally good although frequently marked by a degree of underlying tension. For not only were the traditionalists, as they came to be called, concerned about the antipathy towards classical scholarship displayed by the Modernists, they were also offended by their rejection of many traditional Javanese Islamic practices as being Islamic.

Despite the underlying tension, Muhammadiyah and NU were able to cooperate reasonably successfully during the Japanese occupation and subsequent struggle for independence to the point where they entered the independent era working together in one political party, Masyumi. These good relations didn't last very long however, and in 1952 NU broke from Masyumi and set itself up as an independent political party. The main reason for the split appeared to be frustration within NU with the Modernist domination of Masyumi. What they perceived to be a Modernist assessment of NU members as being unsophisticated and ill-equipped to play a leading role in modern, democratic politics enraged them. The final trigger was the failure of the NU faction to have its candidate selected for the post of Minister of Religious Affairs. Had the Masyumi Modernist traditionalist alliance been maintained a united Masyumi would have dominated in wake of the 1955 election. As it happened both Masyumi and NU received around 20 percent of the votes each, placing them among the leading four parties.[2]

Islam and Communal Politics under Sukarno

The experience of Islamic politics in the 1950s is particularly pertinent to today's situation. During the second half of 1998 a large number of new political parties were formed, many of which were expressly styling themselves as being Islamic parties. Most of these parties, however, gained less than 1 or 2 percent of the votes in the June 1999 general elections. Nevertheless, the two big "Islamic" parties, PKB and PPP, polled reasonably strongly in the June 1999 election finishing in the top four much in the same way as did NU and Masyumi in 1955. This is because the great majority of NU members appear to have supported PKB,
while many Muhammadiyah members seem to have supported PPP. Consequently many observers in 1998 spoke of the reemergence of 1950 style communal politics. A view reinforced by the groundswell of popular support for Megawati Soekarnoputri and her PDI Perjuangan mirroring the charismatic following for her father Sukarno, Indonesia's first president, and the party he was closest to, the secular-nationalist PNI.[3] The fact that the period following Indonesia's first and only free election in 1955 was marked by con-

siderable political instability and a succession of short-lived coalitions, culminating in Sukarno's pronouncement of Guided Democracy, is seen by many as a grave lesson as we witness the re-emergence of communal politics in the late 1990s.

Sukarno's declaration of guided democracy, and his increasingly authoritarian style provoked sharp opposition from Masyumi and led to a number of senior Masyumi leaders becoming involved in several ill-fated attempts at regional secession in West Sumatra and Southern Sulawesi. Not surprisingly, this was met with a sharp response from Sukarno and in January 1960 he moved to officially ban Masyumi. The final half-decade of Sukarno's regime saw Indonesian society increasingly polarized. Finally, the steadily accumulating tensions erupted in a horrific display of violence.

On the October 1, 1965 it was alleged that a small group of Communist leaders had mounted a coup attempt against Sukarno. General Suharto became the man of the hour taking charge and foiling the coup attempt. Because of Sukarno's close relations with the Indonesian Communist Party he came under a cloud of doubt and was finally forced to officially hand over power to Suharto who then became Indonesia's second President. Regrettably, the shift in power that occurred in October 1965 precipitated a violent wave of reprisals against Communists and alleged Communist sympathizers. Several hundred thousand people were killed, mostly by civilians and many by their neighbors and fellow villagers. Undoubtedly, much of the killing involved the settling of old scores, although those involved in the attacks on the Communists sought to justify their actions by saying that "if we did not kill the Communists the Communists would have killed us." Both Muhammadiyah and Nahdlatul Ulama members were actively engaged in the anti-Communist reprisals, particularly in strongly Muslim areas such as East Java.

The Modernists in particular, who had so fallen from grace during the Sukarno regime, hoped that Suharto's so-called New Order regime, backed as it was by the military, would be more supportive of their political aspirations and allow a reemergence of Masyumi. These hopes were quickly dashed, however, and while the Suharto regime did allow a formation of a Masyumi successor by the name of Parmusi they were not willing to allow the old Masyumi leadership an active role in leading Parmusi. The military, perhaps even more than Sukarno, was fearful of giving too much opportunity for the Mod-

ernists to fulfil their political ambitions. For by this stage, some of
the Modernist leaders previously active in Masyumi sought to define their political platform in terms of greater recognition of the
Syari'ah, or Islamic law, and they spoke loosely about the merits of
forming an Islamic state.

This meant that some Modernists, including some of the former
Masyumi leadership, came into the Suharto period increasingly ob-
sessed, and driven by, the prospect of establishing an Islamic state.
The traditionalists, however, continued to operate much as they had
always done, regarding the preservation of religious and personal
freedom as the highest political goal, and one to be achieved as
expediently as possible. The more radical of the Modernists, for their
part, regarded the NU politicians to be opportunists, lacking in political and religious principle. Many Modernists, of course, continued to be active within Muhammadiyah and to focus their energies
on the ideas of social welfare and education programs. A small group
of Modernists, clustered around the late Muhammad Natsir, the
former Masyumi leader founded the NGO Dewan Dakwah (Missions Council).

The 1971 general elections were contested by eleven political
parties and NU once again polled well, gaining slightly less than
twenty percent of the votes. But by the time of the next election, in
1977, Suharto had moved to consolidate the eleven political parties
down to just three. Suharto's Golongan Karya, or Golkar for short,
nominally a grouping of functional groups representing the whole
of Indonesian society, gained the majority of the vote. NU was forced
to join PPP, the so-called United Development Party, which was made
a receptacle for all Islamic political interests. The third party was
PDI, or the Indonesian Democratic Party. Needless to say the deft
hand of Suharto reached into the leadership of both parties and ensured that neither of them became the basis for a genuine political
threat.

Suharto's New Order

The Successful Developmentalist Regime

Suharto's manipulation of the political process served him well.
The use of Golkar as a political vehicle proved to be extremely ex-
pedient. The five yearly national elections maintained a modest cha-

rade of democracy while presenting none of its risks. At the same time, these so-called "festivals of democracy," as the five yearly elections were known, served as convenient escape valves for pent-up emotion and frustration. Golkar always gained around sixty to seventy percent of the votes but even the votes that it lost represented good value in terms of channeling dissent along ineffectual lines.

The Suharto regime was always an authoritarian regime but many regarded it as being reasonably benevolent in many regards. Unlike, say, the Philippines' Ferdinand Marcos and his cronies, Suharto and his technocrats did a relatively good job managing the economy and encouraging growth. For almost three decades Indonesia enjoyed an annual rate of growth of around 6 percent to 8 percent. While much of the wealth generated was soaked up by corruption and nepotism there was still sufficient distribution of the fruits of growth to encourage Indonesians towards optimism about the future and the conviction that things were getting steadily better. And indeed, things did get steadily better. Over three decades, up until late 1997 when the economic crisis hit, all of the major standard of living indices showed substantial improvement. Infant mortality rates declined dramatically just as average longevity improved significantly. At the same time Indonesia did a reasonable job of controlling population growth without, for the most part, resorting to draconian interventions. The Indonesian educational system in particular enjoyed rapid gains and Indonesia in the late 1990s had obtained levels of literacy and general education higher than comparable developing nations.

The urban middle classes in particular, benefited greatly from these decades of growth. And while in many ways the poor remained poor while the rich got richer, many individuals were able to break out of the cycle of poverty and enjoy remarkable social mobility through the opportunities offered by education and an expanding economy.

ABRI and Dwifungsi

Where the "carrots" of growth and development proved insufficient inducement to produce a quiescent citizenry there was always the "stick" of a well organized and widely distributed military. The Indonesian military, of which the police were a part, had been steadily developed along lines of territorial warfare so that at every level in society from the local suburb or village or neighborhood sub-district up to the provincial level the military was closely engaged in the monitoring and running of society. In the mid-1960s when the Suharto New Order regime was still new and struggling with rocketing inflation and badly undeveloped infrastructure, the involvement of the military in managing society and managing business was in many ways very beneficial. The official name for this doctrine of military engagement in social and political life was Dwifungsi, or dual function. Considering the size of Indonesia, the Indonesian military was not particularly large and never very well funded, and the doctrine of Dwifungsi was not unconnected with the military's need to raise money for its own budget. Given the prevailing level of social order, and the intricate system of citizen surveillance that supported Dwifungsi, however, Indonesia's relatively small and poorly equipped military was more than able to check dissent. And where orthodox methods of control proved inefficient or ineffectual the army was fully capable of using less orthodox, though all too common methods, to keep the citizenry in line.

Managing the Threat of Islam

Suharto's masterful management of Indonesian affairs ensured that he did not face any major source of opposition that he was unable to control. The Indonesian press, for example, remained resiliently committed to investigative journalism and political reform but was nevertheless effectively controlled, if not gagged, by what was politely referred to as the "telephone culture." All that was needed to bring an errant magazine or newspaper into line was a quiet telephone conversation suggesting that it was "unwise" or to run the story that they were planning to run. Occasionally when this sort of advice failed to be sufficiently effective a publication would be closed down. Press freedom waxed and waned throughout the thirty-two years of the Suharto regime but the regime's control over the press meant that it was never a serious threat or one that could not be handled.

The only area of civil society that was to a significant extent outside the control of government was Islam. Muhammadiyah and Nahdlatul Ulama were the only mass based organizations to have truly national networks and significant sections of the population under their influence. (The same is true of the churches but they represent a much smaller section of the population.) The Suharto regime was clever enough to realize that direct attempts to control Islam could easily be counter productive and sought by various indirect means to influence the discourse of Islamic expression along lines conducive to supporting government policies. In part the regime did not need to exercise an ordered degree of control over either Nahdlatul Ulama or Muhammadiyah because in many ways both were moderate organizations that were responsive to moves that involved government development initiatives. In the 1960s both the Modernists and traditionalists initially supported Suharto's new order. In the 1970s this support turned to criticism particularly after the regime showed the extent to which it was prepared to go to suppress dissent.

Even when it was most critical of the government, however, NU did not pose a great threat. Culturally NU followed a traditionally Sunni approach of quiescence on political matters. Throughout its past independent history, NU had consistently given priority to maintaining the religious and personal freedom of its members over any other political ambitions. It spoke of "finding the middle path and of avoiding harm," calling on traditional Sunni maxims about approaches to political engagement that emphasized pragmatic cooperation with the regime of the day. Muhammadiyah was also relatively quiescent with respect to national politics. Like Nahdlatul Ulama, Muhammadiyah is fundamentally a religious organization concerned with cultural and social matters.

Pancasila and the Secular State

One of the first actions taken by Abdurrahman Wahid when he became National Chairman of Nahdlatul Ulama in December 1984 was to withdraw Nahdlatul Ulama from PPP, the United Development Party, the official Islamic Party's New Order regime. He did this for a number of reasons, not the least of which was that Nahdlatul Ulama was not having a great influence on affairs through PPP, but importantly he did it also because he argued that party political activity was not the right or appropriate sphere for communal or religious sentiment. In other words it was a good thing for Muslims to be engaged in politic but to argue politically in the name of Islam is dangerous and leads to sectarianism, and increased inter-communal tension. Consequently, to embrace Pancasila, and to acknowledge that as a viable basis for the modern state, he concluded, was a wholly sensible option.

This option became a very important and contentious issue in the early 1980s when President Suharto began to push for all organizations in Indonesian society to acknowledge Pancasila as their Asas Tunggal, or sole basis. In other words, the President was asking that all organizations acknowledge that the fundamental doctrine underlying their organization was to be Pancasila. At first many Muslim groups took offence at this, and suggested that to ask this was to ask them, in some way to deny their faith and to put Pancasila, this artificial human creation above their faith. Other leaders such as Abdurrahman Wahid, argued that there was no contradiction in adopting Pancasila as a basis for interacting in public life. Consequently, NU was one of the first organizations to adopt Pancasila. This went a considerable way to gaining good will for Abdurrahman Wahid as the new chairman of NU. It meant that for the first few years of his term as chairman he was able to establish reasonable relations with government and army figures, and to have access to levels of power within the military and the government which meant that he could influence the outcome of the decisions that were affecting members of NU.

Moreover, he was been widely used by the army whenever there have been problems of inter-religious, inter-communal tension or violence, and has been instrumental in tempering the approach of government and the army towards religious matters. In due course, all of the other groups followed and embraced Pancasila, essentially, because they did not have the choice of doing otherwise. Consequently, for the last fifteen years of the century Pancasila has played a very central part in public discussion about the nature of the Indonesian state and the ways it should evolve and change.

Crisis, Chaos, and the Fall of Suharto

Economic Meltdown

At the beginning of 1998 the Rupiah reached a mid-January low of Rp17,000 to the U.S.$ before recovering to 10,000 to 12,000 for the next six months. With domestic interest rates three times higher than those available on the international market, Indonesian businesses had become highly dependent on foreign borrowing. Unfortunately, most borrowing was unhedged and short term and much of it was channeled through the poorly regulated and inherently corrupt domestic financial system. Suddenly, Indonesia found itself with U.S.$30 to 40 billion of short-term loans which it could neither repay nor refinance (Hill, 1998).

Once the collapse had begun Indonesia's crisis, soon known as Krismon (*krisis moniter*—monetary crisis) was compounded at every turn. Not only did foreign capital flee the archipelago, so too did billions of dollars of local capital. Already for some years the focus of rioting by the frustrated poor, Indonesia's favorite scapegoats, its minority ethnic Chinese population, were made to feel increasingly nervous. A small group of Indonesian Chinese, lead by figures such as Liem Soe Leong and Bob Hassan, had been favored by Suharto in large-scale conglomerate business deals. In return for special import licenses and effective monopolies they had entered into complex cross-ownership deals with members of the Suharto family and other key figures of the New Order elite. This small group is said to control 70 percent of the corporate economy. The majority of Indonesian Chinese have no such links with the high end of town but many have made modest fortunes through traditional small-business endeavors, including the distribution of basic foodstuffs, including rice and cooking oil. Consequently, these traders came to bear the brunt of community anger at the inevitable rapid inflation of virtually all goods in Indonesia (in post-Green Revolution Indonesia even locally produced goods such as rice and mass-farmed chicken require imported inputs, whether fertilizers or poultry feed).

Following the anti-Chinese violence of mid-May 1998, the worst in decades, in which hundreds of Chinese shops and houses were torched in Jakarta and Solo, many Indonesian Chinese fled the country. As a result, the Indonesian economy suffered a huge loss, not just in terms of billions of dollars of capital, but, perhaps more importantly, in terms of highly skilled human capital. The return of confidence among Chinese investors in Indonesia, both locally and intra-regionally, should it be possible, will play a key part in Indonesia's recovery.

Suharto's Denouement

On March 10, 1998 Suharto was sworn in for a seventh five-year term as President, despite enormous community disquiet. Also the cause of considerable disquiet, particularly among international investors, was Suharto's choice of Vice President for his seventh term.

Suharto's choice was his long-term confident, and protégé, B.J. Habibie, previously the spendthrift Minister for Research and Technology with wild ideas about economic advancement through massive investment in high-tech schemes, such as aircraft manufacture. When seventy-seven-year-old Suharto first announced his intention to appoint Habibie in January, the Rupiah immediately plummeted in response. According to the Indonesian constitution, if the President is incapacitated by death or illness, power is transferred directly to the Vice President. The prospect of B.J. Habibie becoming the President filled most observers with horror.

On May 9, Suharto flew to Cairo for the G-15 summit. Three days later, on the May 12, four students from the upper-middle class Catholic Trisakti University were shot dead by snipers using high-powered military weapons while returning to their campus from a peaceful demonstration. Footage of the demonstrations and shootings was aired around the world by CNN. The following day the students were buried and a "second Statement of Concern" demanding Suharto's resignation was issued by 109 LIPI intellectuals (the first being issued on January 19, 1998 by nineteen LIPI staffers).[4] The next day, May 14, Jakarta erupted in bloody rioting on a scale not witnessed since the fall of Sukarno in 1965. Over 1,200 people in Jakarta and the central Java city of Solo died, most were burnt alive as Chinese shop houses were set on fire and shopping centers full of looters were systematically torched. Jakarta descended into chaos. Curiously, the normally conspicuous security forces were nowhere to be seen.

Late on the 14th General Wiranto, Commander of the Armed Forces and Minster for Defense, confronted Major General Syafrie Syamsuddin, Head of the Jakarta Garrison, and ordered him to send his troops out onto the streets. Informed opinion in Jakarta in May argued that Lieutenant-General Prabowo, Suharto's son-in-law, and close friend of Syafrie, was behind both the Trisakti shootings and the May 14 riots. Prabowo, who had previously commanded operations in East Timor, was said to have employed a combination of crack Kopassus (Special Forces) loyal troops and thugs (*preman*) to bring to the national capital the sort of military terror tactics previously only deployed in far-off military controlled provinces such as East Timor, West Papua (previously known as Irian Jaya) and Aceh. Prabowo, who was later demoted, and then discharged and sent to stand trial, over the events of mid-May, was evidently attempting to simultaneously discredit Wiranto and justify a military crackdown on political dissent against Suharto. In the end his gamble, if that is what it was, misfired badly.

Suharto flew into Jakarta early on the 15th only to see his city in flames. Desperately seeking to negotiate his way out of difficulties he proposed a cabinet reshuffle, but with a community outraged and tens of thousands of students peacefully occupying the parliament building (protected by troops loyal to Wiranto) his support was rapidly ebbing away. No one was willing to join a new Suharto cabinet and former sycophants overnight become outspoken "reformers." A group of nine Muslim leaders including Abdurrahman Wahid and the leading liberal, progressive, intellectual Nurcholish Madjid, met with Suharto and told him that he had no choice but to resign. Late on the evening of the 20th Suharto announced to his advisers that he was handing over power to Habibie.

Islam, Communal Politics, and Civil Society

The Emergence of Islamic Liberalism

Before examining some of the more worrying aspects of Islamic political and social activity in Indonesia at the present time it is important to gain an appreciation of the historical context and dynamics of Islam and Indonesian society. Most observers who come to study Islam in Indonesia after first studying other Muslim societies are struck by the evident liberality of Islam in Indonesia. And indeed compared with Islam in many other societies there is good reason for characterizing Indonesian Islam as being liberal.

This is not to say that Indonesian Muslims are not serious about their faith. Like all religious societies Indonesian society is very mixed and those Muslims who diligently carry out all the requirements of their faith, the so-called *santri*, represent a minority within Indonesian Muslim society. In some other societies political pressure to conform to the expectations of religious conservatism may make this proportion appear greater but Indonesian society is probably no less pious overall than most other Muslim societies. What is really significant though, is that among those in Indonesia who are most influenced by liberal, progressive, religious ideas and social application are many pious intellectuals.

One of a number of reasons why Indonesian Islam is so oriented towards progressive and liberal ideas is the influence of what was initially a small liberal movement of Islamic thought that began in the late 1960s and early 1970s and which today has become broadly influential. This new movement of Islamic thought is sometimes referred to as neo-Modernism, the nomenclature of the Pakistani American academic Fazlur Rahman previously from the University of Chicago.

The influence of this movement through intellectuals such as Abdurrahman Wahid, Nurcholish Madjid and others, together with the basically open and tolerant character of Islamic society and culture has meant that a vigorous and reasonably healthy civil society has developed in Indonesia in which liberal Islamic intellectuals play a key role.

As we have noted above, President Suharto's so-called New Order regime which was established in the wake of the toppling and the elimination of the Indonesian Conservative Party (PKI) and subsequent demise of the first President Sukarno, was very much backed by the Indonesian Armed Forces, or ABRI (now TNI). In part, ABRI's incentive in seizing power in 1965 derives from a strong cultural orientation towards the avoidance of social chaos. Many senior ABRI officers, Suharto included, were alarmed by the increasing polarization of Indonesian society in the last four years of the Sukarno period. In particular, they were alarmed about the rise of the Indonesian Communist Party and what they felt to be its undue influence on government policies, including the emergence of a strident anti-Westernism.

ABRI was assisted, often quite enthusiastically, in its elimination of the Communist Party by members of both Muhammadiyah and Nahdlatul Ulama. And generally speaking student groups across the nation supported the emergence of the new government, hoping that it would bring an end to the years of chaos and instability and would bring development and improved living standards for all. To a significant extent these aspirations were not completely disappointed, although the new government proved to be even more authoritarian than the one that it replaced.

One of the groups most bitterly disappointed by the behavior of the New Suharto regime were the Islamic Modernists, particularly those who had been politically active in pushing for the legislative recognition of the role of Islam in Indonesian society. They had nurtured the hope that having assisted ABRI and Suharto to come to power they would be rewarded by being allowed to re-establish Masyumi or at least to make its successor, Parmusi into a fitting replacement. Instead, the new government refused to allow any of the old Masyumi leaders to be actively involved in Parmusi and moved deftly to constrain the prospects for Islamic politics. As a result many of the older Modernists became increasingly disillusioned and embittered. Perhaps the most notable example was former Masyumi leader, Mohammed Natsir who went on to form the so-called Dewan Dakwah or Council for Islamic Propagation and the Building of the Faith. Although initially Mohammad Natsir was reasonably moderate, the experience of political estrangement had embittered him and as a result he became increasingly conservative. Moreover, he succeeded in attracting around him a number of younger people whose views were even more extreme than his own.

Despite the fact that its policy outraged many of the older Masyumi Modernist leaders, the New Order government's strategy of containment was generally successful. It did, however, have a number of other consequences, some intended and some unintended. One of the most significant side-effects of the government's policy of constraining and containing Islamic politics was that it provided a fertile and sheltered environment for the development of a new movement of Islamic thought, neo-Modernism. It also generally provided an environment in which liberal-minded younger thinkers were able to freely explore new ideas and exchange them without either being stopped by their peers or seniors or being challenged by government agencies.

These ideas began to develop in the late 1960s among a generation of young thinkers who had been born around 1940, and were now in their late twenties. With their tertiary education having been previously interrupted by the turmoil of the late 1960s, they were completing their studies while simultaneously engaging in discussion groups and student activity. Most of them were involved in the peak Islamic student body HMI and were based either in Jakarta at the State Islamic Institute (Institut Agama Islam Negeri – IAIN) or at the IAIN in Yogyakarta. The leading figure in Jakarta was Nurcholish Madjid who also happened to be the National Chairman of HMI. In Yogyakarta the main figures developed into a small group clustered under the mentorship of Mukti Ali, a lecturer at the IAIN and later to become Minister for Religious Affairs. The chief figures in Yogyakarta were Djohan Effendi, Ahmad Wahib and Dawan Rahardjo.

Generational Change and the Appeal of Liberalism

These young liberal thinkers soon congregated in Jakarta and were joined in the national capital by Abdurrahman Wahid, son of the former Nahdlatul Ulama leader and former Minister of Religious Affairs, KH Wahid Hasyim and grandson of one of the founders of NU, KH Hasyim Asyari. From 1963 to 1970, Abdurrahman was studying, albeit in a slightly unconventional fashion, in Cairo and Baghdad. In Cairo he spent much of his time reading in the library of the American University and watching films in the French cinemas than at his official place of study at Al Azhar University. In Baghdad he studied Islamic society and civilization, before returning to Jakarta via Europe in 1971.

These young intellectuals met regularly together in Jakarta and were involved in a series of discussion groups, the leading figures being Abdurrahman Wahid, Nurcholish Madjid, Djohan Effendi, the late Ahmad Wahib and, to some extent, Dawam Rahardjo. Earlier, as members of HMI they enjoyed good relations with their more conservative seniors from Masyumi. Indeed Nurcholish Madjid had been described as the young Mohammed Natsir, implying that he would follow in the footsteps of their well-known former Masyumi leader. As their ideas became better known, however, they were met with a sharp reaction from many of the former Masyumi seniors. Many of the older generation of Modernists were critical of these young liberals with their active antipathy towards Islamic politics and their passion for the redevelopment of Islamic thought.

At the same time as these ideas were being hotly debated in Jakarta society, their mentor in Yogyakarta, Mukti Ali, was made Minister of Religious Affairs and embarked on a program of reform within the State Islamic Institutes (IAIN). The State Islamic Institutes were intended to supply functionaries for the Department of Religious Affairs and senior Islamic intellectuals, teachers and community leaders. Under Mukti Ali as Minister and in particular under the leadership in Jakarta of Harun Nasution, the IAIN particularly in Jakarta and Yogyakarta were steadily transformed. Emphasis was given to synthesizing classical Islamic learning with modern Western critical

thought. The efforts of Mukti Ali, Harun Nasution and other reformist leaders were not without fruit and beginning in the 1970s a large
number of *santri* educated youth from Traditionalist backgrounds
experienced a personal transformation as they struggled to integrate
modern Western thought with classical Islamic learning. Many of
these became strongly influenced by the neo-Modernist movement
led by Nurcholish Madjid despite the fact that others, under the influence of older Modernist leaders, were outspokenly critical of these
ideas.

Many of the IAIN graduates went on to become active in civil
society either through joining established NGOs, setting up new
NGOs or through becoming active in public life as journalists, activists, academics and public intellectuals. The result of this was that
civil society was greatly strengthened in Indonesia during the 1970s
and eighties through the influx of a number of the IAIN graduates
and other Muslim intellectuals who sought to integrate a liberal understanding of Islam with traditional civil society concerns for social and political reformation and transformation.

Civil Society and a Culture of Public Intellectuals

Even before this influx of liberal-minded younger intellectuals
there already existed a tradition of liberal intellectual engagement in
civil society in Indonesia. In part this was a legacy of nationalism.
Unlike Malaysia, for example, young Indonesians had had to fight
actively to achieve independence through four years of armed
struggle against the Dutch and much emotional and political turmoil
thereafter. Perhaps as a result of this, a cultural activism and certainly a romance of political engagement and struggle were developed in the psyche of the young nation. Leading the national struggle
in the late 1940s and the political developments of the 1950s were a
number of Islamic leaders, most of whom were naturally sympathetic to Western notions of democracy, progress, and development.

Partly as result of this, partly as result of the dynamics of state
formation in a former colony, and partly because of cultural charac-
teristics, Indonesia developed a society with a strong culture of public intellectuals. Under the Dutch, Indonesian society had been lead
by a small indigenous elite and after independence this pattern continued for several decades, and to some extent continues today. Far
more attention was, and is, given to a small elite group of public

intellectuals in Indonesia than is the case in most societies in the English-speaking world. These intellectuals are often also Islamic intellectuals and the majority are deeply engaged in the development of civil society.

Another factor influenced the development of civil society in Indonesia. This was the need to quickly develop a range of social services for community development, education, provision of health and welfare and so forth. Many of the individuals and groups involved in this, saw their activity as being part of their religious commitment and service to society.

The Track Record of NU and Muhammadiyah

In ascertaining the contribution of Islam to the development of civil society in Indonesia it is important to consider the track record of the two peak organizations Nahdlatul Ulama and Muhammadiyah, comprising as they do such a large proportion of the Islamic community. Overall the track record of the large organizations is reasonably clear and unambiguous. Both organizations have made a significant and consistent contribution toward moderating attitudes and behavior in Indonesian society. Both have supported the government's application of Pancasila ideals of a secular state and both have actively supported the cultural religious pluralism, which is a feature of Indonesian society today. They have worked closely with the Department of Religious Affairs and generally shared in Indonesian national development even while they have been critical of certain aspects of both the Sukarno and Suharto regimes.

Both organizations have also made significant contributions in producing a number of reformist intellectuals and NGOs. As far as NGOs are concerned it is in NU circles, particularly during the Abdurrahman Wahid period, that the greatest contribution has been made. Since the mid 1980s a significant number of NGOs have more or less spontaneously emerged as young IAIN graduates and others have sought to become engaged in the transformation of Indonesian society, most of these have come from a traditionalist background. Furthermore there is something about the nature of NU culture which facilitates and even encourages such spontaneous formation of NGOs.

In Muhammadiyah circles, things appear to be significantly different, not least because it is the culture of Muhammadiyah to do things in a centralized fashion, under the direction of the

Muhammadiyah central board in Jakarta. Even so, a number of Muhammadiyah students and intellectuals have come to the fore as activists in civil society in recent years. Some, like their traditionalist colleagues, have become engaged in critical journalism while others have joined established NGOs.

It is important not to forget, however, the contribution made by NU and Muhammadiyah themselves as mass-based organizations. In particular the contribution of Muhammadiyah through the national school network, through its orphanages and its hospitals has been particularly significant in the provision of social services. In as much as this provision of social services lays the foundation for the basic structure of civil society, Muhammadiyah, then, has made a considerable contribution to building civil society in Indonesia.

In some respects, both NU and Muhammadiyah can be regarded as conservative organizations, in as much as their prime aim is the preservation of the interests of their members, in particular, their religious faith. Under the Suharto regime they needed to act with considerable wisdom to avoid confrontation with the government. Nevertheless a significant number of leaders with these organizations have been involved in pushing for reform. Even at their most quiescent stage both Muhammadiyah and Nahdlatul Ulama were able to exert a degree of reformist influence over the government simply by way of their masses and the need for the government to be mindful of the opinion of their members. In the mid-1980s members of both organizations became increasingly outspoken, albeit within the limits of what they judged to be possible and advisable under the Suharto regime. In the final years of the Suharto regime, however, much of the natural self-censorship and checking that constrained clear criticism of the government has been overcome and they have engaged in direct and at times strident criticism of the government. This is particularly true of leaders such as Abdurrahman Wahid and Amien Rais and will be discussed in greater detail below.

Economic Crisis and Social Relief

Since the economic crisis began to bite hard in Indonesian society towards the end of 1997, Muhammadiyah and Nahdlatul Ulama, along with a number of other non-government groups, many of them linked to these mass organizations, began to seek ways in which they could provide food and shelter to those hit hardest by the economic recession. While the overall contribution of these Muslim groups in absolute terms could be described as modest, their influence and general goodwill should not be overlooked. The contribution towards those most hard hit by the economic turn down has been considerable if limited but more importantly the establishment of good relations between religious communities and across the nation as a direct result of this crisis has been most significant.

Ironically, just as the economic crisis has led to increased social tension and at times, inter-communal conflict, it has also spurred Muslim groups on to pursue better relations with their Christian Chinese and Hindu neighbors. As a consequence of increased social tension over the last three years and particularly through the period of economic crisis, both Muhammadiyah and Nahdlatul Ulama have worked hard to improve their relations with each other and with other communities.

Outbreaks of Violence

As was alluded to at the onset of this chapter, since mid-1996, Indonesia has suffered an unprecedented series of sporadic and apparently spontaneous outbursts of violence, many of which seem to be religious and ethnically based. Frequently the targets of violence have been members of the Indonesian Chinese community, who all too frequently become scapegoats when conditions become difficult in Indonesia. At times the violence has appeared to be clearly religious in nature with churches or mosques being burnt and open conflict taking place between Muslims and Christians. A striking example is the violence in north Jakarta between Christian Ambonese youth and local Muslim youth in late 1998 which provoked an outbreak of violence later in West Timor in which a series of mosques were attacked and burnt down.

Questions need to be raised however about the true nature of this violence for several reasons. Firstly there is considerable anecdotal evidence to suggest that some of the violence had been deliberately set off by agent provocateurs. One of the earliest incidents of violence in this period saw churches burnt in the East Java city of Situbondo. Situbondo lies in the heartland of Nahdlatul Ulama territory and was not an area known previously for poor relations between Christians and Muslims, so the violence surprised many. Though the full facts surrounding the incident remain unknown it is significant that many local witnesses reported seeing trucks packed full of young men coming into town. Moreover, their distinctive accents suggested that these people were from a different part of East Java as did the fact that they were asking for directions through town. Other anecdotal accounts of the incident suggest that it is possible that well organized outside elements deliberately provoked the violence.

While some of the worst cases of violence appear to have been orchestrated, or at least deliberately provoked, there are a number of other incidents where the violence does in fact appear to be spontaneous. One example is the violence that occurred in Rengesdenklok on the eastern fringe of Jakarta in early 1997. The incident is said to have begun when a local Chinese shopkeeper protested against Muslim youths loudly announcing the time for the early-morning prayer time during the fasting month of Ramadan. This violence resulted in a large number of Chinese shop houses being destroyed. A significant factor appears to be that relations between Chinese shopkeepers and the local community was said to be poor.

Another example of apparently spontaneous violence is the conflict that occurred in early 1997, one of half a dozen similar incidents over the past three decades, between ethnic Dayak in West Kalimantan and Madurese transmigrants who had begun settling in the district in the 1970s. There is a considerable history of antagonism between the two communities and also between the Madurese and local ethnic Malays. Tensions between the latter two erupted in March 1999 resulting in some of the worst violence yet seen in West Kalimantan, although so far the death toll did not reach that of the 1997 fighting when over 300 people were killed. Even so, reliable sources indicate that at least 260 people were killed, over 2,300 homes burnt to the ground, and over 24,000 people forced to flee their homes.[5]

The initial trigger for the violence was said to have been a struggle that broke out after a local Malay passenger refused to pay his bus fare to the Madurese driver. Others claim, however, that the real trigger was Malay frustration at the failure of police to act against the 200 or so Madurese who attacked a Malay village in January, killing four villagers. Whatever the case, the Malay retaliation was terrifying in its ferocity. By late March, after almost a week of fighting, over 16,500 Madurese transmigrants had fled their homes seeking refuge in makeshift military camps in the city of Pontianak. As both the Madurese and Malays are Muslims, religious differences do not seem to be a factor in this recent violence. In fact, in March 1999 the Malays were joined by some of their Christian Dayak and Chinese neighbors.

The real issue driving tensions here, it would appear, is local resentment towards the attitude and behavior of recently arrived Madurese. The Madurese who arrived initially in the 1970s were participants in a government sponsored transmigration scheme. This meant that they were given small plots of land and settled into the district as subsistence farmers, much like the rice farming Malays and Dayak. These Madurese were later joined by so called "spontaneous transmigrants" who made their own way to the district and became involved in non-farming activity. It is the later group who are said to steal rice harvests and engage in other acts of petty crime and intimidation and against whom local resentment is directed. Madurese are known to be staunch in their faith but it was the irreligious behavior of some Madurese rather than religion, which was at issue here. Similarly, even though the majority of the West Kalimantan Dayaks involved in the 1997 fighting were Christians, religion does not appear to be a significant factor in this conflict either.

To a certain, extent the inter-communal conflict in West Kalimantan can be explained in structural terms, in as much as it results from social tensions caused by massive outflows of people from the crowded "inner islands" of Java, Madura and Bali to comparatively lightly populated outer island destinations such as Southern Sumatra, Kalimantan, the Maluku, West Papua, and East Timor. For example, the violence witnessed in Ambon (the capital of the Maluku) throughout the first three months of 1999, in which over 1,000 people were killed, is thought to derive, at least in part, from resentment about the extent to which migrants to the city from Sulawesi dominate the local economy. Similar scenarios can be described regarding West Papua and East Timor, although there the resentment towards the newcomers is also fuelled by the terror and suffering that the local peoples have experienced at the hands of the Indonesian Armed Forces.

Even if religion is not a prime cause of the outbreak of conflict, however, it does not mean that religion is not an important factor. If nothing else, the use of religion to reinforce a sense of ethnic identity means that it is relatively easy for religious imagery to be used to bolster group solidarity and provoke outrage. In Ambon, where the population is split almost fifty-fifty between Ambonese Roman Catholics and Muslim transmigrants this certainly appears to be the case. This is graphically illustrated by the way in which the combatants resorted to the language of "jihad" and "holy war" to bolster their support.

Not surprisingly, the Roman Catholic Church in Indonesia is deeply troubled by the violence and has made a point of carefully investigating every aspect of it. As yet, however, the Church has not released its findings, but when it does it will be interesting to see to what extent there is conclusive evidence of the violence being deliberately provoked and orchestrated. The lack of conclusive evidence for the "engineering" (*merekayasakan*), as it is often put in the Indonesian press, of the violence has not stopped prominent figures such as Abdurrahman Wahid from asserting that the violence is not entirely spontaneous.

The most awful outbreak of violence so far was the violence that occurred in May 1998 that led to the resignation of Suharto. In this case as many as 1,200 people were killed many of them through being trapped in burning buildings in Jakarta and Solo in central Java. Here there is considerable evidence that the violence was deliberately provoked and that sections of the military were involved. On the morning of the violence local witnesses reported seeing truck loads of military or paramilitary like figures, disembarking and in some cases setting fire to shopping centers. Adding to the horror of the situation, in many cases local residents, including school children returning from school had been informed that the shopping center was going to be burnt and that they should run inside and loot what they could before the building went up in flames. In some cases the lower floors were set alight before the looters had time to flee.

There is also considerable speculation over who fired the bullets that killed four demonstrating students returning peacefully home to their campus of Trisakti University several days earlier. Initial investigations and charges blamed police but there is evidence to suggest that other elements, possibly Kopassus troops acting under orders from Prabowo were involved.

Unfortunately since the violence of May 1998 there have been a number of similarly mysterious outbursts of violence. One of the most unusual and sinister incidents was the killing of Muslim *ulama* and other community leaders in the town of Banyuwangi in East Java. The killings are blamed on a group of black clad assassins referred to by the local people as *"ninja."* It appears that the *ninja* were initially engaging in the activity against black magicians operating in the area but increasingly their victims included a number of pious Muslims mostly from Nahdlatul Ulama. Many people, including a number of NU leaders, have suggested that these people were acting out of sympathy with, or possibly under direction from former President Suharto. Whatever the case, there does appear to be clear evidence that a deliberate attempt was being made to provoke serious violence, although this does not mean that the violence was not multi-causal in nature. Unfortunately the activities of the *ninja* did result in a harsh and heated response from locals who themselves engaged in vigilante activity as they sought to capture and summarily execute a number of alleged *ninja*. That the incident did not get completely out of hand and the whole region erupt in violence is a credit to the moderating influence of the local and national leadership of Nahdlatul Ulama.

The Re-Emergence of Communal Politics

While the outbreaks of inter-communal violence had been going on for several years in the last years of the Suharto period, the sudden re-emergence of communal politics is something that only became possible after the fall of Suharto. Immediately after Suharto's resignation on May 20, 1998, discussion turned to the formation of new political parties even before these were officially approved. Perhaps not surprisingly, the majority of new parties proposed and established, appeal for support along communal lines.

Some of them, such as Megawati's PDI, and the new National Mandate Party (Partai Amanat National—PAN) had a broadly centrist and inclusive agenda. Others, such as the National Awakening Party (Partai Kebangkitan Bangsa—PKB) linked to Nahdlatul Ulama, although inclusive in character, had clear community links. Most worrying, however, were a number of small Islamic parties which appeared inclined to encourage sectarian sentiment and turn it to political advantage. New parties such as the Moon and Star

Party (Partai Bulan Bintang—PBB) and the Justice Party (Partai Keadilan) are clearly seeking to appeal to conservative Muslims, frustrated with the status quo and desirous of change along the lines desired by many Masyumi leaders in the 1950s.

Not surprisingly, many community leaders such as Abdurrahman Wahid initially spoke out against the re-emergence of communal politics and bemoaned the fact that it appeared that Indonesia was returning to 1950s style communal politics. After further consideration however, others concluded that the situation was not quite as bad as it appeared on the surface. They argued that the communal flavor of much of the new party political activity can be explained simply in terms of societies relative inexperience with party politics, as a result of repression during the Suharto period and the naive enthusiasm of many of the numbers of new parties which sought to quickly cement a membership base. Certainly in the case of parties like Partai Kebangkitan Bangsa (PKB) there appears to be little to fear as regards the promotion of sectarian sentiment. Nevertheless with groups such as Partai Bulan Bintang (PBB) and Partai Keadilan (PK) and to a lesser extent Partai Persatuan Pembangunan (PPP) there appears to be grounds for concern. Not least because many of the individuals involved in PBB, PPP and PK have links with Dewan Dakwah and with KISDI. If it seemed that these parties were likely to gain a large share of the votes then there would be very grave concerns for the future indeed. As it is however, the June 1999 election result is clear that these groups only appeal to a very small section of voters. Nevertheless as will be discussed below, they still have the potential to leverage up a degree of influence disproportionate to their primary constituency.

One of the consequences of the renewed political activity is an understandable resurgence in pre-election campaigning and positioning as party leaders and other hopefuls sought to position themselves and establish a support base. Partly because of this and partly because of the continuing economic crisis and the social tension associated with that and because of the vacuum of power that existed in the interregnum between the fall of Suharto and the election of the new government, a number of hard-line elements have become emboldened and outspoken in expressing their views

Modernist/Traditionalist Tension

One of the most disturbing aspects of the re-emergence of communal politics in 1998 was the way in which long-standing tensions between Modernists and Traditionalists, primarily between members of Nahdlatul Ulama and members of Muhammadiyah, once more become inflamed. In particular much attention was given to the relationship between Abdurrahman Wahid and Amien Rais and the question of whether or not these two men would be able to work together for reform or whether they would remain implacably opposed to each other.

NU, PKB and Abdurrahman Wahid

1998 and Reformasi

1998 was a year of unprecedented challenges for Abdurrahman Wahid, already the subject of considerable criticism early in the New Year because of his political manoeuverings. Abdurrahman's troubles were only just beginning when he suffered a near-fatal stroke on the evening of Monday, January 19, 1998. The stroke left him hospitalized for many weeks and then practically housebound for much of the rest of the year, as well as robbing him of his previously extraordinary stamina and what was left of his eyesight.

Needless to say, Abdurrahman's illness was an enormous blow to the organization. In practical terms it meant that the ambiguity already mounting about NU's involvement in the reform process could not be resolved, or at least not in the decisive way that it would have been possible with Abdurrahman at the helm. One consequence of this was that the nagging doubts about Abdurrahman's tactics in negotiating peace with the regime in late 1996 and early 1997 were able to flare up without being addressed. Exacerbating this was the fact that the long hoped-for meeting between Megawati Soekarnoputri, Amien Rais, and Abdurrahman Wahid was slow in eventuating. This resulted in sharp criticisms particularly by many younger activists, some of whom alleged that Abdurrahman had dumped Megawati, and that he harbored a grudge against Amien Rais, possibly even out of envy for his high-profile position within the reform movement.

Even when several months later Abdurrahman had regained some measure of good health, doubts remained about his commitment to the reform process. His emphasis on moderation and the avoidance of confrontation with the army at all costs, was widely misunderstood. So, for example, when he advised the students occupying the parliament building in May to disperse and return home lest confrontation occur, many saw this as a betrayal of the students. Abdurrahman's argument at the time was that the very large student gatherings were in danger of being infiltrated by *agents provocateurs*, a fear later proven to be well grounded. His greatest fear, he said, was that certain elements in the military would exploit the situation to engage in brutal repression of the students and other reform activists.

Although Abdurrahman's approach was consistent with his earlier policy of avoiding confrontation with the Armed Forces, many were highly critical of him for not supporting the student movement more strongly. Some even argued that NU had contributed little to the process of reformation that eventually toppled Suharto.

Ironically, the fall of Suharto and the sudden efflorescence of a myriad of new political parties dealt another blow to NU's credibility as an agent for political reform. Even before being made executive chairman of NU in December 1984, Abdurrahman had argued that NU needed to return to its original position as a *jamiyah diniyah*, a religious organization, meaning that it needed to return to its original charter and to turn away from party-political activity. In part this position was taken because reform-minded leaders in NU could see no benefit in being involved with PPP and taking part in the charade of Suharto-era "democracy." But the decision was styled as being much more than simply a pragmatic one and Abdurrahman and many younger leaders argued that it was not healthy to have direct links between religion and party politics.

Consequently, the emergence of a plethora of new political parties vying to represent NU, eventually coalescing into one very large party, PKB, came as something of a shock and even a disappointment to Abdurrahman and other like-minded liberals within NU. For many years Abdurrahman had argued strongly against all forms of sectarianism in politics and of the use of religion for party-political purposes, indeed, this was the main reason he gave for opposing ICMI (Ikatan Cendekiawan Muslimin Indonesia—the Association of Muslim Intellectuals) and it represented the cornerstone of his approach to politics.

When President Suharto lavishly backed the formation of ICMI in December 1990, including bestowing upon it the patronage of Senior Minister B.J. Habibie, Abdurrahman was both alarmed by its potential to divide Indonesian society and cynical about Suharto's motives. He saw in the President's new eagerness for rapprochement with conservative Islam a willingness to put personal political expediency ahead of social harmony. It was this that led him, together with Djohan Effendi and a broad cross section of community leaders, including a number of Chinese, to establish the ginger group, Forum Demokrasi, in the following year.

The Emergence of PKB

The emergence of PKB, however, left him, and many others with something of a dilemma. Other liberals, however, such as Nurcholish Madjid, argued that it was only natural, and indeed desirable, that the largely poor and long-suffering masses who made up the bulk of NU's membership should have a party of their own, and at least in the short term. In the end it was clear that it was fruitless to oppose the formation of PKB and that the important thing was that the new party should be inclusive, liberal and non-elitist in character. While these principles were broadly agreed upon and became the stated position of PKB, many younger people within NU were disillusioned by these developments.

Further adding to this disillusionment was the re-emergence of anti-Modernist sentiment within NU and PKB. In particular, the failure to forge an interim alliance with PAN troubled many younger people within NU who feared that the optimism expressed by those setting their hope on a NU-PDI Perjuangan alliance was dangerously naive. While many shared Abdurrahman's apprehension about whether PAN leader Amien Rais had really undergone a profound personal transformation and become a genuine liberal, they argued that many of the leading figures within PAN were liberals of sound credentials. Moreover, PAN's policy-platform, they pointed out, mirrored the values of NU, making alliance, at least in the short-term, a genuinely desirable possibility. Moreover, they argued that there was a real risk that PKB and PDI Perjuangan by themselves may not gain sufficient votes in the 1999 general election to form government.

NU's Pursuit of the Middle Path

NU has displayed great flexibility and many liberal tendencies throughout its long history. Nevertheless, by the early 1980s the organization was rapidly ossifying, and was in danger of collapsing into obscurity and irrelevance under the weight of endemic conservatism. Abdurrahman Wahid and his fellow reformists such as Kiai Achmad Siddiq were able to work a gradual but profound reformation within NU, both in terms of theological thinking and its social application. They did this by expanding the intellectual horizons of several new generations of NU members and *ulama*, and by encouraging them to combine modern western learning with traditional Islamic scholarship in a way which equipped them to respond meaningfully to the challenges of modernity. In previous years it had often been suggested that the liberalism of Abdurrahman Wahid and his friends was an elite phenomenon not widely accepted within the organization.

In an organization full of charismatic, eccentric figures Abdurrahman Wahid still manages to stand out as one of NU's most enigmatic figures. NU itself has been consistently criticized throughout its history for being accommodationist and even opportunistic because of the ways in which it adapts to the prevailing political circumstances. Defenders of NU retort by explaining that the organization's prime goal has always been improving the welfare of its members and protecting their liberty to follow the convictions of their hearts without interference from government or other sources. Even during the 1950s and 60s when it was a political party, they point out, it remained a religious organization. Another element in NU's character and behavior is that it follows traditional Sunni Muslim practice of seeking a middle way in resolving political and social problems and of avoiding harm even if that means engaging in compromise. Through the late 1960s into the 70s the organization had become rather moribund not least because of poor management.

When Abdurrahman Wahid was swept to the leadership of NU in 1984 there was an understanding that his election gave him a mandate for the reform of the organization so that, in the eyes of some at least, it might be saved from a slow but certain death. And indeed over the fifteen years of his leadership Abdurrahman Wahid was a significant force for reform both within Nahdlatul Ulama and within wider society. Throughout the 1990s he was a bold critic of President Suharto and resisted all efforts to be manipulated into supporting Suharto's rapprochement with Islam through ICMI. His detractors respond to this by saying that he has been a very inconsistent critic of the government, seeking accommodation with it when it suited and resisting it when it did not. Indeed, in recent years the strongest criticisms of Abdurrahman have concerned his initiatives in negotiating rapprochement with the Suharto regime. In late 1996 he met with the President and they shook hands after several years of open conflict between the two men. Then, not long afterwards, he invited the President's eldest daughter Tutut to join him on a tour of NU branches, where before large crowds he introduced her as "somebody of great importance" and "possibly one of the nation's future leaders" and therefore somebody the organization needed to come to know. Many of his old critics saw this as a clear case of once again selling out and opportunistically choosing his own way of negotiating compromise with the regime. Even his supporters were in large measure baffled and perplexed by the strange turn of events. Nevertheless, Abdurrahman himself described what had happened as being "a remarkable political bargain."

As an individual and as an organization Abdurrahman Wahid and Nahdlatul Ulama had been up against the wall and had come very close to open confrontation with the government and with ABRI, confrontation that may well have destroyed them both. In those circumstances, Abdurrahman Wahid argued, he had no choice but to sue for peace. The fact that peace came at such a relatively low price, he maintained, meant that he and the organization had procured a great victory.

In support of this view it is significant that Abdurrahman was uncharacteristically careful in choosing his words to talk about Tutut. Never at any stage, he argues, did he voice support for either her or father or family in political pursuits, rather he was merely noting the fact that she was an important person on the national scene and somebody that the organization needed to know. In time, many within NU came to accept this. Nevertheless, some of his supporters and erstwhile allies outside of the organization remained skeptical. The problem was compounded by his apparent desertion of Megawati.

In early 1996 Abdurrahman had supported Megawati as leader of PDI but then by the end of that year, following the infamous July storming of the PDI headquarters and subsequent rioting in the national capital, he appeared to have abandoned her. Abdurrahman's response to this is that he had always desired to support Megawati but had warned her in early 1996 to avoid confrontation with Suharto, and to pull back because there was little to be gained from pushing on but that she had neglected this advice. Moreover, he had not abandoned her, he argued, rather he had simply recognized that there was no point in making a public alliance when Suharto was so strongly entrenched. In fact, if he and Megawati and, as many had asked, Amien Rais had come together in a formal, open alliance it would have led to a severe backlash from the regime. By way of supporting this he tells of how when a senior General questioned him as to the nature of the alliance between Megawati, Amien Rais, and Abdurrahman, he replied that there was an informal understanding to work together but nothing was formalized. At this point the general reportedly replied, "well that's good because if there was a formal alliance we would be obliged to crush it."

More recently Abdurrahman once again confounded his critics, and even his supporters, by meeting with former President Suharto, shortly after a meeting with interim President Habibie. This was done, he explained, in the context of a push for what he calls national reconciliation. And involved a series of meetings of high-profile leaders, politicians and public intellectuals in order to avert the way conflict and rising violence threatened to envelop the nation. He explained his meeting with the former president to reporters very carefully, saying that there was still a danger that many people could act out of a sense of loyal support to the former President even though they received no direct orders from Suharto and that driven by such a sense of loyalty they could engage in acts of violence and the provocation of violence.

What he had in mind very clearly were the "mysterious" killings in Banyuwangi, East Java. Abdurrahman Wahid did not make clear whether he thought Suharto had been directly involved or if it was simply a case of his loyal supporters second-guessing his intentions and desires. But he did make it clear that his meeting with Suharto in late 1998 was an effort to find a circuit breaker to avoid further violence and confrontation. Interestingly, this time Abdurrahman's actions met reasonably quickly with acceptance from other leaders such as Amien Rais who accepted his push for national reconciliation. Abdurrahman Wahid added to this in December 1998 by holding an open house for twenty days during the Ramadan fasting month which was followed by a period of open house at the house of President Habibie. The notion being that members of society from whatever level or whatever unity could approach him and President Habibie to vent their concerns and grievances so that hopefully some solutions might be found. All in all this process appears to have been reasonably successful.

So how then does one explain Abdurrahman's behavior? The first point to make is that he styles himself as a democrat and a liberal in all of his writing and in his public comments and private discussions. More importantly in his actions he consistently gives weight to this assertion. Moreover, while much of his behavior is baffling and enigmatic it is certainly reasonable to take the interpretation that he is searching for a middle way, giving a higher priority to conflict resolution through compromise than to the esoteric notion of theological purity in politics. Whilst very much opposed to the use of religion for party political purposes Abdurrahman has excellent political instincts and well understands the demands of realpolitik. Certainly in recent years there is much evidence to support the view that Abdurrahman as a significant influence for moderation, for reconciliation and for avoiding conflict. That he had a charismatic aura of authority within the organization has been put to good use and is clearly evident in the way in which he steered Nahdlatul Ulama away from confrontation and inter-communal tensions and towards the peaceful resolution of tensions. Even in his support of PKB there is evidence to suggest that he was steering the new party away from sectarianism towards a more open and inclusive nationalism.

Muhammadiyah, Pan, and Amien Rais

Muhammadiyah's Moderate Orientation

Muhammadiyah is undoubtedly one of the most significant organizations in the Muslim world. While not quite as large as Nahdlatul Ulama it is easily larger than any other Islamic organization outside Indonesia. Moreover, it is the single most successful example of Islamic Modernism worked out in organizational form. Its success is not just limited to its membership, numbers or its scale of operation. Equally significantly it has been successful in maintaining something of the original spirit of Islamic Modernism and not, as an organization, degenerating into the kind of reactionary Islamism, found among similar organizations in other countries.

It can be argued that Muhammadiyah lost much of its intellectual momentum over the course of the twentieth century, no doubt largely because it has tended to neglect religious education in favor of secular education and to neglect religious initiatives and activities in favor of practical endeavors, such as the running of schools, orphanages, and hospitals.

Nevertheless there is much about Muhammadiyah that remains true to the original Modernist vision. It continues to take a positive view of the future and to eschew backward looking fixations with a long lost "golden age." It continues to be positive about development, provided that it is done in an equitable fashion, and positive about modern technology, science, and learning, provided that they are used in a moral and ethical fashion. Moreover, Muhammadiyah continues to support the notion of individual interpretation through *ijtihad* giving primacy to the authority of the Qur'an, and to a lesser extent the Hadith when interpreted according to one's conscience and according to sound principles rather than blind submission to the orthodoxy of preceding generations.

Just as significantly, however, Muhammadiyah retains the original Modernist vision of an inclusivistic approach to life in modern society and an acceptance that pluralism is part of society and as a consequence political authority must be shared. To some extent, the experience of Masyumi in the 1950s and in the frustration of the former Masyumi leaders in the 1960s and 70s has lead to Muhammadiyah being a more moderate and politically quiescent organization. This quiescence has come about, in part because of necessity, but also too because it is in accordance with the original Modernist vision that gives greater importance to improving society than it does to political campaigns.

Muhammadiyah's record of engagement with other groups and society since its formation in 1912 has been remarkably consistent. While it is true that many associated with Muhammadiyah, involved in their own campaigns, both political and ideological, which have emphasized an extremely conservative, if not reactionary side of Modernist thought, the organization itself has never supported such views. Instead Muhammadiyah has always had good relations with its neighbors, although at times they have been somewhat strained particularly in the case of its relationship with Nahdlatul Ulama. Nevertheless it has proven itself more than able to negotiate practi-

cal matters such as schooling or healthcare in conjunction with Christian and other groups in Indonesian society.

Amien Rais's Record of Extremism

Whereas Muhammadiyah's record is relatively unblemished and
unambiguous, the same cannot be said for its erstwhile leader Amien
Rais. While a popular leader of Muhammadiyah for many years until
his resignation in the middle of 1998, when he left to take up leadership of the new political party PAN, the former chairman of
Muhammadiyah has not necessarily reflected the views of the organization in every respect. Amien's popularity derives from his charisma and force of character, both of which are in short supply in
Muhammadiyah. In an organization that, relative to its size, is lacking in significant public intellectuals and fiery personalities Amien
stood out as a figure of whom the rank and file could be proud if for
nothing else than for his prominence and increasingly bold outspokenness.

Nevertheless many in the organization expressed disquiet over
Amien's frequently provocative statements. Others expressed apprehension and concern over Amien's enthusiastic involvement in
ICMI, either because they felt that Suharto was using him as a political instrument, or because they feared it would lead to increased
sectarianism. Still others pointed to some of Amien's companions
and the circles in which he moved, and in particular expressed concern about his connections with Dewan Dakwah and KISDI personalities. Those who held such concerns, both within Muhammadiyah
and without, referred to his not infrequent outbursts and public statements that smacked of racism, prejudice and ignorance.

For example, Media Dakwah the periodical published by Dewan
Dakwah ran an article against American academic William Liddle
claiming that he was part of a Jewish conspiracy seeking to undermine the interests of Islam in Indonesia and around the world. Amien
Rais in public referred to Liddle as a "stinking Jew." Some years
later he sought to retract that statement claiming that he had been
misquoted and had merely called Liddle a "stinking American"! The
evidence in support of the earlier version however, is difficult to
refute. And certainly if Amien were concerned about being linked
with anti-Semitism he then would have been concerned about his
colleagues in Dewan Dakwah and KISDI who not infrequently spoke

of threats to Islam in the form of Jewish conspiracies, anti-Islamic business groups and secret plans to Christianize Indonesia.

PAN's Secular/Moderate Modernist Coalition

In the weeks after the fall of the Suharto regime attention quickly turned from the euphoria of being able to speak out against the abuses and corruption of the old regime to the question of what came next. It was widely recognized that it would not be possible to organize an election during 1998 because of the extent of legislative and political reforms that were required before an election could be held. For example, the Suharto regime had permitted the existence of only three political parties, Golkar, PDI, and PPP, and time would be required to establish new parties to contest elections, to organize campaigns and to revise election procedures and rules. Even though the interim Habibie government did not move as quickly as might have been hoped to overturn the legislation of Suharto's regime with respect to elections, including permitting the formation of new political parties, this did not stop a variety of groups from moving ahead with plans for party formation. Literally within weeks of the Suharto regime collapsing there was news of plans for dozens of new political parties, and by the end of 1998 over eighty new political parties had been formed.

Admittedly, it was clear from the outset that many of these new parties would never go on to claim a large share of the votes but that only a few had the potential to become major parties. Some of the new parties were very predictable, for example it was fully expected that either the coup that had ousted Megawati from PDI would be reversed and Megawati would be reinstated as leader of PDI or else Megawati's PDI would become in effect the new PDI and the old Suharto regime PDI would quickly fade from view. This is exactly what happened, with Megawati's party forced to adopt the name PDI-Perjuangan (the PDI of the Struggle) to distinguish itself from the old PDI. Similarly, it was not all that surprising that a party was formed to represent the interests of Nahdlatul Ulama.

There was considerable speculation that Muhammadiyah might do the same and that Muhammadiyah, or even a new Masyumi, might emerge on the political scene to represent the interests of Modernist Muslims. What happened instead was that Partai Amanat National was formed. On the face of it, it might appear as if PAN is simply the

Modernist Muslim equivalent PKB, in other words the "Muhammadiyah political party." In fact the reality is rather more complex. From the outset PAN, was formed as a non-sectarian cross-communal party. Moreover it set itself up as a non-elitist party aiming to get the support of all sections of Indonesian society. The various constituent elements contributing to the party's formation come from a broad spectrum of Indonesian society. Nevertheless, Modernist Muslims do tend to predominate and even those who don't come from that background are largely middle-class and urban, suggesting from the outset that PAN would struggle to gain votes in the rural areas where seventy percent of Indonesians live.

Whether even urban voters would pay a great deal of attention to PAN's policy position was a further area of uncertainty even though policy formulation appeared to be one of the party's strengths. Indeed the policy platform of PAN was arguably altogether more complete, more clearly articulated and more unambiguously liberal than that of any of the other political parties, including PDI Perjuangan and PKB. Some of Indonesia's best secular nationalist figures as well as some of its leading liberal Muslim thinkers contributed to the formation of PAN and not all of the Muslim figures came from the Modernist side of the Ummat.

For example a number of younger Nahdlatul Ulama people made a significant contribution to the formulation of PAN and the elaboration of the PAN platform.[6] Another leading figure associated with PAN, although not formally a member, was Gunawan Mohamad, editor of Tempo magazine (banned by the Suharto regime in 1994). While Tempo's and Gunawan's linkages with Modernist Muslims have always been strong nevertheless he was generally seen as belonging more to the *abangan*, or "secular Muslim" position. Gunawan declared that he would not formally join PAN because he believed that as the editor of a major newsmagazine it was best that he had no partisan linkages. Nevertheless he remained closely involved in its formation.

Given the range of liberal figures involved with PAN it is perhaps somewhat surprisingly that in the end the figures behind PAN sought to woo Amien Rais to become its chairman. In fact, it seems from the outset that Amien Rais was their favorite choice for chairman. In many ways this seems incongruous given Amien's background and known penchant for extremist utterances and conservative if not reactionary views. Clearly, the principal figures behind PAN decided that for PAN to have any success in becoming a major political force it would need a significant and well-known charismatic leader with a national reputation. Seen in this light, Amien was the obvious choice, all the more so, given his drift to the canter since mid-1996, and his willingness to admit to having been wrong.

Putting aside for the moment, the question of Amien, it is worth considering the potential of PAN to contribute to Indonesian politics. PAN's major weakness has already been alluded to; namely that it is a largely urban and middle-class party and that it is not at all clear how this can translate into political success outside the major cities. This was demonstrated very clearly in the results of the June general elections with PAN gaining little more than 7 percent of the overall vote. This was a deeply disappointing result for PAN and confirmed that the party has yet to establish a major presence outside of the major cities. Nevertheless, in the longer run it is possible for PAN to gradually turn this result around. PAN's biggest rivals politically will be PKB and PDI Perjuangan. PKB will compete with PAN in securing Muslim votes particular in the rural areas, and not just from traditionalist Muslims. It is likely that many *abangan* Muslims will consider choosing PAN over PKB or PDI Perjuangan depending upon the credibility of the latter two parties during the first post-Habibie government. In terms of their natural constituencies however, PAN will be competing directly with PDI Perjuangan, that is appealing not just to *santri* Muslims but to *abangan* secularists and Democrats from an urban and middle-class background.

Amien's Journey to the Middle

Many people even today mistakenly believe that Amien Rais comes from the region of Aceh in North Sumatra, where people are known to be frank and outspoken. In fact Amien Rais comes from the central Javanese royal city of Solo, also known as Surakarta. The reason that Amien's identity is often mistaken is that his manner seems at odds with the stereotypical image of the Central Javanese. Amien has long been known as somebody who "shoots from the hip," who is outspoken, and who expresses what is on his mind, in the plainest of terms. Moreover, he has also long been known as somebody who, even within Muhammadiyah circles represents a more conservative, or even reactionary, position than the mainstream.

Like many Muhammadiyah people, in fact like the majority of Muhammadiyah leaders and intellectuals, Amien grew up studying very little classical Islamic scholarship and learning little Arabic. His basic education was essentially secular although, as is typical in Muhammadiyah families, it included basic religious instruction but not of the kind that afforded him an in depth understanding or insight into Islamic thought. This contrasts strongly with the experience of the majority of traditionalist Muslims who are members of Nahdlatul Ulama. Most NU members are schooled for at least several years in a *pesantren,* where they learn not only fluency in classical or Qur'anic Arabic but also study basic commentaries, Sufi texts and other classical works which gives them an insight into the complexities and shades of gray involved in Islamic scholarship.

Given his previously anti-Western demeanor, some people are surprised to learn that Amien was educated in the West and received a Ph.D in political science from the University of Chicago. Most Indonesians with Western Ph.Ds develop considerable admiration for the society in which they undertake their postgraduate studies and return to Indonesia with a new degree of sophistication and complexity to their thought. Indeed this is the very reason that the Department of Religious Affairs encourages bright young IAIN students to complete Masters and PhD studies abroad, so that they will return home as sophisticated and nuanced thinkers with an appreciation of modern "western society." Amien was in Chicago at the same time as liberal thinker Nurcholish Madjid who was also doing his PhD at the University of Chicago.

By all accounts though, Amien, unlike Nurcholish, did not avail himself of the opportunities to mix more broadly and learn about American society. Whereas Nurcholish travelled widely across the U.S. and mixed with a broad range of people, Amien reportedly kept to himself and concentrated on his studies. To the extent that he was involved at all in the local communities, he mixed mainly in Muslim student circles. Whereas Nurcholish developed a deep and abiding affection for America, even today Amien continues to be rather cynical at best about the U.S. and the West in general.

Since 1997, however, Amien has undertaken a number of international visits and conference appearances and has been unusually open and warm to the national media. Where not that long ago he was a man with a reputation for being impatient with foreign jour-

nalists and scholars he has suddenly become almost warm and wel-
coming. Moreover, he now styles himself as a liberal thinker who
appreciates the plural nature of modern Indonesian society and recognizes the need for working cooperatively with all groups across
society.

Consequently, we have two Amien's, the "new Amien" and the
"old Amien," how can this be explained? Even Amien himself uses
the language of "undergoing a conversion" to explain the transition
between the "old Amien" and the "new Amien." Perhaps even more
surprising is the fact that Amien's explanation has an air of credibility about it. He describes himself as having previously moved in
very narrow circles and not having had much practical exposure to
other groups in Indonesian society, much less the broader world. He
explains how in recent years, as he began to deal with the other
groups in society and began to understand in a global sense the
problems facing Indonesia, he developed a new appreciation for the
diverse nature of Indonesian society. He occasionally even uses
phrases of himself such as "well I saw the light, I changed, I was
wrong, now I understand."

Nevertheless, Amien still carries the burden of suspicion against
him. Many people remain yet to be convinced that the "new Amien"
is anything more than the "old Amien" with new clothing. Even so,
many others are prepared to publicly take him at face value, while
privately reserving judgment, on the basis that his current role in
Indonesian society is so important that to alienate him or cut him off
would be counterproductive to the process of reform. This approach
is also shaped by the fact that many judge PAN to be, on the whole,
a liberal minded party with a clear, democratic agenda for reform
and that whatever their personal reservations it makes sense to work
with Amien. Still, it is important for us to ask the question if Amien
has changed why was this so and what does it mean? At the very
least we need chart his personal journey and try to put it in some
broader context.

It is only fair to Amien to acknowledge the fact that he had a long
history of being outspokenly critical of the Suharto regime. Consequently to dismiss him as a latecomer to the reformist cause (like so
many other members of the Jakarta elite, including members of ICMI)
is to ignore his earlier history of courageously railing against the
regime. Indeed, it was precisely because Amien stood at the locus of

Islamist or right wing Islamic criticism of the regime that Suharto targeted Amien and his circle in his grand move towards rapprochement with the formation of ICMI in December 1990. Suharto, through Habibie and ICMI, sought to court Amien and his friends to bring them on side. For his part it would be wrong to say that Amien was easily convinced of Suharto's good intentions. Nevertheless he saw an opportunity for Islamising Indonesian society from within, through the opportunity presented by ICMI. In particular he saw an opportunity to change the culture of the technocratic and bureaucratic classes through a sophisticated modern organization like ICMI with the ear of the government and the clear backing of Senior Minister Habibie and the President himself. In other words, (and this is precisely the expression sometimes used), "ICMI could be a Trojan horse," the main thing was that the regime was transformed and that if it could not be transformed from without, then let it be transformed from within.

Amien was made chairman of the board of experts that directed ICMI and worked closely with B. J. Habibie. During the first half of the decade Amien appeared essentially happy with the opportunities afforded by ICMI. Adding to a sense of momentum, the formation of ICMI coincided with a resurgence of interest in Islam in Indonesian society. Consequently ICMI was able to ride the wave of increasing interest in Islam and displays of piety, particularly among previously rather nominally Islamic members of Jakarta's upper middle classes, including the governing elite.

It is clear that for the first five or six years the relationship was mutually beneficial. Suharto had bought off his old critics and the Islamists, for their part, felt that whatever compromises were involved in working with the government they were greatly outweighed by the opportunities. Then in 1996 things began to go wrong. Some speculate that following the death of his wife Ibu Tien in April that year Suharto's judgment began to show signs of significant impairment. Certainly, his order to storm the Jakarta PDI headquarters occupied by supporters loyal to the ousted Megawati in July 1996 was widely seen to have been a grave mistake. The use of organized thugs followed by heavy-handed police intervention was widely seen as being excessive and the fact that it gave rise to the worst rioting in Jakarta in decades, added to the view that Suharto's normally excellent political instinct was slipping.

This point appears to mark the beginning of Amien's recent dis-
enchantment with Suharto. Towards the end of the year he began to
speak out against various abuses occurring in Indonesia. In particular he highlighted what he saw as endemic corruption and poor management in the Freeport mining contract. Amien visited the Freeport
mine in West Papua and on his return reported that "ninety percent
of the wealth" under the current contractual arrangements was being expatriated, and that the remaining ten percent was going largely
to "a couple of families" with the result that little benefit came to the
nation as a whole. Not surprisingly, given the reference to "a couple
of families," Suharto was furious with Amien.

Amien was warned through Habibie to tone down his language.
His response, true to form, was that he became even more outspoken. Finally, Suharto is reported to have had a heated session with
Habibie demanding that Amien be sacked. Habibie then confronted
Amien and Amien finally tendered his resignation from ICMI's Board
of Experts. If Suharto felt, however, that this was the way in which
Amien would be kept quiet and the problem dealt with, he was very
wrong indeed. Whereas in the early 1990s his ICMI plan to buy out
a small group of noisy critics had succeeded brilliantly, the ousting
of Amien resulted not just in Amien becoming even more outspoken
but also in the entire body of Muhammadiyah openly questioning
the approach taken by the president.

Perhaps if Suharto had been able to remove Amien from influence within Muhammadiyah, as indeed he had often been able to do
deftly and skillfully in the past with other organizations in Indonesia, he might have been able to emasculate Amien. As it happened,
however, from the beginning of 1997 Amien was brazenly critical
of the Suharto regime in a manner that inspired increased public
support.

For the first time in many years, activists, students, and other critics of the government began to speak openly of the potential for a
coalition between Megawati Soekarnoputri, Abdurrahman Wahid and
Amien Rais. By this point Amien had, at least in the eyes of the
general public, clearly entered the ranks of the reformers.

For his part, however, when questioned about the potential for a
coalition between Megawati, Amien and himself Abdurrahman
Wahid was consistently evasive. In private, he explained that there
were two obstacles to such an alliance. Firstly, he recounted how he

had been clearly warned by elements within the military that a formal three-cornered alliance between these three high-profile public critics of the regime would meet with swift and decisive repression from the military.

The second reason given by Abdurrahman Wahid for his reluctance to enter an open alliance with Amien was Amien's personal background. He argued that Amien's history of narrow and reactionary comments against certain sections of Indonesian society, such as the Christians or the Chinese and, indeed, his public endorsement of Islamist conspiracy theories involving Jewish bankers and so forth, left him with a serious credibility problem: "it is very hard for people to forget all the things that Amien has said." As a result, Abdurrahman Wahid noted, many non-Muslims do not trust Amien and even many traditionalist Muslims feel uncomfortable with his views. Even the possibility that Amien may have undergone some degree of conversion, Abdurrahman argued, did not completely ameliorate these concerns, indeed if Amien was to convince people that he had truly changed it would take considerable effort and quite a bit of time. Given this, it was not possible for him to form an open alliance with Amien.

Critics of Abdurrahman, including even those who admired him point out that there was a considerable degree of personal animosity between the two men. Consequently, it is difficult to separate Abdurrahman's objective judgment of Amien from his personal antipathy towards him. Whatever the case, it certainly remained true that many non-Muslims and many traditional Muslims felt a great distrust for Amien and even with clear and decisive leadership from Abdurrahman Wahid this cannot be easily overcome. Nevertheless, Amien greatly strengthened his credentials as a reformist when in the early part of 1998 he continued to speak out against the Suharto regime, calling for Suharto's resignation at a time when it appeared that both Megawati Soekarnoputri and Abdurrahman Wahid had gone to ground.[7]

Amien became a critical figure leading many activists, particularly students, to move against the Suharto government. He, in the eyes of many, is perhaps the single most outstanding reformist figure. As a result, many of those who had been earlier critical of Amien were prepared to give him a new degree of support. At the very least, they argued, it is necessary to work with Amien since he more than ever represents a large part of the community.

At the same time, even within Amien's own circle, it was clear that a degree of transformation was occurring. A number of liberal-minded Muslims who had good relations with Amien sought to encourage him to shift from the right to the center. Amien is said to have responded at one point in mid 1998 by saying that he did not realize his potential to be a statesman on a larger stage or to represent a much larger constituency. It appears that this new vision dawned on Amien rather slowly. On the one hand he was clearly reluctant to sever his ties with the Islamist Right, on the other hand he could see there was conceivable scope for broader political involvement through taking the middle path. In the end what proved decisive was the formation of PAN.

At the time that PAN was formed, Amien had confirmed in writing to the leaders of PPP that he was willing to take up leadership of PPP. This went on the public record and it was widely known that Amien was joining forces with PPP. Consequently, Amien's ascension to the leadership of PPP was regarded as a foregone conclusion. Presumably had Amien become chairman of PPP, PPP would have vied to get the backing of a large section of Muhammadiyah members but by no means would they have been guaranteed of obtaining broad Muhammadiyah support. Some may have perceived PPP to be too narrow and too sectarian to appeal to them. More importantly, PPP under Amien, would very likely have been an essentially communal party appealing to conservative Muslim voters.

At the eleventh hour, however, those close to Amien who possessed a broader and more liberal vision than his own and were involved in establishing PAN were able to persuade him that he personally, and PAN as a party, had a greater future if he should take the PAN chairmanship. By all accounts, even at the very last moment Amien oscillated between going with his agreed leadership of PPP or taking up the chairmanship of PAN. In the end of course, he chose PAN. He explained this decision as being a decision to move to the center of Indonesian politics and represent a non-elitist, non-communal party. Even so much of the backing for PAN came from Modernist Muslims most of whom are members of Muhammadiyah. Despite working hard to present itself as a non-communal party it is not at all clear whether it succeeded in gaining a significant amount of the Chinese Christian and *Abangan* vote.

Since becoming chairman of PAN, Amien has increased his efforts to sell himself as a reformed character, somebody with a new understanding and new vision. While occasionally he shows signs of visible annoyance when asked about his past views, on the whole he has done a credible job of selling his new image. Nevertheless, some worries remained. Not least of these have to do with occasions when, even after announcing his former position and even subsequent to his taking up of the leadership of PAN he has made statements which hark back to his previous sectarian views. For example on a trip to Malaysia in 1998 he spoke once again of the problem of Jewish conspiracies, although when questioned about this he later denied having made such comments. As is to be expected a cloud of doubt remains over Amien personally as to the degree of genuine reform that has occurred.

What is perhaps most interesting about PAN and Amien Rais is not the question about whether Amien has genuinely repented of his previous position and changed his views or, as it were, has undergone a conversion and become a liberal but, rather, the extent to which his own views, whatever they might be, will be given any scope at all within PAN. There is good reason to believe that whatever the change of heart that Amien has experienced as an individual, that as chairman of PAN he must continue to espouse a liberal non-sectarian view.

Hard-Line Islamists and Regional Unrest

Muhammadiyah's "Right Wing"

Muhammadiyah is essentially a moderate organization and certainly, in its stated position, consistently supports the Pancasila doctrine of the modern Indonesian state, with its emphasis on pluralism and the acceptance of difference. Nevertheless, like any large organization, Muhammadiyah represents a spectrum of opinion. Muhammadiyah has what might be called a right wing, a grouping of conservative or reactionary Modernist Muslims who push for issues which the organization as a whole has long since renounced. For example, there are still some people within Muhammadiyah, though admittedly not many, who openly speak of the need to strengthen Islam's legisled status within the Indonesian state. For them the example of Malaysia, where Islam is the official religion of the state, represents a desirable model to follow. Normally, however, such opinions are articulated in circles other than Muhammadiyah itself. Even so, some of the people who are involved in the more radical Islamic Modernist organizations continue to remain members of Muhammadiyah.

A good example is, or was, the old Amien Rais. Amien had close contacts, as was noted above, with more conservative groups such as Dewan Dakwah while at the same time, continuing to lead Muhammadiyah. To some extent, this could be explained in terms of his involvement with ICMI. Even so Amien seemed naturally drawn to a more conservative group of thinkers and activists. There are a number of Muhammadiyah members who moved in those same circles who continue to be involved in the organization though none so prominent as Amien Rais. To speak of Muhammadiyah's right wing is to recognize that at the extreme end of the spectrum some Muhammadiyah members are quite at odds with the mainstream Muhammadiyah outlook, but as a whole Muhammadiyah does not harbor a significant number of extremist thinkers.

Perhaps slightly more common, and in some ways, much more dangerous than the ideological right wing of Muhammadiyah are those whose political tactics and behavior cannot be nailed down to any one ideology but who have consistently employed right-wing extremist ideas for opportunistic political advantage. A good example of this was the late Lukman Harun. Lukman was an old foe of Amien and the two clashed frequently. It probably makes sense to put Lukman in a different category from Amien despite the fact that at one point in time anyway, both represented the political right of the organization.

In defense of Amien, it can be said that he has consistently displayed integrity in his thought and there is good reason to believe that his views are linked strongly to his political and ideological convictions. In the case of somebody such as Lukman Harun and his colleagues it is difficult to make the argument that they acted out of some intellectual integrity. Lukman was extremely radical in his pronouncements on some occasions but on other occasions was very compliant with the Suharto government. In many other respects too his behavior suggested that he was somebody who responded to political circumstances rather than being strongly driven by ideology.

During 1998 and 1999, up until his death in May 1999, Lukman spoke of supporting groups such as Pemuda Pancasila and other right-wing militant activist groups representing an extreme right position. Through his long career with Muhammadiyah, Lukman never showed any reluctance to invoke religious sentiment for his own advantage. In particular he has often spoken out against the danger of Christianization, frequently making the link between the Chinese and Christianization, and the danger of international Jewish banking conspiracies and other alleged Western endeavors to undermine the interests of Islam. In these matters he was clearly not an original thinker and was simply buying in to the prevailing rhetoric of Islamism around the world. It frequently suited him to set himself up against Amien Rais as either, in earlier years, being more loyal to the regime, or at other times, as being more critical of it, styling himself as representing the true values of Islam as opposed to those who are willing to compromise them.

Unfortunately, because there appeared to be few moral scruples involved in this political behavior and because the issues are often explosive the potential of such political actors within Muhammadiyah to do damage is still considerable. Nevertheless, it is important to recognize that this group represents a vocal minority. The mainstream of Muhammadiyah in fact seems to find such views distasteful in the extreme.

Dewan Dakwah, KISDI, and the New Islamic Parties

Muhammadiyah is not only Indonesia's second-largest Islamic organization but also the world's largest, and by that definition most successful, Modernist organization. It was established in 1912 and activities have focused increasingly around practical welfare, educational initiatives for schools, orphanages, hospitals, and more recently, universities. So because of its importance in Indonesian society it is not surprising that some within the organization will express more radical views and that the politics of the organization will attract a degree of fierce struggle on occasion.

On the whole though, when considering hard-line Islamists in the Indonesian context, one needs to look outside of Muhammadiyah and look at some of the smaller, single-issue organizations. It is significant that virtually without exception all extremist Muslim voices in Indonesia come from a Modernist background. There are, to be sure, some traditionalists who speak out on certain issues but it is rare for a traditionalist to adopt a truly radical position. The dominant ethos of Sunni traditionalism, is one of compromise and finding the middle path. Even within Muhammadiyah true radicals become frustrated with the mainstream conservatism of the organization. For example, the disgruntled former Masyumi leaders who maintained their rage against the Indonesian government throughout the 1970s and 80s, increasingly broke with Muhammadiyah and became active in separate organizations.

Perhaps the single most important organization is Dewan Dakwah. Dewan Dakwah was formed in the late 1960s by Muhammad Natsir as a result of his frustration with New Order government initiatives designed to so weaken Parmusi that Parmusi would be unable to serve as a channel for the political aspirations of the Masyumi generation. The name Dewan Dakwah literally means the Council of missionary activity. "Dakwah" is otherwise not a term commonly used in Indonesia. The notion of Dakwah is of working to strengthen the faith both of those outside the fold of believers, particularly of those who are lax in their faith. In practice the activities of Dewan Dakwah became increasingly concerned with pushing the convictions of Natsir and his colleagues about the need to form an Islamic state and to resist the attempts of the New Order government to water down the political vision of Islam Modernists.

Dewan Dakwah never attracted a large following as most of those who were involved in Masyumi tired of the political struggle and many in any case were not strongly convinced about what it meant to struggle for an Islamic state. So while most former Masyumi figures went on to become active in more mundane pursuits within Muhammadiyah, Muhammad Natsir and colleagues worked to maintain the political issues. Sadly Muhammad Natsir himself, who as young man was known to be quite a sophisticated and even liberal thinker, became increasingly bitter as he grew older. Moreover, some of his disciples, as is so often the case, became much more extreme than he was. As a result Dewan Dakwah today is frequently given to extremist and reactionary statements through its publication Media Dakwah.

To some extent, it is difficult to work out how much of this is theatrical posturing and how much of it is genuine conviction. Anecdotally it is interesting to note that some who have passed through

Dewan Dakwah as young people and become disillusioned as they grew older, speak of it as being the product of youthful romantic idealism. In other words those, at least, who leave the organization reflect on their experience as being born in part of ignorance and misunderstanding. Nevertheless there are no doubt some hard-liners within Dewan Dakwah who given the chance would promote sectarian violence to advance their objectives.

Sadly, there has been considerable evidence in recent years, that groups linked to extremist elements within Dewan Dakwah have been involved in encouraging groups of organized thugs or hooligans to agitate and provoke violence, to break-up meetings and generally disrupt the activities of those whom they regard as their political enemies. Prompted by the start of the Palestinian Intifadah in 1987, Muhammad Natsir met with like-minded friends to discuss what could be done within Indonesia to help the causes of Islamic groups around the world. As a result they decided set up "The Committee for Islamic Global Solidarity" better known by its Indonesian acronym KISDI. And it is in KISDI that we see the sharp edge of right-wing reactionary Islamist thought in Indonesia. While it is reassuring to know that those who associate themselves with KISDI represent a very small minority of Muslims in Indonesia and that the vast majority of Muslims, whether Modernist or traditionalist outlook, find the views of KISDI abhorrent, it is worrying to see the opportunities afforded such groups in the post Suharto renaissance of democratic parties.

It is significant to note that Yusril Mahendra, the leader of Partai Bulan Bintang, is widely viewed as being a charming, urbane and sophisticated figure. When questioned about his willingness to associate and to include in the ranks of his party leadership, people known for their sectarian views, he explains his behavior as being tactical in a move to try and win over the hard-liners. Nevertheless, a question mark must remain over Partai Bulan Bintang and so, too, with other similar parties such as Partai Keadilan, that are openly willing to link themselves not just with KISDI and Dewan Dakwah but with the use of force to advance the particular Islamist political agenda, even at the risk of considerable social disharmony and violence.

Whatever the real ideological position of PBB there seemed to be little doubt that Golkar could count on its support when it came to forming a coalition. In an interview with the *Van Zorge Report* in

January 1999, M.S. Kaban, Secretary General of PBB and close con-
fidant of Yusril Mahendra, confirmed that PBB had no problems in
forming an alliance with Golkar, saying that: "If they can agree with
us concerning the priorities of our struggle, then we can work together."[8] Given the background of Yusril Mahendra this is hardly
surprising. Yusril is known to be a close friend of BJ Habibie and is
employed by him as a special assistant to the president's office. Under
Suharto Yusril worked for a number of years in the Secretariat of
State where, among other things, he wrote speeches for the president. He was rewarded for his efforts by being made a professor in
law at the University of Indonesia.[9] He continued his presidential
speech writing duties under President Habibie.

While PBB is certainly politically conservative it appears that it is
also relatively moderate. In the same interview MS. Kaban responded
to the question of "How does Indonesia need to change to become
the ideal system for an Islamic party?" by asserting: "One thing is
certain, we are not bringing up the issue of an Islamic state. We
don't want to go there. We still acknowledge the Pancasila as the
national consensus of all the groups in Indonesia. We don't want to
get trapped with the image of a state being ruled by Islamic law."[10]

Acehenese Separatism

One of the areas of concern that is frequently raised with regard
to the political and social future of Indonesia is the problem of regional unrest and the desire on the part of some, at least, for independence. The question of separatism though, seems to be very much
overstated. While it is clear now that East Timor is likely to be independent or at the very least enjoy an extreme form of autonomy
from Jakarta it is by no means clear that Indonesia faces a Balkans
scenario. It is difficult, for example, to conceive of West Papua breaking away from Indonesia. If the eastern half of the island is barely
viable despite the years of monetary and human aid that New Guinea
has received, it is hard to conceive how the western half, West Papua,
can possibly have an independent future. And yet there is no denying that there is considerable antipathy towards Jakarta on the ground.
Similarly, in Ambon and their eastern islands there is strong antagonism towards Jakarta just as there is a degree in Sulawesi. Perhaps
the most extreme case though, is Aceh on the northern tip of the
island of Sumatra.

Aceh has a long history of antipathy to Jakarta and Batavia before that. It was only very late in the colonial history that the Dutch succeeded in bringing Aceh under their control. Even then it occurred at great cost with considerable loss of life and a great deal of uncertainty about the level of practical control the administration Batavia had over the province of Aceh. Through the Sukarno Old Order period there were murmurings of a desire in many regions to separate from the new Indonesian state. Such murmurings, however, even in Aceh failed to produce credible separatist movements.

The botched PRRI rebellions in West Sumatra and South Sulawesi in 1958 represented the high water mark of separatist endeavors. During the Suharto regime, ironically it is the pace of economic development, which has once again inflamed tensions between the center and Aceh on the periphery. The exploitation of significant oil and natural gas fields off the East coast of Aceh has lead to considerable anger on the part of the Acehenese that more of the wealth has not been repatriated and reinvested in the province.

Because of this brooding antipathy, Jakarta responded by stationing large numbers of troops in the Acehenese province. The result of this throughout the Suharto regime was a series of human rights abuses and ongoing political repression by violent means through intimidation and organized terrorism which have left deep scars on the psyche of the Acehenese people. It is not at all surprising, then, that as more and more evidence of these abuses has come to light in the post-Suharto period, Acehenese anger is once again boiling over. This was particularly so during the period of interregnum after the fall of Suharto when ABRI/TNI seemed unsure of its place or role in Indonesian society. Tragically, the circle of violence was constantly repeated in Aceh. As local resentment boiled over into demonstrations and into symbolic gestures of resistance, military presence was stepped up and terrorists hunted down, justice is enforced by the armies in a harsh fashion and the resentment increases waiting for an opportunity to boil over again. Throughout 1999 the activities of ABRI troops in north Aceh in rounding up separatist so-called terrorists led to greatly inflamed tensions in the region.

Adding to the sense of tension and brooding danger in the Acehenese situation is the fact that the Acehenese historically have been fiercely proud of their ethnic identity and have seen a strict observance of Islam and pervasive piety as being evidence of the strength of Acehenese character. As a consequence, the Acehenese express their ethnic nationalist sentiment in religious terms. For centuries Aceh has been referred to as the verandah of Mecca suggesting that Aceh is the place in Indonesia closest to the conservative orthodox world of the Middle East. In some ways of course this stereotypical picture is quite mistaken, because Acehenese Islam is still markedly different than Middle Eastern Islam. Nevertheless because of the link between religious sentiment and expression and ethno-nationalist sentiment the religious imagery in Aceh has often been reactionary and extremist even if the practice of Islam in personal lives does not matched the imagery. Given this, it is not surprising that many observers are fearful of what will happen in Aceh.

The formation of a national identity in the Indonesian psyche and the level of practical interaction and engagement in the New Order state have been highly successful in creating among younger Indonesians at least a strong sense of Indonesian identity. Much as young Europeans are more inclined to see themselves as European as much as they are French, German or whatever, so too, but even more so, young Indonesians increasingly see themselves as Indonesians first and as Chinese, Malay, or Javanese second. Increasingly intermarriage and interaction and geographical mobility have added to this feeling. To some extent, however, it has been undermined by the rate of out migration from Java to the outer islands and the dominance of Javanese migrants in the local business and the civil service and government.

East Timor—A Case of Religious and Ethnic Violence?

In terms of the sheer scale of numbers the most significant outbreak of violence in the Republic of Indonesia in the late 1990s occurred in East Timor after the result of the August 30 referendum was made known. The news that 79.5 percent of the voters had elected to choose independence rather than autonomy within Indonesia led almost immediately to violence across the region. This violence as was already beginning to be the case in the lead up to the referendum, was marked by a disturbing new trend or characteristic. For the previous two and a half decades the Catholic Church and its servants and property had always been considered sacrosanct in East Timor even by outsiders who were not themselves Catholic. In August and September something new and awful happened where priests and nuns were killed and church property burnt to the ground. Given the scale of the violence, the intensity of the ferocious attacks by the militia and the clear targeting of religious institutions, it is only reasonable to ask the question as to whether what was happening was the product of ethnic and particular religious sentiment.

In many ways this was an old question. Many people have been tempted to see East Timor's suffering at the hands of the occupying Indonesian forces in terms of the religious conflict. Indonesia is after all the world's largest Muslim nation and East Timor is almost totally Catholic. To make this rather simplistic assumption however ignores the fact that, until recently at least, there has been relatively little sign of religious coloring to the violence that has occurred in East Timor over the past two and a half decades. Indeed, the vast majority of the violence appears to have been a combination of Indonesian army attempts to suppress the East Timorese resistance and Indonesian military initiatives to terrorize and subdue the East Timorese population to deter them from backing the resistance. In this respect, East Timor is remarkably similar to Aceh. Whereas in Aceh the language of militant Islam is joined together with the push for a referendum and independence, and Islam forms an essential element of Acehenese ethnic identity, there is no reason to believe that the basic dynamics are greatly different. In both regions the Indonesian military has responded to guerilla activity by cracking down hard on the civilian population. In both cases a consequence of this has been that civilians more than ever have been turned against the military and the government in Jakarta and inclined to take the dangerous risk of siding with the guerillas in the mountains. In both regions the Indonesian military has systemically used methods of organized terror against civilian populations including systematic rapes, tortures, abductions and so forth, as a means of intimidating and subduing the population. It would appear, that the Indonesian military under Suharto and even more recently under Habibie, has been as willing to take harsh action against Muslim separatists in Aceh as it has against the East Timorese campaigning for independence.

In seeking to understand the East Timor situation it is important to consider its historical and political context. The impetus behind the Indonesian invasion and annexation of East Timor is deeply bound up with Cold War geopolitics. Indeed, the initiative did not come originally from Indonesia.

It was the U.S. that was most concerned about the prospect of an independent newly freed former Portuguese East Timor becoming a "Cuba" in the South-East of the archipelago. This concern was not simply some general antipathy towards the notion of a small socialist state emerging in a relatively sensitive part of the world, it was in fact far more distinctly linked to particular concerns about Cold War nuclear deterrents.[11]

Given that Indonesia's annexation of East Timor has more to do with Cold War geo-politics than it does with Indonesian expansionism why then has the Indonesian military been so reluctant to relinquish East Timor? Answering this question in a comprehensive fashion is not at all easy. For to speak of reasons is to imply rational behavior and it is clear that the Indonesia military, like so many militaries tied to authoritarian regimes, has an internal logic that is out of step with the outside world. Just as the TNI can never hope to bring peace to Aceh or West Papua by simply stepping up military operations in these troubled regions so too it is unclear how it could possibly have thought that intimidation and violence would serve to restrain East Timor from breaking away. Ironically, perhaps if there had been a much-reduced military presence in East Timor since the 1980s and a much more humane local administration operating then possibly things may have been very different.

In terms of immediate causes, it is clear that the timing and circumstances of the August 30 1999 referendum were less than ideal. As early as May 1999 there were signs that the TNI was not going to facilitate a violence-free referendum. For the Indonesian military retention of East Timor was as much a point of pride as it was a rational cause. East Timor, after all, was the main "operational zone" for the armed forces, one which had afforded the opportunity for rapid promotion for many officers and one which had also cost the lives of hundreds of military personnel as well as many thousands of East Timorese.

Anti-Semitism

One indicator of the degree of radicalism in Islamic movements around the world is their expression of anti-Semitic sentiment. It needs to be noted at the outset, that Indonesia is probably as a country, less anti-Semitic than any other Muslim nation. This is encouraging given that it is the world's largest Muslim nation. To some extent this is not surprising given that there is no significant Jewish community within Indonesia and even within Southeast Asia as a whole the number of resident Jews is not great nor has ever been at any point through history. Therefore there is no local reason for anti-Semitism being a particular issue. Nevertheless to the extent that reactionary or extremist Islamists in Indonesia buy into the globalized language of Islamic extremism they refer to imagined dangers such as Jewish banking conspiracies, alleged Jewish involvement in U.S. State Department, the Pentagon and White House policy and so on and so forth. Mercifully such expressions are conspicuous by their absence in Indonesia. No mainstream Islamic groups countenance such ideas, they have been entirely the province of extremist groups such as Dewan Dakwah and KISDI. Even there it is difficult to know what is meant by the regular invocation of Jewish conspiracy theories.

It is important to note that Media Dakwah quite regularly carry stories that show strong anti-Semitism. For example, as was noted above, Amien Rais accused the American academic William Liddle, several years ago of being a stinking Jew and the story was reported in Media Dakwah. Even long after Amien himself has backed away from such statements, Media Dakwah continues to keep the issues alive. Consequently liberal Islamic figures such as Djohan Effendi and Abdurrahman Wahid are occasionally referred to as being involved in the Jewish conspiracy to undermine the interests of Islam. If these views were widely held they would be worrying in the extreme. The fact that they are only held by a very small minority of Muslims in Indonesia does not make them any less worrying in themselves, but the fact that every mainstream Islamic group rejects them and regards them as the sign of crazy extremism is an encouraging response.

One of the real tests of the genuine liberalism found among Indonesian Islamic leaders revolves around response to the state of Israel. Leading the way of the liberal thinker in Indonesia in this regard is Abdurrahman Wahid. Abdurrahman's political and social thought is consistently democratic, liberal and extremely sophisticated. He closely follows the events of the Middle East and is concerned about many developments. Nevertheless, he strongly believes that Indonesia should move to formerly establish diplomatic relations with Israel and he holds passionately to the hope that Indonesia, as the largest Muslim nation in the world, ought to play some role in brokering peace between the Palestinians and Jewish Israelis. Abdurrahman argues very cogently that for Indonesia to diplomatically recognize Israel is not to say that everyone endorses every aspect of policy carried out by various Israeli governments. Rather it is to acknowledge the existence of the state of Israel and the presence of many people of faith and goodwill and the desire to work together to achieve peace. From his point of view the failure to establish diplomatic relations is an obstacle to constructive efforts to engage various parties in the building of peace.

It is very illuminating then to consider the reaction met by Abdurrahman Wahid to his efforts as leader of Nahdlatul Ulama, the world's largest Islamic group to the establishment of diplomatic relations between Indonesia and Israel. Before becoming President, Abdurrahman Wahid has made three visits to Israel and on each occasion he received a degree of official backing from the Indonesian government. For example, his first trip received the personal endorsement of Moerdiono, Indonesian Secretary of State. On this trip, Djohan Effendi accompanied Abdurrahman and the two of them encountered considerable antagonism at home as a consequence of their activities.

The degree of antagonism they met with then is a good barometer of the level of anti-Semitism in Indonesia, given that it draws out the full range of extremist views. Within Nahdlatul Ulama, Abdurrahman met with significant but not overwhelming opposition. It would appear that more than anything else the opposition was based around political maneuvers against him and that the reference to his visits to Israel were opportunistic rather than rooted in deeply held convictions. More important is the fact that when he explained his position to the NU *ulama* and the broader membership his explanation was well received. For example after his first trip he had an opportunity in November 1994 at the five yearly National Congress of Nahdlatul Ulama to explain his actions.

The context of this address was a highly charged political struggle in which Abdurrahman narrowly defeated his rival Abu Hassan who was being backed by the Indonesian government or at least by forces close to Suharto, in an effort to topple Abdurrahman from the NU leadership. Not surprisingly then, Abdurrahman's involvement with Israel and his recent trip were used as a way of attacking his leadership. When he explained before the assembled masses of *ulama* leaders and ordinary members from across the nation the reasons for his trip, he stressed the need for Indonesia to show leadership in the Islamic world and the need to be active in brokering peace. Earlier it was evident that some had misunderstood what he was doing. Once was it was explained, they expressed the view that they now understood and supported his actions. After a second trip, Abdurrahman had another opportunity at a National gathering, this time a five-yearly special meeting of Ulama in Lombok in November 1997. Once again Abdurrahman's opponents raised the issue of Israel and once again Abdurrahman's careful and cogent explanation for his activities met with wide approval and indeed even a sense of pride on behalf of many members that NU, through Abdurrahman Wahid, was so active on the international stage.

The June Elections and the Strength of the Secularist-Nationalist/Moderate-Islam Alliance

Rapprochement between Islamic Traditionalist and Islamic Modernists

By the fourth quarter of 1998 many analysts saw the future for democratic reform being bound up with an Alliance between secular nationalists represented by Megawati's PDI P. and by moderate Muslims in the PKB led by Abdurrahman Wahid and in Amien Rais' PAN. The real fear was that Golkar though under pressure and undoubtedly destined for a slide in fortunes at the June ballot would nevertheless retain enough votes to form government at least in conjunction with its old allies. In this respect PPP represented a strong threat for while it was positioning itself as an independent political party it was clear that it was most likely to be an ally of Golkar. It was also expected that many people who in the past had habitually voted for PPP would continue to do so in the belief that it represented the interests of Islam and an alternative independent voice to Golkar. There was also some concern about the New Islamist parties such as Partai Bulan Bintang and the seven or eight other parties clearly established on an Islamist platform. So while many put their hopes in this secular-nationalist/moderate-Islam alliance many regarded it as hoping against hope and despaired of the chance of the alliance really taking hold and proving to be lasting.

The main reason for doubt was not the relationship between Abdurrahman Wahid and Megawati Soekarnoputri but rather the relationship between Abdurrahman Wahid and Amien Rais. Abdurrahman and Megawati had long been allies and had worked together over many years to challenge the Suharto regime. Abdurrahman and Amien on the other hand had long been rivals, frequently bitter rivals at that, and Abdurrahman had continued to be outspoken in his criticism of Amien Rais' sectarian track record. Nevertheless, there were grounds for hope in the second and third tier leadership of the various parties where there appeared to be individuals with a genuine desire to foster cooperation and smooth over difficulties.

As it happened, in the period from the formation of PAN through to the election of the Indonesian president one of the remarkable turnarounds has been the way in which the traditional rivalry between traditionalist Muslims represented by PKB and Modernist Muslims represented by PAN was largely overcome. On the ground a new relationship developed between Muhammadiyah and Nahdlatul Ulama resulting in genuine rapprochement. The months leading up to the election and the second half of 1999 saw a profound thawing of relations often spearheaded by the youth divisions of Muhammadiyah and Ulama. At the same time at the upper leadership levels the relationship between Amien Rais and Abdurrahman Wahid went from strength to strength. It appeared as if eventually Abdurrahman Wahid was persuaded that Amien Rais had genuinely changed his position and had become a committed democrat opposed to his former sectarian standpoint.

The Souring of the Abdurrahman and Megawati Alliance

One of the surprising developments during the same period was the way in which the relationship between Megawati and Abdurrahman continued to deteriorate. There were signs of this occurring reasonably early. On May 17 a historic agreement was signed between the three reformist parties to work together to form a "common front" in order to topple Golkar. In order to announce this important development a joint press conference with Megawati, Abdurrahman and Amien, was planned for 10.30 PM on Monday the 17th of May. The press conference and the statement finally went ahead two hours behind schedule but Megawati failed to show. At the time Abdurrahman calmly excused her absence explaining fatigue and the fact that she had an early morning departure to Lampung, Sumatra. Nevertheless, behind the scenes, there was considerable anxiety at the reticence of Megawati to co-operate publicly.

Anecdotal accounts suggest that the relationship continued to suffer erosion from that point forwards and did not begin to show genuine recovery until early October. Specifically the first signs of a turn-around in their relationship came with the election of Amien Rais to the chairmanship of the MPR. This was followed two days later by the election in the MPR of Akbar Tanjung, Golkar's reform-minded parliamentary head to the chairmanship of the DPR. In both of these votes PDI-P did badly, with its traditional ally PKB deserting it. Moreover it was clear that Abdurrahman Wahid and Amien Rais were able to marshal the support of some sections of Golkar and the military and of more conservative Islamic parties against Megawati.

This posturing finally achieved its aim and a breakthrough in the relationship was marked with Megawati accepting a long-standing invitation to join Abdurrahman on a pilgrimage to the tomb sites of their fathers in East Java. The breakdown of the relationship through the middle of 1999 is difficult to explain except in terms of personal conflict and perhaps also false sense of confidence on the part of PDI-P.

PDI-P's Significant Success at the June Polls

The only party to enjoy runaway success at the June 7 polls was PDI-P, and even they did not enjoy the full success they had predicted. Nevertheless, with 33.7 percent of the vote, PDI-P was clearly ahead of all other parties by a long measure, with Golkar its closest rival trailing by a full 12 percent. In part this success can be explained as a phenomenon of the relative success of old parties versus new parties. The three old parties Golkar, PPP, and PDI-P (that is if PDI-P can be considered a continuation of PDI which in the eyes of most it was) all enjoyed significant success whereas the new parties struggled to make their mark. Given the short time available for campaigning, the relatively low level of education and general awareness among voters and the fraught circumstances, it was not surprising that the old parties should do best. Golkar of course suffered a massive erosion of its base, achieving less than a third the number votes that it had in previous elections. Even so, the fact that it was able to get as much as 22 percent of the votes surprised many and can probably be explained partly in terms of the inertia of tradition with many traditional Golkar voters, particularly those in the outer islands such as Sulawesi which were relatively unaffected by the economic crisis, continuing to vote for their old party of choice. Similarly, while PPP was predicting a vote of the order of that which it had enjoyed in previous elections (that is in excess of 20 percent,) it ultimately gained only half that number of votes. Nevertheless, this result too surprised many. The majority of urbane professional commentators saw PPP as nothing more than a stooge for Golkar populated largely by professional politicians of the Suharto era. Many voters however, evidently saw PPP differently. Specifically it appears that many people who had habitually voted for the old Islamic party continued to do so. Significantly, many of these voters were from NU, and in many made their decision based upon charismatic NU personalities within PPP. Similarly, it is possible to see PDI-P's almost 34 percent of the vote as a vote for a known "brand name" both in terms of the connection with the old PDI and of Megawati's association with her father, Sukarno.

The Modest Success of PKB and PAN at the June Polls

All of the other parties struggled to make their mark. PKB of course did best, no doubt helped in large measure by its endorsement by the Central Board of NU and by the charismatic authority of Abdurrahman Wahid. Even so PKB polled way below the expectations of many independent commentators and of many within the party. Where many had hoped for at least 15 to 20 percent of the national vote PKB got only 12.4 percent. This was way below the expectations of many although not necessarily below some in the party who had kept their eyes on the polling booth. It was certainly, however, below the expectations of Abdurrahman Wahid who had spoken confidently, perhaps for reasons of psychology and confidence building, of getting two or three or more times that amount of votes. Indeed, on occasions he even spoke of PKB gaining a clear majority, although it is not clear that even he believed this to be possible.

The biggest disappointment among the reformists, however, was experienced by PAN which garnered barely 7 percent of the national vote. In many ways, PAN had the most difficult road to hoe, being a completely unknown entity probably only saved in terms of profile by the leadership of Amien Rais, who was more widely known in urban centers than in the rural heartland of Indonesia.

Many people within PAN were deeply disappointed by its election result, none more so it would appear, than Amien Rais himself. There are good reasons, however, for arguing that PAN did as well as could be reasonably expected for a new party with no track record, no established profile and a platform which must have seemed confusing and uncertain to the majority of Indonesian voters. Unlike PKB, with its strong relationship to NU reinforced by the charismatic authority of NU chairman Abdurrahman Wahid, PAN could not count on automatically drawing a large section of the Muhammadiyah vote. Indeed, it appears that many Muhammadiyah people voted for PPP, perhaps as they'd always done while many others similarly, voted for Golkar, while a further section representing the right wing of the organization, voted for parties such as PBB.

PDI-P Draws Away, PKB and PAN Draw Closer

The relative success of PDI-P and relative lack of success of PKB and PAN left the relationship in an awkward position. Flushed with success Megawati and much of the PDI-P leadership behaved in a manner suggesting that they no longer needed to rely upon their old reformist partners PKB and PAN, or at least that they were assuming these now clearly much smaller partners would have to work with them on their terms. Abdurrahman Wahid was said to have been bitterly disappointed when having approached Megawati shortly after the election and being told that PKB could expect "to be given one minister and that was all." The already difficult relationship between Abdurrahman and Megawati became considerably more frosty from that point forwards.

Immediately following the election Amien Rais appeared to go into a state of deep depression and shock. As he recovered from the initial shock of PAN's relatively poor polling, however, a change came over Amien that considerably facilitated the improved relationship between himself and Abdurrahman Wahid. In what appeared to be a fit of honesty and self-reflection Amien declared himself to be out of the presidential race on the grounds that his party had polled so poorly, and he immediately began to look for ways in which to make a contribution. At first PAN spoke of going into the role of opposition party but was eventually persuaded that this would mean siding with Golkar and in the short term would probably achieve very little. Instead, Amien decided to back Abdurrahman Wahid.

At the same time, Megawati and other senior figures and PDI-P added to their a pre-election gaffes with a series of moves that while probably not calculated to insult the Muslim majority in Indonesia nevertheless had that effect. In the run-up to the June 7 national elections many people were deeply disappointed by PDI-P's insensitivity to the electorate in appointing a disproportionately high number of non-Muslim candidates and then justifying the decision in a very off-hand fashion. While most commentators respected the nonsectarian stance of PDI-P they nevertheless expected that good sense would guide Megawati and her team to be sensitive to Muslim feelings, particularly at a time of great uncertainty in which Islam was being manipulated for political reasons on all sides. Instead PDI-P went blithely forwards. Flushed with confidence after the June elections it continued to take actions that angered its erstwhile allies. One particularly difficult point came during the Jakarta Council local government elections when PDI-P for voted in favor of TNI candidates over against their own PDI candidates. This odd move was justified by PDI-P on the grounds that the party needed the support of the military in the coming October presidential elections.

In the lead up to the June 7th national elections there was considerable unease and uncertainty as to whether the relationship between PAN and PKB, specifically between Amien Rais and Abdurrahman Wahid could be made workable. It was thought that even if cracks in the relationship could be patched over, in the long run the differences between the two men and their past mutual antagonism would be the undoing of the alliance. As it happened, the relationship between Amien and Abdurrahman went from strength to strength through the third quarter of 1999 while at the same time, and quite unexpectedly, the relationship between Abdurrahman and Megawati continued to deteriorate. The result of this deteriorating relationship was that these former allies began to act as if they were rivals.

Abdurrahman Joins the Central Axis

The most generous interpretation to be made of Abdurrahman Wahid's behavior in this context is that he was deliberately engaging in a blocking maneuver against Habibie and Golkar in order to protect Megawati. There is clear evidence, however, to suggest the relationship between the two had reached an all-time low and that the perceived rivalry had a very genuine element. As discussed above, the reasons for Megawati's confidence are obvious, her party was the outstanding success story from the June 7 ballot. Abdurrahman Wahid's poorer than expected electoral results, however, were not, in themselves, the basis for forming a power base in competition with Megawati. The vehicle for Abdurrahman's political maneuvering through the third quarter of 1999 came from an unexpected quarter. While the relationship between Amien and Abdurrahman represented rapprochement between traditionalists and Modernist Muslims, those who ultimately came forward to indicate support for Abdurrahman came from a very different orientation.

By August 1999 Abdurrahman was being proposed as an alternative presidential candidate supported by the so-called Central Axis force (*poros tengah*) comprised of the parties most clearly linked with Islam including PBB and the Justice party. This so-called Central Axis members said that they would find an alternative to both Habibie and Megawati in order to break with what they saw as an emerging deadlock between the two traditional rivals. As we have already noted, early on Amien Rais had declared himself as unsuitable for presidential candidacy on the basis that PAN polled so overly badly in the election. Surprisingly, Amien turned around and nominated Abdurrahman as his preferred presidential candidate. Even more surprisingly, however, was the fact that this nomination was eventually backed at least ostensibly, by the whole of the Central Axis including Yusril Mahendra's PBB and the Justice party. The final element in this Alliance and its support for Abdurrahman was the official shift in position by PKB which previously had been wedded to supporting Megawati. By early October the Central Axis, to the surprise of many, came to represent a credible third force. For by early October it appeared to both be serious about its nomination of Abdurrahman Wahid and to have the means to back this nomination up within the MPR.

How can this serious fallout between Megawati and Abdurrahman Wahid be explained? In part it has its origins in the unhealthy sense of over-confidence developed in PDI-P ranks following the June 7th results and in the subsequent disappointment that was widely felt by many who had previously supported Megawati's nomination.

The Fall and Fall of B.J. Habibie

Mainly because of ICMI Habibie had come to be seen in the late 1990s as a champion of Islam. As was noted above, this was the basis for his campaign for Golkar at the national election and it was also seen to be the basis for locking in support from PPP and especially from the small Islamist parties, for his presidential election in October 1999. Unfortunately for Habibie, however, the second half of the year saw things go badly wrong. Never a particularly credible or inspiring president at the best of times, Habibie began to hit the wall in the second half of 1999. Habibie suffered two major defeats. The first was his failure to combat corruption. In particular, Habibie was widely seen to have failed to bring the corruption of former President Suharto and his extended family to account. When finally on October 11 the official inquiry into Suharto was scrapped on the grounds of lack of evidence no one was surprised. The failure was seen to be all Habibie's. He was seen to have never been serious about putting his erstwhile mentor on trial. Even more damaging, however, was the so-called Bank Bali affair involving Indonesia's second-largest bank. It came to light that a "consultancy fee" of $80 million U.S. had been paid to a group of men close to Habibie and his younger brother Timmy. It was widely surmised that this "consultancy money" would be used to bankroll money politics for the presidential campaign.[12] The outcry against Habibie was immediate and widespread. The protestations of Habibie's office that the scandal had nothing to do with him personally was believed by virtually no one and he suffered an enormous further erosion in his credibility in an area in which he was already considered extremely namely the reigning in of corruption, collusion and nepotism.

The second major blow for Habibie came with the East Timor debacle. It had been Habibie who had pushed for a referendum in East Timor, apparently without consultation with the military or even with his Minister for Foreign Affairs, Ali Alitas. And it had been Habibie who had pushed for that referendum to be an all or nothing scenario in which the East Timorese either voted in favor of remaining within Indonesia with greater autonomy or, by inference, rejected the idea of being part of Indonesia altogether and, following ratification by the MPR, be immediately declared independent from Indonesia. This policy initiative horrified many within Habibie's own cabinet. It also horrified the military. It was hardly surprising then, that the military failed to actively work towards insuring peace in the run-up to the referendum and in the weeks that followed. The military was widely seen to be involved, at least at the local level and possibly at much higher levels in supporting, encouraging and even directing militia units in East Timor to initially block the referendum vote through intimidating the East Timorese and then to raze to the ground the infrastructure build-up in East Timor during the Indonesia period before its hand-over as an independent nation. While the military was able successfully at least in the short term, to manipulate media coverage within Indonesia and find an external scapegoat in Australia and in the international peacekeeping force, the damage done to Habibie's reputation was nevertheless enormous.

On Thursday, October 14, the embattled president delivered his Accountability Speech. Rejection of this speech would effectively kill his prospects for re-election and so the stakes were high. Nevertheless Habibie completely failed to use the occasion to garner at least a modicum of sympathy, much less redeem his reputation. On the contrary, he sailed forth with surreal confidence into a speech true to form, being long on decorative detail but short on substance. Critical responses, from both within the MPR and from without, started virtually as soon as the president sat down. Unfortunately for Habibie his critics found much of a concrete nature to fault in his speech. Leading economists, such as PDI-P's Kwik Kian Gie for example, found it to be riddled with errors, and not just at the level of general analysis but even in the use of basic statistics and numerical measures. Sunday, October 17, saw Habibie compound his earlier mistakes when his official response speech was widely seen as evidence that the president had but a slender grip on reality. Finally, when his running mate, General Wiranto, announced the next day that he was declining his nomination for the vice-presidency Habibie's lame duck status was confirmed.

A Liberal Democratic Future for Indonesia?

A Bumpy Road Ahead for the New Government

The new government now faces an extremely difficult task in 2000 and for some years to come. Indonesia's economic recovery is not likely to take place overnight and even conservative estimates have a full recovery not picking up until late 2001, or maybe even 2002 and with the likelihood of the economy not returning to 1997 levels until 2003 or 2004. Moreover, the new government will face a range of pressing social problems. Not only will serious poverty, unemployment, and social frustration continue to be a reality for the next several years, the current level of "sectarian violence" is not likely to disappear in the short term. Even if much of the violence was initially engineered there is still a sense in which "the genie is out of the bottle" and it could be difficult or impossible to put it back. In other words now people have learnt how to vent their frustration by scapegoating certain sections of the community it is likely that such actions will continue even without any further inducements over the next several years. The best that can be hoped is that the extent of such violence is constrained within reasonable limits and that the broader community sees the sense in turning its back on such action and checking violence where it occurs.

Civil Society, Islam, and Democracy

It should be evident by now that the potential for Islam in Indonesia to make a positive contribution to Indonesian society, specifically to the development and growth of civil society and democracy, greatly outweighs its potential to make a negative contribution. Or more accurately, the likelihood of Islam making a negative contribution is greatly outweighed by its likelihood of making a positive contribution. Clearly the area in which Islam can best be said to make a positive contribution can be generally described as the building and strengthening of civil society. This takes a number of aspects. Firstly, there is the general aspect of civil society, that voluntary associations contribute to the general well-being of a society through performing tasks or providing services that otherwise would not get done by government agencies. In that sense then, Muhammadiyah's program of schools, hospitals orphanages and so forth and the Nahdlatul Ulama *pesantren* network and charitable foundations, are making a clear contribution as voluntary agencies to the strengthening of civil society. This, however, is a fairly basic understanding or at least a fairly basic aspect of civil society and if this is all that is provided then the result does not give the sort of rich society envisaged by the term.

Another word that comes to mind talking about religion's contribution to civil society is that of moral leadership. In Indonesia's case it is very clear that at its best as Daniel Lev suggested, Indonesia is capable of considerable moral authority and moral leadership. This is not simply some esoteric or abstract matter but can clearly be seen in the events in Indonesia over the last several years. Specifically, without the moral authority of leaders in both Muhammadiyah and Ulama it seems highly likely that Indonesia would have experienced much worse violence on a much broader scale than has been the case.

So the contribution of Islam through voluntary associations to broader social services and in terms of moral leadership to moderating and guiding society, both represent contributions to the building of civil society in Indonesia. A third contribution which is readily evident is the potential for religious associations such as Nahdlatul Ulama and Muhammadiyah to encourage a sensible understanding of democratic processes, a desire for reform and a moderate and sophisticated approach to achieving the reform. Once again, it is possible to argue that neither Muhammadiyah nor Nahdlatul Ulama seem very sophisticated in terms of their approach to democracy. And indeed, the campaigns by PKB and PAN leave much to be desired, for the most part being reasonably superficial and symbolic and lacking a suitable number of experienced leaders.

Nevertheless, the contribution over many decades through the *pesantren* and other educational institutions and affiliations in encouraging in people an understanding of justice and democratic processes and a realistic sense of what can be achieved and in the context of needing to seek a solution to compromise, these organizations achieved a great deal. And when one looks at the major figures in civil society, this becomes even more evident. Not only do figures like Abdurrahman Wahid and Amien Rais, stand as key figures in shaping public opinion, through their role of public intellectuals, a large number of Indonesia's best investigative journalists and NGO activists come from a religious background. Moreover, there is good reason for believing it is not mere rhetoric when these people claim that their inspiration for moral engagement comes directly from their convictions as Muslims about justice and about the way that they should engage in society.

So in general terms then, it could be argued that Islam has made a significant contribution to the establishment and development of civil society in Indonesia. Given that optimistic reading though, it must be acknowledged that the greatest test for Muslim leaders, Islamic intellectuals and civil society generally in Indonesia lies ahead, particularly in the immediate future. To the extent that Indonesia hangs together, avoids separatist conflict, class pressures, inter-communal clashes and general anarchy, much of the credit should be directed to the moral authority and leadership of religious leaders. The challenges facing Indonesia are enormous. Looking at figures such as Abdurrahman Wahid it is clear that considerable responsibility and potential for good is concentrated in the hands of a few individuals. It can only be hoped that they will have sufficient wisdom, presence of mind, maturity and greatness of character to rise to the occasion. We can realistically take heart from the fact that in the past they have demonstrated that there is reason for having confidence in this regard.

The Way Ahead for the Wahid Government

Abdurrahman and Political Islam

As has been outlined above the reasons for feeling positive about Indonesia's medium and the long-term future are due in large part to the fact that the new government is seen to be formed on the basis of a genuinely democratic process. Notwithstanding the fact that there are many reasons to question the ability of Abdurrahman to always act decisively and wisely it seems reasonable to expect from his presidency a stable and reformist government.

One of the key factors influencing the success of Abdurrahman's government is social stability and for that he needs the backing of all, or at least most, sections of Indonesian society. Certainly, in the short term at least, he cannot afford to alienate any of the diverse political factions that bought him to power. For this reason the short-term future and possibly long-term outcomes are very much influenced by the extent to which Abdurrahman can negotiate consensus and build confidence, while not neglecting the need for immediate and consistent implementation of reforms.

There is no question that the new president faces enormous challenges but his position was enormously strengthened by the election of Megawati Soekarnoputri as his Vice President. Despite difficulties in the second half of 1999 Megawati and the PDI-P continue to enjoy the general support and goodwill of PKB and Nahdlatul Ulama.

A further encouraging sign is the greatly improved nature of relations between traditionalists and Modernist Muslims. As a result of the Amien-Abdurrahman, PAN-PKB Alliance, relations between Muhammadiyah and Nahdlatul Ulama are better than they have ever been. This is most evident at the level of youth wings of the organizations but does seem to have genuinely permeated the organizations as a whole. This is a fact of crucial importance in lending stability to the new government.

It remains to be seen whether Abdurrahman's dalliance with the Central Axis grouping will have achieved lasting value in terms of his ability to influence conservative Muslims. There is good reason, nevertheless, for expecting that if nothing else, relations between Nahdlatul Ulama, Muhammadiyah and the more extremist elements of the Islamic community have been improved at least at the level of mutual understanding and appreciation. Given the way in which he was able to turn the support of the Central Axis to his own advantage there are even good grounds for hoping that figures such as Yusril Mahendra in PBB and the various other conservative Muslim leaders will not have too much scope to exploit religious symbolism and sentiment for party political purposes. Indeed, it was an astute move for Abdurrahman to offer Yusril a cabinet post. In doing so he gained an able colleague and the good will of conservative Muslims. Even more importantly, however, it might well serve to limit the efficacy of Islamism as a tool for political opposition.

For Indonesian democracy to mean anything it is important that a strong and credible opposition emerge well before the next election. Nevertheless it is also important that neither the government nor the opposition use religion to differentiate their political position. Consequently, it is important that Abdurrahman avoids completely alienating conservative Muslims by keeping them "on board" his new government while at the same time constraining their ability to influence policy.

Handling Regional Unrest and Past Injustices

But all this is no guarantee that the government will not face challenge from religious extremism. This is not because religious extremism or inter-communal unrest should automatically arise of its own accord, has been argued earlier in this paper but rather that the underlying causes of unrest in Indonesia, as witnessed in recent years have to do primarily with social and economic issues. Consequently if the new government fails to address these issues head-on it risks seeing this cycle of violence not only continue but very possibly escalate. Since the fall of Suharto, Indonesians have been looking forward to the prospects, firstly of elections that were free, democratic and then the formation of a new government and then the addressing of long-standing grievances. 1998 and 1999 were marked by occasional outbreaks of violence, especially in areas such Maluku and Aceh, on the whole though, there was a significant degree of collective goodwill as people looked forward expectantly to better times. Quite likely this goodwill will continue into the early days of the new government. If however, the new government fails to deliver on reform and on attending to long-standing grievances, then it is possible this mood of general patience and forbearance could quickly give way to agitation and anger. In large measure this is tied up with reform of the military, not an easy exercise in the best of circumstances.

On the one hand the new government has to gain the confidence of the military and work towards their support and on the other hand it has to generally tilt things in favor of reformist within the military and away from hawkish conservatives. To a large extent the international community will also assist in this endeavor but it certainly requires astute political management in Jakarta. If the military can be persuaded to pull back from areas such as Aceh and to actively work to curtail militia activity coming out of west Timor into East Timor for example, there is every chance that these areas of unspeakable violence in the past will relatively quickly find a new and lasting peace.

More than this however there needs to be some process akin to the Truth and Reconciliation Commission process in South Africa. Those who have lost husbands, sons and daughters need to have their stories heard and to be able to close the chapter on their personal tragedies by finding out what happened to loved ones. To the extent that its possible, the perpetrators also need to be brought to account and justice needs to be seen to be done, but possibly the hearing and knowing of the truth is even more important. The progress of South Africa's Truth and Reconciliation Commission even with the wise influence of figures such as Nelson Mandela has been less than perfect. Nevertheless, if Indonesia enjoys even moderately similar success a great deal of good can be achieved. If these issues of the past cannot be dealt with relatively quickly, the old sores that have seen increasing violence in Aceh will continue to fester. If however, these are addressed quickly, and military brutality stopped in the first year of the new government and if a clear process of beginning to deal with what has happened in the past is seen to commence then there is every chance that the current groundswell of movement against Jakarta and in favor of extremist and separatist voices will be quickly quelled.

All of this, however, is still insufficient if the underlying economic and social concerns are not addressed. Even without military brutality continuing, unless the so-called outer island communities see their economic grievances dealt with through greater fairness in regional development through the local re-investment of a greater proportion of the wealth extracted from their provinces then the disaffection with Jakarta will continue. Clearly what is required in this area is twofold in nature. Firstly, there needs to be greater economic justice in terms of the way in which local wealth is returned, reinvested and local development takes place. Throughout the Suharto era the pace of development in major urban centers such as Jakarta was astounding, but traveling a short distance outside of Jakarta and certainly outside of the island of Java, produced a starkly contrasting picture. If Kalimantan, North Sumatra and West Papua and the Maluku do not begin to experience some of the same development as has occurred in Java then its to be expected that there will be continued disaffection with Jakarta and in some areas at least the question of separation will remain a live issue.

Secondly, the new government needs to look at the question of regional political autonomy. For reasons of history and bitter experience, particularly from the struggle against the Dutch in the run-up to independence, many Indonesians are uneasy with the concept of federalism. But in effect the Republic of Indonesia will need to develop a kind of federated state system if local aspirations and sensitivities are to be dealt with in a fashion which is satisfactory in the long-term. Not only does the military have to be taken completely out of politics at both the national and local level but the current domination of outer island provinces by politicians originating from Java, Bali and Madura needs to be turned around. People need to have a sense that when they vote for local government, that local government both represents them and has real ability to bring about change in the region. Many analysts have observed that in almost every case of healthy democracy around the globe there are second and third tier democratic elections for local governments in various forms and this is an essential element in satisfying the aspirations of regional populations to have people they know and recognize made accountable for decisions made in their region.

The Long Road to Liberal Democracy

If all of these things above can be tended to, and there is no reason why they can't because none of them is, at least in themselves too difficult, then there is every reason to expect that the large scale inter-communal unrest which Indonesia has witnessed since the mid-1990s will begin to fade away. Perhaps it's inevitable that there will be occasionally incidences such as that in Sambas, West Kalimantan where conflicts of a local nature arise between different groups of people. But hopefully the sort of conflict and violence witnessed in Aceh could quickly be dealt with. There is no reason to believe that there is some deterministic logic to the disintegration of Indonesia. Nor is there any reason to believe that just because Indonesia is a multi-faith, multi-ethnic society that there should automatically be ethnic and religious tensions and violence.

What is required, however is a government of consistently reasonable wisdom and transparent accountability. The June 1999 elections surpassed pretty much all expectations in the extent to which they were fair and just. Similarly, the session of the MPR in October 1999 and the election of the new president and formation of a new government proceeded reasonably smoothly and there were encouraging signs of nascent democracy at work. There is every reason then, to expect that this modest early success will continue.

Even with good government however, one of the deciding factors will be the contribution of civil society. In Indonesia's case civil society is largely influenced and shaped, strengthened or weakened by religious sentiment, religious communities and religious figures. In particular Islam in Indonesia has demonstrated the surprising extent to which it is able to make a positive contribution to civil society. Provided that the new government is reasonably wise and accommodating of a diversity of interests and able to bring community leaders on side, and also, of course, providing that Indonesia does not suffer any great external shocks, there is every reason to believe that both civil society and democracy will continue to develop in Indonesia.

In conclusion then, it has to be acknowledged that Indonesia's immediate past is extremely complex and will probably not be understood at all well for some years to come. We are simply too close to the events at the moment and have too little hard data to be dogmatic in drawing conclusions. And if the immediate past is difficult to understand then the immediate future is even harder to fathom. While the possible scenarios for the election's likely outcomes were made with a good basis and have a reasonable likelihood of being realized, it has to be acknowledged that all such talk is ultimately speculative and that it is entirely conceivable that events may go down an entirely unforeseen path.

One thing that is clear, however, is that we need to have realistic expectations. Indonesia is not going to become a liberal democracy overnight. In that sense then one would have to acknowledge that the developments of the last twelve months in certain ways far outweigh even the wildest, most optimistic predictions of analysts in early years regarding the transition to a post-Suharto era. While the Habibie government has in many respects proven unsatisfactory much has been achieved, not just by the government but by the Indonesian people as a whole and in many ways it is much better than anyone had hoped for. Against this background it seems reasonable to continue to be optimistic.

Even so, it has to be acknowledged that the Wahid government, even though it is a reformist government led by an extraordinary man, is going to have many failings and weaknesses. Indonesia has a number of experienced and well-educated people well able to contribute to the formation of government along democratic lines but it has an insufficient number of such people. And this is even more so in the civil service. Most Indonesians have never experienced democracy in their lifetime and have little intuitive feel for how it should work in their day-to-day life whether they be civil servants, businessmen or politicians. It seems realistic then to acknowledge that not just the Habibie government of 1998-1999 but also the new Wahid government has to succeed and it will be transitional government. Even if Indonesia moves well on course towards liberal democracy it will not be achieved in a complete sense during the lifetime of the Wahid government.

The considerable challenges facing Indonesia, specifically the challenge of rebuilding the economy that overnight lost decades of growth, cannot be overstated. In some ways, the situation in which Indonesia finds itself can be said to be entirely unfair, but there is no getting around the fact that for the economy to recover and be re-established Indonesia needs to regain the confidence of not just the international community but of domestic business and government circles. And it needs to do this at the same time as maintaining a reasonable social order and encouraging patience on the part of many Indonesians who have been suffering and are due to suffer hardship for some years to come.

If what occurred in Indonesia had occurred in any other country, it is fair to say that one could be considerably less sanguine about the prospect of that country to recover, but Indonesian society has shown itself to have many remarkable qualities, not the least being a considerable capacity for tolerance and moderation and even wisdom. In large measure the fact that this exists as a cultural trait is a contribution made by Islamic leaders and Muslim society over many generations, particularly over the past generation. If Indonesia is to face a brighter future then it will depend very much upon the continued wisdom of such leaders. This is not denying that one of the greatest threats facing Indonesia is that religious extremism may ratchet up social tensions to the point where social unrest reaches such a scale that even the armed forces cannot contain it. A more modest scenario is that ill will and prejudice may so dominate national life that it is not possible for stable governments to perform and enter cooperatively into the ongoing process of nation building and nation rebuilding. In this sense the dangers of an extremist Islam of a political and activist variety, which is often called Islamism, are real. But seen in context, however, it should be acknowledged that the overall contribution of Islam so far has been overwhelmingly positive and one can look confidently to that continuing to be so.

Making Sense of President Wahid

Throughout this chapter the name Abdurrahman Wahid has come up repeatedly. The reasons for this are obvious. He was, and remains, one of the most influential Islamic leaders in Indonesia and certainly represents one of the nation's most significant intellectuals. And now, contrary to all expectations, he is Indonesia's fourth President. It is does not seem right to finish this study without reflecting on what it means for Indonesia to have Abdurrahman Wahid as President.

As we have seen above, there are good reasons for believing Abdurrahman Wahid to be a genuine democratic, someone committed to empowering civil society and making government accountable to the people. When he became President, however, he inherited a political structure which gave tremendous power to the person of the President. Indeed the essential principle of Suharto-era politics was the concentration of power and the unaccountability of the President. As a civil society activist he railed against this. But now he is President and at this time of enormous flux and uncertainty it is neither possible nor advisable for him to dismantle the strong powers of the presidency too quickly. We have therefore something of a dilemma or a paradox. Abdurrahman Wahid, reformer and liberal democrat, becomes President of a nation in transition from authoritarian rule to democratic government. As a reformer, if he is to succeed in the enormous task of reform before him, he needs to be a strong and bold. At the same time he risks his stance as a liberal democrat being seen to be totally hypocritical if he doesn't begin to dismantle the very system that gives him power.

There is reason to believe that under "normal" circumstances Abdurrahman would not be an ideal candidate for the presidency. Ordinarily, a President should be an able administrator and a good manager. It is important, of course, that they have vision but it is just as important that their actions are clearly explicable and are implemented it in a consistent and predictable fashion so that the President might be held accountable. Abdurrahman is the quintessential political maverick. Ordinarily, his eccentric approach to leadership would mean that he was ill suited to ruling a nation of 220 million people. There is nothing ordinary, however, about Indonesia's present circumstances. What Indonesia needs now is not so much a normal government and a normal president as it does bold and visionary leadership backed by wisdom and courage.

The Habibie period is generally seen as representing a period of transition. So too a strong argument can be made that the Wahid government is also a transitional government if by transitional it is meant that this government bridges two cultures. It is charged with transporting the nation from one system and culture of politics unto another very different one. It can be argued, and generally is, that under such circumstances Abdurrahman Wahid clearly represents the best of all possible presidents.

Abdurrahman Wahid's strengths as President can be summed up by describing him as a realist-idealist. During his first six months as President he has demonstrated that he remains wedded to the ideals that he has fought for since his youth. It has also been equally apparent that his approach to politics is a realistic and pragmatic one. For Abdurrahman politics is quintessentially the art of the possible.

Wahid's Idealism

The sources of the President's idealism have already been discussed above. The first source is his faith. As should by now be clear, Abdurrahman's understanding of Islam is that of a religion which is committed to tolerance and compassion. There is ample evidence to argue that his liberal view of Islam is supported by the primary texts and sources of that faith. There is of course, as with all world faith, also ample evidence to suggest that these principles have all too often not been put in place by the governments and societies that espouse them. Nevertheless it is important to consider these principles and recognize that the convictions of liberal religious figures such as Abdurrahman have real force behind them. For Abdurrahman Islam is a religion in which all people are equal before God, whether male or female, whether rich or poor, whether Asian or Western and indeed whether Muslim or non-Muslim.

A second source of Abdurrahman's idealism comes from his environment. He grew up in exceptional circumstances. As the son of a leading nationalist and greatly admired liberal Islamic thinker and grandson of two of the founders of Nahdlatul Ulama he was born into a remarkable family. His mother too was a remarkable women and great influence over him. Following the death of his father in a car accident in 1953, when Abdurrahman was only twelve years old, his mother imparted to him a strong sense of mission. He was destined, she felt, to continue the work of his father and grandfathers. He spent the early years of his childhood partly in rural Jombang, the world of the *pesantren*, and partly in urban Menteng, the home of a government minister filled with books and interesting people.

It was his good fortune to enjoy a remarkable childhood environment and, in particular a remarkable home environment, one which communicated to him the importance of ideals and principles as well as the importance of being able to mix equally with all people. As a teenager and young man, in the years preceding his studies in the Middle East and following his return to East Java in the 1970s, he was greatly influenced by his mother's father Kiai Bisri Sansuri and by his uncle Kiai Wahab Chasbullah. These men, though related through marriage and good friends, were as different from one another as can be imagined. Bisri Sansuri was a straight forward, serious, man well known for his mastery of Islamic jurisprudence and his pious application of it in his own life. His was an unaffected piety. He was also respected as an innovative farm manager and stalwart community leader. Kiai Wahab, in contrast, was a flamboyant and idiosyncratic figure. He was as eccentric as Kiai Bisri was straight. He married over twenty-one women and during the was a famous sight around Jombang during the 1950s and 60s riding his Harley-Davidson motorcycle with his characteristic white turban flapping in the wind. Abdurrahman grew up deeply influenced by both these men. Both by the earnest and sincere piety of Kiai Bisri Syansuri and by the liberal and intuitive approach to interpreting Islam of Kiai Wahab.

He was also clearly shaped by his reading. From an earlier age he read a wide range of literature, both fiction and non-fiction. He was an usually precocious reader for a young boy from a *pesantren* background in Java in the 1950s and 60s. He read widely in Marxist/Leninist thought as well as reading extensively on American politics, European philosophy and history. As young man in his twenties he developed a love of the great European novels of the nineteenth and twentieth centuries. He explains the power of attraction of these novels, whether French, Russian, English, or American, as being bound up in the way in which good literature describes the complexities of human nature. For the same reason he was drawn to the traditional Javanese shadow theatre, the Wayang Kulit. Similarly, he early on became a fan of French cinema because of the way in which a good film can portray the complexities of human nature and human society. His wide reading represents a great resource for the development of his thought. It has been readily evident in his speeches and addresses as President, for example, just how much his broad reading has shaped his thought.

Finally his idealism was also shaped by his friendships not only within family circles but across society and around the world. He has a broad, and indeed eclectic, range of friends. It is significant that as President he has continued to maintain the friendships that he has enjoyed throughout his life. It seems to be almost a matter of principle to him that he draws his friends from a wide range of social classes, backgrounds and religious faiths. Since Abdurrahman become President, traditionally dressed East Javanese *kiai* have been a common sight at the Palace. But so too have various of foreign friends, as well as Chinese business people, and ex-political prisoners jailed during the crackdown on Communism in the mid 1960s. Abdurrahman argues that he is shaped by all his friendships and certainly there appears to be good reason to believe that this is the case. In conversation he frequently displays a keen desire to learn and get feedback from those he is talking with. It would appear as if there is a genuine broad-mindedness at work and that through these interactions his thinking is constantly refreshed and developed.

These claims might be regarded as overly romantic in some circles and indeed they have been disputed frequently in the press since Abdurrahman became President. And yet there is good reason for believing that his idealism is genuine, not least because of his performance over 15 years as leader of Nahdlatul Ulama and before that as a public intellectual of some standing. His commitment to political dissidence throughout the Suharto era is almost unparalleled. Although he has frequently been criticized for his pragmatic approach to such dissidence and his often bewildering tactical manoeuvrings, his courage and conviction were widely admired.

Nor was his dissidence simply confined to criticism of the government. He was also an able, and at times a courageous, defender of the weak and the powerless. In particular he consistently spoke up for minority groups, most notably Indonesia's Chinese. He is drawn irresistibly to defend the underdog and at many times went out of his way to defend groups and communities in ways in which it is difficult to see any direct political benefit to himself.

But not only was he a consistent defender of minorities and the disempowered and impoverished he also worked actively for reconciliation. His idealism was frequently translated in practice in a practical approach to seeking compromise and dialogue between opposing groups, something that has been readily evident in his approach to the Presidency.

What then is the nature of his vision? What are the concrete implications and ramifications of his idealism? The first element of his idealism relates to justice. In the vision of Abdurrahman Wahid, justice should apply across society in all sectors and for all people. And indeed not only across Indonesian society, but also across the global community. He is committed to redressing north-south relations globally, as much as he is committed to seeing greater justice for the persecuted and impoverished in Indonesia. Related to this is commitment to egalitarianism. He has repeatedly stated and there is every reason to believe that this is his serious intention, that he wants to see a more equitable distribution of wealth in Indonesian society and the global society. He is also however, committed to growth and development.

His is a forward-looking vision in which it sees the future and modernity and modernisation generally as offering much. He works, driven by an irrepressible optimism, by the belief that things can and must get better. But this optimism is ready to embrace the better aspects of capitalism and globalisation and recognize that the creation of wealth is necessary if there is to be wealth for all. Finally, he is committed to democracy and to empowering civil society. As suggested at the outset of the section, he has been criticised in his first six months as President for being too interventionist and too much committed to having his own way. Arguably such strong leadership is necessary but it has certainly been a bone of contention for many active within civil society. On the other hand, there is much evidence in his political actions as President that he is steadily reforming the government system as a whole, and particularly the civil service and the military, in order to permit greater accountability, transparency and ultimately the development of democracy. For example, one of his first actions as President was to dismantle the Department for Information. There was no need, he argued for the government to regulate and control the flow of information, rather this should be the business of the media and independent press. He followed this up several months later by replacing the head of the government news agency Antara with an old friend and civil society activist, Mohamed Sobary, and charging him to make Antara a critical and open agency for the dissemination of information and not one beholden to the government and committed to defending the government position.

Realism

Abdurrahman's idealism is at every turn shaped in its application by his realism. This is the source of most of the criticism that has been directed against him as President. Indeed it is the source of most of the criticism that has been directed against him throughout his career as a public intellectual and religious leader. Abdurrahman's approach to reform has always been to push were it is possible to push and to pull back and wait where he thinks nothing more is to be gained, or that proceeding any further may be dangerous. This has been readily evident in his approach to the reform of the Indonesian military as President. And even though he has worked realistically to try and build confidence in the military for his leadership and to cajole them as much as confront them, this middle-of-the-road approach has not greatly slowed his progress in reform. In fact a strong argument can be made to the contrary.

His reform of the military during the first six months of his Presidency was remarkably rapid. It began with the promotion of General Wiranto, previously head of the Indonesian Armed Forces, out of a direct chain of command position and into a civilian portfolio. It then saw steady pressure bought to bear on Wiranto culminating in his resignation in February 2000. Wiranto's resignation was followed with the overhaul of senior command positions in the restructure of the Indonesian military. This push to reform the military was been accompanied by a realistic approach to engagement in which he sought to build his relationship with the military and to reward good behavior as well as to punish bad behavior.

What are the sources then of Abdurrahman's realism? The first source is his understanding of human nature. Arguably his religious understanding shapes this as much as it is shaped by his reading and life experience. Abdurrahman has an ambivalent view of human nature. On the one hand he has a great love of life build upon a love of people and on the other hand he has an awareness of the potential of human beings for great folly and evil.

He is also committed to a staged, evolutionary, approach to reform. As a young man he studied Marxist thought and whilst in Egypt as a student worked part-time for the embassy in Cairo during the anti-Communist crackdown in Indonesia. His position in the embassy meant that he had good access to information about what was happening at home and what he learned horrified him. Like many other Indonesians, the nightmare circumstance of the anti-Communist purge of the mid-sixties has left an indelible mark on his thinking. He has ever since shown a commitment to evolutionary rather than revolutionary change.

In his leadership of Nahdlatul Ulama and his criticism of the Suharto regime, he was always seeking a middle way, a compromise approach that would involve more negotiation than confrontation. Inherent in his approach was always an element of incremental change. In this approach to evolutionary change he is clearly greatly shaped by traditionalist Sunni thinking about politics. Sunni political philosophy is often essentially quiescent and guided by the principles of avoiding harm and promoting the greatest good. In traditionalist Sunni political philosophy this means being prepared to work with all manner of governments and political figures where there is the prospect of either avoiding harm or promoting good. This was the source of much of the modernist angst and anger towards Nahdlatul Ulama during the 1950s, 60s, and 70s. NU was always seen as all too willing to compromise and to dance to the government's tune. From the NU point of view this was precisely how politics had to function. Abdurrahman extended this approach and refined it over more than two decades of engagement in public life. An important principle for Abdurrahman has always been the minimisation of harm.

Whilst this realism and pragmatism may seem to have within it the seeds of fatal compromise, for Abdurrahman it is clear that a profoundly realistic understanding of politics, and a pragmatic approach to governance, is bound up with genuine idealism and commitment to principles. Many of his critics have been surprised by the extent to which he has been able to move towards reform as President. For although he has continued to repeat the mistakes of the past and has draw criticism for his outspokenness and his tendency to shoot-from-the-hip but he has also drawn praise throughout society for his preparedness to tackle hard issues and tough questions.

If he can maintain, even at a much reduced pace, what he has begun in the first six months of his Presidency then there is good reason to believe that over the five years of the Wahid government,

Indonesian society, politics and government will be profoundly trans-formed. This is not to say all problems will be overcome. It is certain, for example, that corruption will take much longer than five years to stamp out. It is also clear that reform of the military requires a staged approach. At the same time there is good reason to believe that the Wahid government will be successful in the decentralisation of the previously highly centralised approach to government under Suharto. This, in fact, may well be a critical element in leading the nation away from fragmentation and dissipation. During his first six months in government Abdurrahman invested considerable energy and time in addressing the Aceh problem. He met behind the scenes both at the Freedom Palace and at his old home in Ciganjur, South Jakarta with numerous Acehenese delegations comprised principally of *ulama* and students, as he sought to negotiate and dialogue.

Aceh and Maluku will continue to be difficult problems because a circle of violence has begun which is now difficult to close. Nevertheless, there are grounds for optimism.

Postscript

After months of deadlock involving the President, the Parliament, the military and a host of other special and vested interests, the self-congratulatory tone of Jakarta MPs at their special session that ousted President Wahid on July 23, 2001 may have suggested that Indonesia's political woes are almost over. If only it were so easy. Building a democracy from scratch is never easy, nor is dealing with the entrenched institutions and powerful, wealthy, and desperate powerbrokers from a discredited authoritarian regime.

Many ordinary Indonesians saw what happened that day as a constitutional coup. They may have been disappointed with the maverick manoeuvres of Abdurrahman Wahid but they were even more disappointed by the sanctimonious, self-serving attitudes of many parliamentarians. However, given Abdurrahman's abhorrence of violence it was not surprising that, despite his anger over his dismissal, he discouraged his many grass-roots followers from taking to the streets in protest. Instead he wisely urged his supporters to channel their energies into the next general elections in 2004 and into the work of strengthening civil-society for the long road ahead. In fact he had spent much of the previous six months traveling throughout Indonesia and appealing to his followers and sympathizers to avoid violence and give up plans to flood into the capital in a show of support.

Abdurrahman also wisely elected not to openly criticize his successor and estranged friend, preferring to describe her as a victim of circumstances. Nevertheless, there is little doubt that he will speak out if she finds herself unable to restrain the hard-line elements who propelled her into the presidency. The challenge now for President Megawati Sukarnoputri is to win back the confidence of the tens of millions who voted for her on the basis of her commitment to reform, while negotiating to share the spoils of power with her new friends, and former opponents from Golkar and the Islamic right. One of her toughest challenges will be standing up to the military. This will not be made any easier by her own conservative style of nationalism. To prove her critics wrong she will have to show that she will not tolerate military adventurism in troubled regions such as Aceh and Papua. Seething ethnic conflicts in Ambon, Sulawesi and Kalimantan will also need to be reined in without resorting to indiscriminate suppression.

The case of Ambon provides a disturbing example of local tensions exacerbated by outside influences, including the military. The bloody clashes between Muslims and Christians have left thousands dead and many more displaced persons, and although massive reinforcements of troops have quelled some of the unrest, rogue elements in the military have colluded in some bloody incidents, leaving a long-term solution to the conflict very much in doubt. An indication of how such clashes can ignite other parts of the nation into religious parochialism was demonstrated in April 2000 when several thousand Islamic militia men were discovered training at a camp outside Jakarta brandishing daggers, swords, and guns, with the clear intention to fight alongside their Muslim brethren in Ambon. President Wahid ordered the group disarmed, but by June the self-styled "Laskar Jihad" had managed to spirit themselves and their arms separately to Ambon virtually under the noses of police, which led to a dramatic increase in violent clashes.

Megawati will also have to take a stand on corruption and allow the Attorney-General's office to pursue investigations in progress. Some of the people that the Attorney-General is most interested in investigating happen to be her close friends and colleagues. The assassination of the judge who convicted the fugitive Tommy Suharto, Justice Syafiuddin Kartasasmita, within days of Wahid's ousting, sent a clear signal that efforts to bring to account corrupt elements of the Suharto regime will face fierce resistance.

She will also be beholden to her Islamist backers, after they relinquished their initial theological reservations about a female Head of State. The election of United Development Party (PPP) head Hamzah Haz as her Vice President underlines how critical maintaining the Government's Islamic credentials will be. As leader of the third largest party in the parliament, Hamzah Haz's nomination was not altogether surprising, given the alternative, Akbar Tandjung of Golkar, would have given the new government a connection with the Suharto era that the PDI-P faithful could not stomach. However, Haz's conservative Islamism could usher a shift in sentiment against the Islamic humanism preached by Abdurrahman. More radical Islamic parties and shadowy vigilante groups like the Defenders of Islam Front will see a tempting opportunity pressure the government to adopt a more exclusionary agenda.

Perhaps most important o all the challenges facing the new administration is the need to fundamentally reform the Indonesian constitution. If a parliamentary style of government is desired, it is important that the checks necessary to sustaining a healthy democracy are properly developed. There needs to be a truly independent upper house and a constitutional court of appeal. Without such reforms Indonesia will have endless political instability and may fail to move to full democracy.

An ominous precedent was set by the move against Indonesia's first democratically elected president. If Megawati and her administration, together with the members of parliament, are not very careful, Indonesian democracy will be limited to the crude dynamics of "might is right" and religious chauvinism for years to come.

Notes

1.   There has been significant academic debate over the scale of the organized raping of Chinese women in May 1998, in large measure because the women involved were justifiably too frightened to testify before antagonistic government authorities. Whatever the precise numbers prove to be, however, there is no doubting the scar that it has left on the psyche of the community.

2.   In the 1955 elections PNI, the Indonesian Nationalist Party (Party Nasionalis Indonesia) gained 22.3 percent of the national vote, Masyumi 20.9 percent, NU 18.4 percent and PKI, the Indonesian Communist Party, 16.4 percent. Four second-tier parties each received between 2 percent and 3 percent of the vote and the remaining 12.5 percent went to a series of minor parties. Around thirty eight million valid votes were cast.

3.   PNI effectively continued into the New Order period as PDI, the Indonesian Democratic Party (Partai Demokrasi Indonesia), though like the other officially sanctioned opposition party PPP, the United Development Party (Partai Persatuan Pembangunan)

the combination of discriminatory electoral laws and regular government manipulation of its affairs meant that PDI could never really present a serious challenge to Golkar, the Suharto government's political vehicle. This began to appear as if it might change, however, when in the 1990s Megawati was successful in taking over the leadership of PDI from Soerjadi, a chairman with whom the government clearly felt comfortable. As the Suharto government waxed increasingly repressive from mid 1994 onwards (when three leading newsweeklies were banned, including TEMPO) official discomfort with Megawati increased. Nevertheless, Megawati only became more outspoken, openly courting confrontation with the regime, despite being urged by friends such as Abdurrahman Wahid to make a tactical retreat. Finally, in July 1996 Suharto retaliated by organizing an internal party coup against Megawati and replacing her with Soerjadi. Because Soerjadi continued to cling to the leadership of the now greatly diminished PDI Megawati's own PDI faction was not permitted to use the title PDI. Consequently Megawati's group is now styling itself PDI Perjuangan (PDI-P) or the PDI of the Struggle.

4. LIPI—Lembaga Ilmu Pengatahuan Indonesia: the Indonesian Institute of Sciences.
5. *Kompas*, "Puluhan Jenazah Ditemukan di Sambas," 25 March 1999, (*http:// www.kompas.com/kompas-cetak/9903/25/UTAMA/pulu01.htm*), Tempo Online, 29 March 1999 (http://www.tempo.co.id/harian/ include/index.asp?file=29031999-jp-2).
6. For example, figures such as the bright and independently minded Ulil Abdulla Abshar, a rising young intellectual within NU.
7. Abdurrahman explained his apparent quiescent during the period as being bought about by the necessity to avoid confrontation with the military. Indeed, it would appear that Abdurrahman had intelligence from military contacts indicating there was a high degree of likelihood of demonstrations meeting with fierce confrontation from the military, and indeed subsequent events tended to bear this out.
8. Van Zorge Report on Indonesia, Issue VII, January 23 1999 [www.vanzorgereport.com].
9. The Indonesian academic system is much like the British one, with the rank of professor being a very high one and professorships perhaps even less common than is the case in the United Kingdom.
10. Op. Cit.
11. In the mid-seventies, nuclear deterrents were judged to turn very much on the ability of nuclear submarines whose location was unknown, to launch inter-continental ballistic missiles. Of course the percentage of all inter-continental ballistic missiles that could be launched by submarines was relatively small but the argument went that as the land launch sites whether in the Soviet Union or in the U.S., were largely known, therefore the only unknown factor would be these submarine launches. In order for the location of the submarines to remain a secret, however, it was necessary to be able to transverse the world oceans and to be able to cross from the Indian Ocean into the Pacific Ocean without being detected by the Soviets. To move from the Indian Ocean to the Pacific Ocean essentially means a submarine had either to go south of Australia or through the Indonesian archipelago. The only safe choice for a submarine wishing to keep its location unknown and undetected was to choose a deep-water strait and the only practical deep-water strait was the Wetar Strait to the east of East Timor. Consequently, the argument went that if East Timor fell into Socialist hands there was good reason to believe that the Soviets may have access to monitoring in the Wetar Strait through seeding microphones or other detection devices and consequently be able to plot the position of U.S. ICBM nuclear submarines.
12. Which was ostensibly paid in gratitude for help in recovering bad debts but which on those grounds should never have been paid as the debts were guaranteed by the central bank.

Bibliography

Anwar, M. Syafi'I, (1995), *Pemikran dan Aksi Islam Indonesia: Sebuah Kajian Politik Tentang Cendekiawan Muslim Orde Baru* (Jakarta: Paramadina).

Barton, Greg, (1994), "The impact of Islamic neo-Modernism on Indonesian Islamic thought: The emergence of a new pluralism," in David Bourchier and John Legge (eds.), *Indonesian Democracy: 1950s and 1990s* (Clayton: Monash University), pp. 143-150.

——, (1995a), "Neo-Modernism: a Vital Synthesis of Traditionalism and Modernism in Indonesian Islam" *Studia Islamika*, vol. 2, no. 3 1995, pp.1-75.

——, (1996), "The Liberal, Progressive Roots of Abdurrahman Wahid's Thought" in Greg Barton and Greg Fealy (eds.), *Nahdlatul Ulama, Traditional Islam and Modernity in Indonesia* (Clayton: Monash Asia Institute), pp. 190-226.

——, (1997a), "Indonesia's Nurcholish Madjid and Abdurrahman Wahid as intellectual *ulama*: The meeting of Islamic traditionalism and Modernism in neo-Modernist thought," *Islam and Christian-Muslim Relations*, vol. 8, no. 3, October 1997, pp. 323-50.

——, (1997b), "The Origins of Islamic Liberalism in Indonesia and its Contribution to Democratisation," *Democracy in Asia* (New York: St. Martins Press, 1997).

——, (1999a), Gagasan Islam Liberal: Telaah terhadap Tulisan-tulisan Nurcholish Madjid, Djohan Effendi, Ahmad Wahib dan Abdurrahman Wahid, 1968-1980 (Jakarta: Yayasan Wakaf Paramadina).

——, (1999b), with Andree Feillard, "What does Nahdlatul Ulama's November 1997 Konbes/Munas in Lombak tell us about NU?" *Studia Islamika*, vol. 6, no. 1, June 1999.

Binder, Leonard, (1988), *Islamic Liberalism: a Critique of Development Ideologies* (Chicago: University of Chicago Press).

Boland, B.J., (1971), *The Struggle of Islam in Modern Indonesia* (The Hague: Martinus Nijhoff).

Crouch, Harold, (1987), *The Politics of Islam in Southeast Asia*, Flinders Asian Studies Lecture 18 (Adelaide).

Effendy, Bahtiar, (1994), *Islam and the State: The Transformation of Islamic Political Ideas and Practices in Indonesia*, Ohio State University Ph.D. Dissertation (Columbus). 1994).

——, (1995), "Islam and the State in Indonesia: Munawir Sjadzali and the development of a new theological underpinning of political Islam," *Studia Islamika: Indonesian Journal for Islamic Studies*, vol. 2, no. 2, pp. 97-121.

Eldridge, Philip, (1995), *Non-Government Organizations and Democratic Participation in Indonesia* (Kuala Lumpur: Oxford University Press).

Eyerman, Ron, (1994), *Between Culture and Politics: Intellectuals in Modern Society* Cambridge.

Fakhi, Mansoor, (1996), *Masyarakat Sipil* (Yogyakarta: Pustaka Pelajar).

Fealy, Greg, (1996), The 1994 NU Congress and Aftermath: Abdurrahman Wahid, Suksesi and the Battle for Control of NU," in Greg Barton and Greg Fealy (eds.), *Nahdlatul Ulama, Traditional Islam and Modernity in Indonesia*

(Clayton: Monash Asia Institute), pp. 257-77.

——, (1996), "Indonesian Politics, 1995-1996: The Makings of a Crisis," a paper presented at Indonesia Update 1996, The Australian National University, 23-24 August 1996 [to be published in *Indonesia Update 1996*, (1997)].

Gellner, Ernest, (1981), *Muslim Society* (Cambridge: Cambridge University Press).

——, (1992), *Postmodernism, Reason and Religion* (London: Routledge).

Gouldner, A., (1979), *The Future of Intellectuals and the Rise of the New Class* (New York).

Hefner, Robert, (1996), "Secularization and Citizenship in Muslim Indonesia," a paper presented at the IRSEA workshop, 2nd EURAMES Conference, Aix-en-Provence, France, 6 July 1996.

Hewison, K. and Robison, R., (1990), *Southeast Asia in the 1990's: Authoritarianism, Democracy and Capitalism* (Sydney: Allen and Unwin).

Liddle, R. William, (1988), *Politics and Culture in Indonesia* (Ann Arbor: Center for Political Studies Institute for Social Research, University of Michigan), pp. 1-55.

——, (1990), "Changing Political Culture: Three Indonesian Cases," unpublished paper.

——, "Islam and Politics in Late New Order Indonesia: The Use of Religion as a Political Resource by an Authoritarian Regime," unpublished paper.

——, (1993), "*Media Dakwah* Scriptualism: One Form of Islamic Political Thought and Action in New Order Indonesia," unpublished conference paper.

——, (1994), "Can all good things go together? Democracy, Growth, and Unity in Post Soeharto Indonesia," in David Bourchier and John Legge (eds.), *Indonesian Democracy 1950s and 1990s* (Melbourne: Centre of Southeast Asian Studies, Monash University), pp. 286-301.

——, (1996), "The Islamic Turn in Indonesia: a Political Explanation," unpublished paper.

Madjid, Nurcholish, (1992), *Islam: Doktrin dan Peradaban* (Jakarta: Yayasan Wakaf Paramadina).

——, (1994), *Islam, Kerakyatan, dan Keindonesiaan: Pikiran-pikiran Nurcholish "Muda,"* (Bandung: Mizan).

——, (1994), "Islamic Roots of Modern Pluralism," *Studia Islamika: Indonesian Journal for Indonesian Studies*, vol. 1, no. 1 (April-June), pp. 55-77.

——, (1995), *Islam, Agama Kemanusiaan: Membangun Tradisisi dan Visi Baru Islam Indonesia*, (Jakarta: Yayasan Wakaf Paramadina).

——, (1995), *Islam, Agama Peradaban: Membangun Makna dan Relevansi Doktrin Islam dalam Sejarah* (Jakarta: Yayasan Wakaf Paramadina).

——, (1995),. *Pintu-pintu Menuju Tuhan* (Jakarta: Yayasan Wakaf Paramadina).

Munawar-Rachman, Budhy, ed., (1994), *Kontekstualisasi Doktrin Islam dalam Sejarah* (Jakarta: Yayasan Wakaf Paramadina).

Nakamura, Mitsuo, (1983), *The Crescent Arises Over the Banyan Tree: A Study of the Muhammadiyah Movement in a Central Javanese Town* (Yogyakarta: Gadjah Mada University Press).

——, (1996), "The Radical Traditionalism of the Nahdlatul Ulama in Indonesia: A Personal Account of the 26th National Congress, June 1979,

Semarang," in Greg Barton and Greg Fealy (eds.), *Nahdlatul Ulama, Traditional Islam and Modernity in Indonesia* (Clayton: Monash Asia Institute), pp. 68-93.

——, (1996), "NU's Leadership Crisis and Search for Identity in the Early 1980s: from the 1979 Semarang Congress to the 1984 Situbondo Congress," in Greg Barton and Greg Fealy (eds.), *Nahdlatul Ulama, Traditional Islam and Modernity in Indonesia* (Clayton: Monash Asia Institute), pp. 94-109.

Rahman, Fazlur, (1982), *Islam and Modernity/ Transformation of an Intellectual Tradition* (Chicago: University of Chicago Press).

——, (1979), "Islam: Past Influence and Present Challenge," in *Islam: Challenges and Opportunities* (Edinburgh: Edinburgh University Press), pp. 315-30.

Ramage, Douglas E., (1995), *Politics in Indonesia: Democracy, Islam and the Ideology of Tolerance* (London: Routledge).

Turner, Bryan S., (1994), *Orientalism, Postmodernism and Globalism* (London: Routledge).

Van Bruinessen, Martin, (1987), "New Perspectives on Southeast Asian Islam?" in *Bijdragen*, Deel 143, Afl. 4e, pp. 519-37.

——, (1996), "The 28th Congress of Nahdlatul Ulama: Power Struggle and Social Concerns," in Greg Barton and Greg Fealy (eds.), *Nahdlatul Ulama, Traditional Islam and Modernity in Indonesia* (Clayton: Monash Asia Institute), pp. 139-62.

——, (1996), "Traditions for the Future: The Reconstruction of Traditionalist Discourse within NU" in Greg Barton and Greg Fealy (eds.), *Nahdlatul Ulama, Traditional Islam and Modernity in Indonesia* (Clayton: Monash Asia Institute), pp. 163-89.

Vatikiotis, Michael R.J, (1987), "A Propagation Problem," *Far Eastern Economic Review*, 31 December, pp. 21-2.

——, (1990), "A Surge in Muslim Activity Despite Extremist Scares: Faith Without Fanatics," *Far Eastern Economic Review*, 14 June, pp. 25-32.

——, (1988), "One Code for All Courts," *Far Eastern Economic Review*, 22 September, pp. 28-30.

——, (1987), "Thoroughly Modern Muslims," *Far Eastern Economic Review*, 10 December, p. 30.

Wahid, Abdurrahman, (1978), *Bunga Rampai Pesantren* (Jalarta: CV Dharma Bhakti).

——, (YEAR?), *Muslim di Tengah Pergumulan* (Jakarta: Leppenas).

——, (1985), "The Islamic Masses in the Life of State and Nation," *Prisma*, pp. 3-10.

Ward, Ken E., (1977), *The 1971 Election in Indonesia: An East Java Case Study* (Melbourne: Centre of Southeast Asian Studies Monash University).

Woodward, Mark R., ed., (1996), *Toward a New Paradigm* (Tucson: University of Arizona Press).

——, (1989), *Islam in Java: Normative Piety and Mysticism in the Sultanate of Yogyakarta*, The Association for Asian Studies Monograph no. XLV (Tucson: University of Arizona Press).

Yamamoto, Tadashi, (1995), *Emerging Civil Society in the Asia Pacific Community: Nongovernmental Underpinnings of the Emerging Asia Pacific Regional Community*, Singapore: Institute of Southeast Asian Studies (ISEAS).

2

Islam, Society, Politics, and Change in Malaysia

Greg Barton

Introduction

What Kind of Islam?

If the Western view of Islam in Indonesia is that of a friendly, non-threatening, but perhaps none-too-serious faith, the corresponding Western stereotype of Malaysian Islam is often rather different. This has been especially so after the Islamic resurgence that first stirred in the early 1970s began to increasingly dominate Malaysian politics. The appropriation of Islam as a legitimizing political force by Prime Minister Mahathir in the 1980s served to further alarm the West. This was against a backdrop in which the West, increasingly on edge about Islamic fundamentalism following the 1979 Iranian Islamic revolution, was beginning to recognize Islam, and religion generally, as important elements in international politics. The collapse of Communism and the elevation of Islamic fundamentalism as the West's new dark other in popular perception, underscored by the serious academic writings of Huntington (1993; 1996) and others, meant that Mahathir's manipulation of Islamic symbolism served not only to boost his domestic profile but also his international one. A consequence that was by no means unintended.

A common view of Islam in Malaysia is that it tends towards fundamentalism and is generally characterized by an anti-Western stance. In certain respects, at least when comparing Islam in Indonesia and Islam in Malaysia, Islam in Malaysia does seem to be rather more narrow and scripturalist, and more suspicious of the influence of

91

modern Western thought. Moreover, Islam is widely used in domestic Malaysian politics both as a way of bolstering support for the regime through direct, and sometimes racist, criticism of the West and of finding fault with it. In its extreme form in the hands of Prime Minister Mahathir, this criticism has occasionally taken the form of rhetorical diatribes loaded with inferences of conspiracy theory and with blatant anti-Semitism.

So what kind of Islam is Malaysian Islam? Is there something different about the Malaysian soil, about the geographical or historical setting that means the liberalism readily evident in Indonesia is not to be found in Malaysia? As is invariably the case with such stereotypes or simplifications, this view of Malaysian Islam is neither completely right nor completely wrong. Islam in Malaysia is on the whole more conservative, or scripturalist, and less comfortable with the West, than is Islam in Indonesia. This does not mean however, that it is difficult to find Malaysians who empathize or agree with an Indonesian outlook nor does it mean that the problems faced by Malaysia in regards to Islam conservatism are completely absent in Indonesia. One of the key points of difference between the two nations is that in Indonesia there are a considerable number of theologically educated Islamic intellectuals who have also studied modern Western thought and social science. These Islamic theologians have synthesized classical Islamic scholarship with modern Western thought in a way that has produced a sophisticated and powerful synthesis. For example, influential thinkers such as Nurcholish Madjid and Abdurrahman Wahid have clearly illustrated the potential for combining these two educational traditions in an immensely creative and productive fashion (Barton, 1997a; 1997b). The liberal thought that results from this meeting of traditions is not liberal merely out of a desire to be flexible or to accommodate, or even to be humanitarian, but rather has its roots in a deep understanding of the core values of Islam as they apply to modern society. In many Muslim societies, indeed in the majority of Muslim societies, the *ulama* or the theologically educated Islamic scholars tend to remain separate from the modern intelligentsia. It is rare then, to find a modern intellectual with a profound scholarly understanding of Islamic thought, just as it is rare to find an *alim* (*alim* is the singular form of *ulama*) with a thorough and intimate understanding of modern Western thought. In Indonesia, however, this combination is becoming

increasingly common, due in no small measure to the success of the
pesantren system of religious boarding schools, and at the tertiary
level of State Islamic Institutes (IAIN), in producing modern Islamic
intellectuals. The fact that the Suharto regime was more than keen to
encourage this development, principally through progressive ministers and technocrats in the Department of Religious Affairs, was extremely consequential.

In this respect, the situation in Malaysia is almost the reverse of
the Indonesian situation. While, the Mahathir government has been
essentially no more keen than was the Suharto regime to encourage
fundamentalistic forms of political Islam, it nevertheless, has done
little to produce the kind of "cultural Islam" so evident in Indonesia.
Even its best initiatives to modernize Islamic thinking, such as the
International Islamic University established in 1983 just outside
Kuala Lumpur, have been less than satisfactory in creating a new,
more liberal, milieu for Islamic intellectuals. The reasons why this is
so are manifold, but prime among them is the fact, that unlike Indonesia, Malaysia does not have a strong recent tradition of independent *ulama* or religious scholars. Instead, the official offices of Islamic authority have been filled by government appointees and the
men who occupy such offices are generally completely beholden to
their government masters.

Islam and Opposition

Given that the root cause of Islam conservatism in Malaysia is
arguably the considerable extent to which the Malaysian government controls the core institutions of Islamic leadership and intellectual production it seems rather surprising then, that we can speak of
Islam and opposition in Malaysia. And yet, this is really the other
side of the government's attempts to control Islam. For while officially all of the important posts in Muslim Malaysian society have
been controlled directly or indirectly by the government this has led
to the emergence of a series of local expressions of Islamic opposition. This opposition comes in part because of political disaffection
and in part because of the disillusionment with the way in which the
Mahathir administration has controlled and contrived most expressions of Islamicity in official Malaysian life. One of the best examples of this is PAS, the Islamic Party of Malaysia. At first glance
PAS appears to be an Islamist party driven by traditional Islamist

concerns to turn the Malaysian state into a properly Islamic state along Islamist lines. One would expect then, PAS members would be in every respect conservative or even reactionary in their views and narrow in their political outlook. The reality is rather more complex. The seat of PAS's power lies in the northern peninsula states of Kedah, Kelantan and Trengganu. And while it is generally true that the Malay population in these states tends to be rather conservative and traditional in outlook, in other respects many of the PAS members do not fit the general Middle Eastern description of Islamists. In part, this is because it is often difficult to make a cultural distinction between PAS members and non-PAS Muslims based upon their expression of Islamicity. This is because PAS essentially represents the locus of political opposition to the ruling regime. The way in which Malaysian politics has been dominated over the last three decades by the Barisan Nasional (National Front) coalition, an alliance between the United Malays National Organization (UMNO) and the leading non-Malay parties of the Malaysian Chinese Association (MCA) and the Malaysian Indian Congress (MIC) means that there has been very little scope to organize political opposition to the incumbent regime. One of the few opportunities to engage in significant political opposition for ethnic Malays, who represent around 59 percent of the Malaysian population, is through PAS. This is particularly true in the northern states of Kedah, Kelantan and Trengganu. The small number of non-Malays voters, and the presence of a large number of independently minded, largely rural Malays critical of the government in Kuala Lumpur, means that PAS has been able to consistently do well in these states.

The other main expression of Islamic opposition in Malaysia has arisen since the 1970s with the resurgence of Islam around the world generally, and within Southeast Asia specifically. One of the most evident products of this resurgence has been the emergence of a series of so-called *dakwah* organizations and other similar non-government bodies.(Jomo & Cheek, 1992; Peletz, 1997; Shamsul, 1997) These *dakwah* and other groups are essentially religious groups concerned with changing the religious culture of modern Malaysian society. In many cases one of the driving forces behind these groups seems to be a youthful disaffection with the apparent hypocrisy and manipulation of Islam for political purposes evident in the Mahathir regime. These groups are primarily concerned with proselytizing and encouraging greater purity among Malaysian Muslims. The Arabic word *dakwah* (literally: to call to action) in fact loosely translates as "missionary activity" and the *dakwah* groups are primarily concerned with changing individuals and society to become more faithful to Islam according to their understanding of Islam. In other respects though, the *dakwah* movement can be read as a kind of opposition to, or rebellion against, the ruling elite, the ruling generation and the prevailing political order, as is the case with many other youth movements around the world.

Up until recently, there has been little planning for alliance between the various Islamic groups critical of the government. Nevertheless it is clear in general terms that Islam represents one of the few avenues available to Malays to oppose the government. Ironically, it is partly because the Mahathir government of the past decade has been so keen to use Islam as a legitimizing political and cultural force that such broad opportunity has been created to employ Islam as a force of opposition. Because the Mahathir government has styled itself as the champion of Islam and a defender of the faith it has found it problematic to clamp down on autonomous expressions of Islamicity, even when those expressions contain a veiled criticism of the government itself. At times it has tried to delineate what it sees as being "responsible Islam" from dangerous, political, or Islamist, activity. In reality, however, it has found it more than a little difficult to argue that it can simultaneously be a defender of the faith and an opponent of spontaneous expressions of Islamic enthusiasm.

Islam and Reformation

Increasingly, particularly since the beginning of the trial of Anwar Ibrahim in late 1998, community leaders and intellectuals in Malaysia have begun to wonder aloud if this natural tendency for Islam to be used as a channel of opposition can be turned along more productive lines and Islam harnessed to the cause of reformation. One of the most striking features of the spontaneous and large-scale eruption of anger towards the Mahathir government for the arrest of Anwar Ibrahim (on apparently trumped-up charges of corruption) in late 1998, was the way in which Malaysian youth so quickly picked up the language of their Indonesian counterparts. In particular the word *reformasi* was widely seen on banners and placards, and heard over

megaphones, during the heady months of late 1998. What was seldom heard however, was a coherent explanation of what *reformasi*
meant in the Malaysian context. It was transparently a term bor-
rowed from the student movements and civil society activism that
led to the downfall of Suharto in Indonesia in May that year. In the
Indonesian context *reformasi* stood for a complete renewal of the
political order, of the justice system and of the way in which the
Indonesian economy and business worked. In the Malaysian case it
was not entirely clear whether those who appropriated the term had
in mind the same sets of issues, although it does seem clear that in a
loose sense the concerns were shared. Certainly the youthful and
angry supporters of Anwar Ibrahim seemed, like their Indonesian
counterparts, to be arguing for a new political system, a new government and a more genuine democratic process, in particular a more
separate and independent judiciary and a more transparent and open
system of government.

While this movement was not using Islam as its primary focus of
opposition it nevertheless did mark the beginnings, at least in a public sense, of a more liberal, pluralist and inclusivistic understanding
of Islam being allied to the *reformist* cause. Particularly striking was
the extent to which the crowds protesting over Anwar's arrest were
multicultural, composed of not just Malays but Malaysian Indians
and Chinese as well. It remains to be seen whether the new political
party lead by Azizah, Anwar's wife, the National Justice Party, will
be able to realize its ideals but its ideals are certainly laudable. Central to them, together with concerns for greater transparency in Malaysian government is a notion of a cross-communal political party
representing the interests of all Malaysians in a direct effort to resist
the abusive use of ethnic difference, and religious difference by the
Malaysia government in the last three decades for the sake of its
own political strength. Moreover, it appears that this inclusivism and
cross-communal vision is allied to a liberal progressive understanding of Islam similar to that found in Indonesia.

Islam and the State in Malaysia—The Legacy of History

The Coming of Islam

Many of the reasons as to why Islam in Malaysia seems so different to Islam in Indonesia have to do with recent history, particularly

the political developments of the past few decades. There is also a sense in which the nature of the relationship between Islam and the state in Malaysia has origins that go back to the coming of Islam to the port city of Malacca in the fifteenth century. Compared with Java, the Malaysian peninsula has had a longer history of Islamization and, in certain respects the ways in which local rulers responded to Islam are also significantly different. More importantly though, is the way in which the British, beginning late in the nineteenth century and early in the twentieth century responded to the Malay sultanate system and used it for their own colonial purposes, reinforcing the position of the sultans as the official guardians of Islam.

That this was possible has much to do with the history of Islam in the Malay world. The earliest records we have of the arrival of Islam in the Malaysian-Indonesian archipelago are of tombstones with Arabic inscriptions dating from the twelfth century and then evidence of Muslim settlements in the twelfth and thirteenth centuries, leading observers to infer that the northern tip of Sumatra was Islamized in the thirteenth century or possibly earlier. While there is little documentary evidence of the way in which Islam came to Aceh and the surrounding area of North Sumatra there is rather more evidence of what took place in Malacca in the 1400s. According to the *Sejarah Melayu*, the official Malay genealogy setting forth the ostensible origins of Malay royal families, the first Sultan of Malacca converted to Islam as a result of a powerful dream. How this relates to the historical circumstances we cannot be sure. Nevertheless it does suggest that early in the 1400s a king in Malacca decided to embrace Islam, presumably as a result of contact with Muslim traders in that famous port city, and hence became known as sultan. Moreover, it seems likely that this conversion came as a result of free choice by that ruler of Malacca and certainly not as a result of conquest, for there is no evidence of the latter. In any case this seems to have set the stage for the Sultanate of Malacca over the next century. Because the Sultanate of Malacca enjoyed great commercial and political success it was able to influence the surrounding regions including the coast of Sumatra, possibly the Western extremities of Java, and parts of the coast of Borneo. The Sultanate of Malacca played an important role in the Islamization of the Malay world. When the sultanate collapsed in the early part of the sixteenth century partly as a result of the Portuguese conquest of Malacca in 1511, the remnants dispersed around the peninsula, carrying with them a tradition of courtly society based on Islam. Consequently, the royal houses of Malaysia trace their origin back to the Malacca sultanate.

Beginning with the Malacca Sultanate Islam quickly became an integral part of Malay notions of ruler-ship and power. In early texts, such as the *Sejarah Melayu*, one can trace a shift between the notion of Hindu-Buddhist "god-king" to a more mortal but nevertheless powerful caliph, or vice-regent of God, the Shadow of God Upon the Earth, as kingship passed out of the Hindu-Buddhist era into the era of Islam. In many respects there was a significant continuity of ideas so that, for example, the earlier Hindu-Buddhist concept of the welfare of a kingdom being closely bound up with the spiritual power of the ruler was transmogrified in Muslim Southeast Asian society so that the notion of the *daulat* or the royal authority, carried with it connotations of mystical power. In many respects this has shaped popular thinking about modern governance in Indonesia and Malaysia.

Because relative to Java, Islam came much earlier to the Malay Peninsula, this meant that Islam in Malaysia has a relatively long and rich history of contact and influence via trade from India and the Middle East. At the same time, however, many of the same ambiguities about the nature of Islam in the state and in the sultanate can be observed on the peninsula as they can be in Java. In some respects, it could be argued that vestigial elements of Hindu-Buddhist notions of power and certainly of earlier superstitious beliefs prevailed. From another point of view one might argue that the situation of the peninsula is not only similar to the island of Java, but is not greatly different to the situation in almost all other Muslim societies including South and West Asia and the Arab world itself. That is to say, at various points in time a common, or folk Islam, which emphasized a more magical or enchanted understanding of the world prevailed over a high, or scripturalist tradition focused on the Qur'an and the Hadith as authoritative sources. In general terms, the high or scripturalist tradition revolved around the authority of the *ulama* who are the guardians of scholarly Orthodoxy, while low, or common, or folk Islam was both the domain of peasant villages, farmers and also at times of members of the royal Court. The reality of course, is much more complex than this simple overview suggests. Suffice to say, however, that when the British came to Malaya, they found that the relationship between the sultans and orthodox Islam was ambiguous.

The Malay State and British Colonialism

In the East Indies the Dutch decided that their interests were better served by using more nominally Muslim aristocrats and members of the lower aristocracy to act as their cultural brokers and political intermediaries. In the case of Malaya, the British decided that they would accentuate the role of the sultans as keepers of the faith. In both cases however, the intention was much the same, namely that colonial authority would be asserted through a policy of divide and rule, and that the local rulers who were employed for this process would be made to represent the interests of Islam. Further, local rulers employed for the purposes of colonialism would be made to act in such a way that a more acculturated or less political, less threatening form of Islam prevailed in royal favor and that the more puritan or Middle East oriented form of scripturalist Islam was constrained and kept outside the power of the court.

In the case of the East Indies this meant that for a long time the dominant state ethos was one of ambivalence towards the high traditional or scripturalist traditional Islam. It also meant, however, that the *ulama* were encouraged to organize themselves independently. This led to a nascent form of civil society even during the colonial period, as the *pesantren* network developed at a local and provincial level finally coalescing into a national organization in Nahdlatul Ulama in 1926. Similarly, the formation of Muhammadiyah in 1912, and the subsequent growth of a nation-wide network of schools, hospitals and orphanages resulted in a one of the nation's most extensive and substantial networks in the civil sphere.

In the case of the Malay Peninsula the details were somewhat reversed. Here the colonial powers made the sultans the official guardians of Islam thus simultaneously ensuring that a more threatening, political Islam was not allowed to emerge and that the sultans were kept busy with things which were largely of no consequence to their colonial overlords. Further accentuating this was the natural geographical and political setting of Malaysia. In Java, a series of powerful kingdoms had dominated large parts of the island for relatively long periods of time. In the Malay Peninsula, following the fall of the Sultan of Malacca in 1511, however, Malay ruling power was divided among a series of sultans spread across the peninsula and indeed around the coast of Borneo and Sumatra.

On the peninsula itself it was a relatively natural development that a series of small sultanates would work together to form a kind of federation rather than a single large sultanate. This was because the natural topography of the peninsula and the cultural orientation of the Malays led to the creation of a series of smaller sultanates focused around port cities up and down the peninsula. Moreover, the peninsula was relatively under-populated, but fertile, and farming and fishing easily produced sufficient food. However Malay society remained essentially water-borne, focusing on fishing and trade, and to some extent wet-rice cultivation in areas such as Kedah where this was easily done. As a consequence Malay settlements were typically ports either on rivers or at the mouths of rivers on the Straits of Malacca, or along the east coast of the peninsula. The larger of these ports developed into centers of power, the seats of the local sultanates. Difficult terrain including dense jungle and relatively rugged mountain ranges meant that it was natural that sultanates should develop locally. At the same time water-born trade meant that communication, including intermarriage between the sultanates, was relatively easily carried out and so the kind of federal system that naturally emerged was easily converted into the official system of government employed by the British. This federal system gave the British the added advantage of being able to play off one sultan against the other. Even the formalized system of electing an overall king or Yang di-Pertuan Agong, through an artificial system of rotation, gave to the colonial overlords considerable scope for political manipulation and control.

In many other respects too, the Malays under the British were encouraged to continue their traditional form of life both in the royal courts and in their villages based on fishing and farming, generally remaining unencumbered by the presence of the colonial overlords. Rather than use the Malays as laborers, the British came to the conclusion early on that it was easier to import either Indian or Chinese labor for specific tasks. This meant that the Malays as a whole, the sultanate as an elite group, and Islam, remained in something of a backwater as far as modern Malayan colonial society was concerned. At the same time the British much like the Dutch, though perhaps more so, undertook to educate members of the aristocracy in a way that ensured they were overwhelmingly European in outlook.

Independence, Emergency, and Political Authority

Another point of significant difference between Indonesia and Malaysia in the development of their respective political cultures has to do with the way in which nationalism and independence were worked out.

The rise of nationalism in the Dutch East Indies saw some members of the *priyayi* or the aristocratic ruling classes become involved in nationalism and others oppose it on the grounds of preserving the status quo, which clearly served their interests. The fact that the Dutch were not willing to allow nationalism to achieve its declared goal of independence following the cessation of hostilities at the end of World War II meant that a revolutionary struggle for independence was necessary. The Indonesian nationalist leaders declared independence on August 17, 1945 in the brief interregnum between the Japanese surrender and the return of Dutch and Allied troops. The nationalists were forced to quickly move into an armed struggle against the returning Dutch forces over a period of four years before finally the combination of their armed resistance and political pressure from nations friendly to the Netherlands forced the Dutch to allow the Indonesian nationalists to claim their independence. During this period of struggle for independence a number of issues were worked out which later colored the shape of the new nation. One of these was that the majority of traditional rulers, sultans, and princes who did not support the nationalists found themselves wiped out during the nationalist struggle with the exception of one or two pro-independence sultans, such as the Sultan of Yogyakarta. In Malaya, however, the British, as they have done in India, decided that in the postwar period they had no choice but to grant independence to their colonies. Unlike the case in India, however, in Malaysia the British and their allies had to contend with communist guerilla resistance before they could grant independence. Nevertheless, when independence came it occurred in a peaceful and carefully planned fashion with political power being handed over to the nationalists and the Malay aristocracy not only preserved intact but in fact called upon to play an important role in governing the newly independent nation.

In many ways, the interests of the new government in Malaysia coincided with interests of the former British colonialists with respect to the sultans and Islam. That is to say it rather suited the new government to leave to one side the question of Islam on the grounds that it was the province of the sultans and need not become concern the new government. In the early years then, Islam did not play an important role in the development of political culture in Malaysia except as a symbol of Malay identity. To the extent that it was involved it was co-opted or controlled by the government, and by the sultans, and was very much an instrument of the state rather than a third force in society. Whereas in Indonesia, Nahdlatul Ulama and Muhammadiyah, as mass-based religious organizations, contested the 1955 elections via the Nahdlatul Ulama Party and Masyumi and continued to function as mass based organizations throughout the independence period, in Malaysia they had no equivalent. All of the important religious postings in the new nation were directly or indirectly under the control of the government. Malaysia lacked an extensive system of religious instruction along the lines of Indonesia's *pesantren* and IAIN system. For while the *pondok* system in Malaysia is in some ways similar to the *pesantren* system, it is also much less extensive and Malaysia does not have an equivalent of Indonesia's tertiary level IAIN network. Consequently, to a significant extent it fell to the government to ensure that correctly trained religious functionaries were produced.

The Issue of Race and Malay Identity

This brief overview obviously glosses over many important and interesting details but in general terms it can be said that religion did not play an important, or at least central, role in the development of Malay political culture until after the issue of race relations emerged in the late 1960s. In many ways it can be argued that the British had left a time bomb ticking away in its former colonies in the form of an explosive mixture of racial and socio-economic conditions. In the West Indies, in Sri Lanka, in India, in Malaya and even in Fiji, the British practice of dividing and ruling along racial and ethnic lines, and in many cases the importing of labor for specific tasks, and the resultant development of stark social and economic differences, created enormous problems for the newly independent nations.

In Malaya the large numbers of Chinese and South Indian immigrants left the newly independent nation with a delicate balance between indigenous Malays and other indigenous races and immigrant peoples. While under the British and even after the hand-over of power the Malays were envisaged as playing a central role in the political process and essentially being the locus of political power, demographically they were left clinging to a slight majority. It was almost inevitable then, that politics in Malaya would develop along racial and ethnic lines. And indeed, it was not long before the Malayan Chinese Association (MCA) and the Malayan Indian Congress (MCI) were vying for power together with UMNO plus a series of other reasonably communal parties. Even the dominance of the Barisan Nasional (BN), or National Front, coalition from the mid-1950s onwards, which served to align the MCA the MCI and UMNO, did little to remove the focus on ethnicity and communalism in Malayan politics. The infamous May 13 incident of 1969, however, which saw hundreds of people die in bitter ethnic violence following MCA's electoral success in the national capital, led to a serious rethinking of politics and race relations in Malaysia.

The Islamic Movements

Introduction

Malaysia has nothing quite comparable with Indonesia's two large mass based organizations of Muhammadiyah and Nahdlatul Ulama, but it does have a number of less extensive Islamic movements which in certain respects parallel these Indonesian organizations. Three categories of Islamic movements can be identified in Malaysia. The first are the so-called *dakwah* or missionary movements including groups such as, Jamaat Tabligh and Darul Arqam. (Jomo & Cheek, 1992; Peletz, 1997; Shamsul, 1998) The second category includes activist organizations that reach into university campuses and involve university graduates. The most prominent organization here is ABIM (Angkatan Belia Islam Malaysia), the Malaysian Islamic Youth movement. Finally there is the category of political parties in which PAS is the singularly most important example. PAS will be discussed below in the following section but first some consideration will be given to Jamaat Tabligh, Darul Arqam and ABIM. Even though for various reasons these groups no longer continue to exert the influence on Malaysian society that they once did, it is difficult to understand the contemporary situation without some appreciation of the contribution of such groups.

Jamaat Tabligh

Of all the *dakwah* groups, Jamaat Tabligh is the most consciously apolitical. Jamaat Tabligh was set up in India in the 1920s and came to Malaysia in the 1950s and initially was active largely within Malaysia's Indian Muslim community. As a consequence it was most strong in those towns such as Penang, Kuala Lumpur, and Singapore where there were significant Indian Muslim communities. In later years, however, it made significant inroads into Malay village communities and attracted a following amongst Malays in general. Like most *dakwah* organizations around the world, Jamaat Tabligh is mosque based. It has either established or taken over mosques across Malaysia and conducts its teaching programs out of its mosques. The message of Jamaat Tabligh in some respects is similar to that of other *dakwah* groups, Darul Arqam in particular. It is notably different, however, in its aversion to political criticism. Indeed, Jamaat Tabligh has often been criticized for being too apolitical to the point that it actually supports the government. For these reasons it is welcomed in some official quarters as a safe and moderate expression of *dakwah*. For example, in places such as a Pattani in southern Thailand (where there is a significant Malay Muslim minority community) the Thai government is said to have actively encouraged its presence. The message of Jamaat Tabligh, which in some respects is the message of all *dakwah* groups, is one of appealing for a return to the purity and commitment of the early Muslim community. Consequently there is an emphasis on personal morality and piety but also an emphasis on what some might regard as the more superficial aspects of Islam. For example, Jamaat Tabligh encourages members to behave in what is thought to be a seventh-century Arabic fashion, to eat in a "Arabic" fashion and otherwise behave in the way which they claim is in accordance with the behavior of the Prophet and his companions. In as much as the organization has a big picture view of social change, its position is simply that as Muslims in Malaysia become good Muslims, the various social ills and problems current in society will begin to disappear.

Darul Arqam

Although it has been some years since Darul Arqam was officially and unambiguously banned by the Malaysia government in

1994, its contribution to the shape of Muslim society in Malaysia endures to the present. Indeed, some would argue that the organization itself endures to the present albeit in an underground form. That Darul Arqam was eventually banned is a direct product of its increasingly critical stance towards the Mahathir regime and its current support among middle-class Malays. In its early phase Darul Arqam was in many respects similar to Jamaat Tabligh in that it was begun by a religious activist for the purpose of making Malaysians into better Muslims. It was founded in 1968 by twelve (a religiously auspicious number as this is the number of Muhammad's companions), Muslim leaders under the overall leadership of Ashaari Muhammad. Ashaari Muhammad was previously a government schoolteacher in Selangor and a PAS activist. The organization derives its name from Arqam, one of the prophet's companions in Mecca who supported the prophet in his flight or Hijrah to Madina. The name Darul Arqam means the abode of Arqam. The motif of migration became a central motif early in the life of Arqam evoking a sense of renunciation from this world.

Darul Arqam, much more so than Jamaat Tabligh and other *dakwah* organizations sought to establish entirely new communities. In 1972 Darul Arqam set up a community on the outskirts of Kuala Lumpur in the village of Sungei Penchala. Here on about eight acres of land they established a mosque, school and series of firms and shops forming a Darul Arqam commune. Much like the case of other *dakwah* movements, Darul Arqam initially drew attention for the manner in which it encouraged its members to live. Not only were they to renounce ordinary society and if possible live in a Darul Arqam commune they were to dress, eat, and generally behave in the way that it was envisaged the Prophet Mohammad and his companions had behaved. Particular emphasis was given to questions of ritual purity with regards to food. One of the first initiatives in business was production of *halal* foodstuffs and other personal items. This was a significant development because the Darul Arqam communities were to be self-supporting. In fact, over time they became very successful businesses and branched out across Malaysia into Thailand, Indonesia, and other countries within Southeast Asia. The organization had a strong appeal among young Malaysians particular among middle-class Malay youth who had grown disillusioned with the superficial materialism, as they saw it, of their seniors.

Consequently, the Sungei Penchala community was successful in attracting many Malay private school students and university students. The initial point of contact was through talks and courses. The distinctiveness too of the Darul Arqam members with their Arab style garb and with women wearing the Purdah or veils exerted a certain appeal to Malay youth as a counterculture, or counter-establishment, movement. Similarly, the emphasis on communal living also must have had a certain appeal. Not only were members encouraged to pray five times daily, as would Muslims, but to do this communally. Marriage and family life also took place in the context of community a point that often caused conflict between young members and their families many of whom were nominal in their faith and suspicious of what they saw as the extremism of Darul Arqam. In many respects the views of Darul Arqam are not extremist, at least not in a profound fashion, that is to say the group never endorsed extreme measures in political engagement or terrorist activism. Nevertheless their religious views could easily be characterized as extremist. For example, they claimed that as the official state education system was not Islamic and the Malaysia government was not Islamic, consequently they set up their own school system. Not just this, they established their own health clinics and medical centers arguing that it was wrong for the female patients to be treated by male doctors or for patients to unwittingly take non-*halal* medication because their doctors were insufficiently versed in the requirements of *halal* food standards.

One of the significant differences between Malaysia and Indonesia is that whereas it was not until the 1980s that Indonesia began to feel the effects of widespread resurgence of interest in Islam, in Malaysia this resurgence of Islam could already be detected in the early 1970s. The 1970s were also the period in which PAS experimented with joining ABIM's national coalition with UMNO. Ultimately PAS broke with UMNO, its period of co-operation was widely criticized as having sold out to the secular and corrupt influences of UMNO. In this absence of established opposition, Darul Arqam, and to some extent ABIM, stepped into the breach. This time Darul Arqam enjoyed rapid growth and at the same time became increasingly critical of both PAS and the Barisan Nasioinal coalition. The criticisms made by Darul Arqam towards PAS were essentially the same as those made at other times by PAS of ABIM and of other sectors of society, namely the criticism of not being sufficiently Islamic in emphasizing Islamic principles. The fact that PAS had not moved decisively to establish an Islamic state in Kelantan even though it ruled that state from 1959 until 1977, was used by Darul Arqam as grounds for arguing that PAS was not serious about its Islamic platform. Moreover, when PAS joined the Barisan Nasional coalition in 1973 it became even easier to argue that it had sold out to secular interests.

Although in certain respects however, Darul Arqam and PAS shared similar concerns, the two organizations were very different. PAS was a modern well-organized, reasonably efficient organization and Darul Arqam was deliberately traditional and esoterically focused. In other respects, however, they appealed to similar constituencies, young mostly middle-class Malay youth disenchanted with the excessively authoritarian and materialistic nature of Malaysia government. One important difference between Darul Arqam and PAS was that PAS styled itself as not just an Islamic party but as a party defending the interests of ethnic Malays. Darul Arqam seized upon this to argue that PAS was being un-Islamic in arguing for nationalist causes. The only true path for an Islamic organization, Darul Arqam argued, was to argue for the greater good of Islam and the greater good of all Muslims. A nationalist agenda contradicts this on at least two levels, they argued. Firstly to push nationalism over and above the interests of Islam is to sell out the interests of Islam at the expense of the interests of nationalism, hence the failure of PAS to establish an Islamic state in Kelantan or its willingness to join a Barisan Nasional government. Secondly to push nationalism is to promote ethnic tension and as such is un-Islamic, since Islam is a religion of justice and fairness for all. Even though Darul Arqam was keen to see an Islamic state established in Malaysia, such a state they argued, would work for the good of all citizens whether Muslim or non-Muslim. A movement that argues only for the interests of Malays then, was a movement at odds with the overall principles of Islam according to Darul Arqam.

To some extent these points of difference were conveniently played up or accentuated because the Malaysia government, particularly the Mahathir regime, was very clever in dividing its Islamic opposition. One real point of difference however, between Darul Arqam and other Islamic movements in Malaysia was that Darul

Arqam appealed to popular Malay notions of Islam albeit arguing that they should be purified and brought into alignment with early Islamic practice. Specifically, it presented a Sufistic understanding of Islam very much in line with the prevailing Sufi ethos of South-East Asian Islam but at odds with the scripturalist high tradition promoted by religious teachers and professionals aligned with the government. In this respect, Darul Arqam is somewhat like Nahdlatul Ulama although the two organizations in other respects differ greatly. Indeed, when Darul Arqam was finally banned by the Malaysia government in August 1994 Nahdlatul Ulama was one of the strongest voices of criticism from within the ASEAN region. The Nahdlatul Ulama leadership made a point of saying that many of the practices for which Darul Arqam was being criticized closely paralleled similar practices within NU. In respect Darul Arqam is a traditionalist organization as opposed to the Modernism evident in ABIM and in most of the government sponsored bodies. This is not a traditionalist organization after the manner of Nahdlatul Ulama or even PAS in that it did not grow out of pre-existing village religious communities but rather was very much a modern response to modern problems, albeit dressed up as a return to the purity of a past age.

For many observers, both within Malaysia and outside, one of the most worrying aspects about Darul Arqam was its consciously anti-Western stance. In denouncing the Malaysia government as being overly secular and particularly in denouncing the essential principles of secularism, of separation of religion from politics, Darul Arqam claimed that the modern Malaysia government had been unduly influenced by Christian and Jewish ideas. Not only should young Malays denounce pop music and other aspects of popular culture that come from the West, and so clearly in their eyes carry elements of moral degradation, they should also, Darul Arqam argued, turn from the whole Western notion of politics which they claim was based on a Jewish-Christian understanding of society.

It is not surprising, then, that Darul Arqam was one of the groups was most vocal in its praise of the 1979 Islamic revolution in Iran. Not only did they support the anti-Western stance of the Islamic revolutions in Iran they supported its emphasis on leadership by *ulama* and indeed were sympathetic to Iranian Shiite Islamic culture in many of its teachings and practices. For example, one of the issues that was to cause some controversy within the ranks of Darul

Arqam members was a later emphasis by the leadership on polygamy. And although it is not widely discussed, a point of difference that caused many to leave the movement was the promotion of the Shiite notion of Mut'ah marriage, or temporary marriage, as a way of alleviating or accommodating sexual tension within the community. This, and the messianic and mystical emphases of the organization's leadership caused many, particularly among older generations of Malaysians, to become suspicious of Darul Arqam. The particular doctrinal position which most incensed those outside the movement was the assertion of the leader, Ashaari, that the group's Sufi master, Sheik Suhaimi would come back after death as a messianic figure to bring renewal and revival.

Nevertheless, many within Malaysia and the surrounding regions were upset and outraged by the way which the Malaysia government moved to crush the organization. The Mahathir government had become increasingly alarmed both by the extent to which Darul Arqam was prepared to be outspoken in its criticism of the government and by the extent to which this critical message received a strong following from Malay youth. In the 1990s the Mahathir government was accustomed to managing and manipulating religious sentiment for its own purposes and it found Darul Arqam an increasingly difficult body to manage. Finally on August 5, 1994 the government played its hand in the form of a statement, from the Mufti, or leader the National Fatwa Council in the form of a ten point fatwah against Darul Arqam.

The first and foremost criticism made was that the Darul Arqam belief that Sheik Suhaimi would be resurrected as Imam Madi, or the Messiah, was a complete aberration from orthodox Islamic belief. Secondly the fatwah pointed to the claim that Sheik Suhaimi had a meeting with the prophet at the Kabah and that he had received the philosophy of Darul Arqam the so-called "Arad Muhammadiyah" directly from him. The remaining ten points contained a similar series of lesser criticisms of Darul Arqam doctrine and behavior. The contravening orthodox Islamic practice including criticizing the claim that Ashaari had godlike powers to decide on matters and to influence the course of creation and also claiming that Darul Arqam had failed to observe State Islamic laws enacted regarding Islamic affairs and it did not to comply with the recognized positions and statements of the government Sunni scholars. The fatwah had the effect of officially banning Darul Arqam in that it forbade Darul Arqam members to adopt or preach its philosophy or to engage in any kind of public circulation of its ideas or even to possess books or recordings, display symbols or engage in religious talks. Moreover, the Malaysian government leaned heavily on ASEAN member states to follow it in banning Darul Arqam, calling for the its banning in Singapore, Thailand, Philippines and Indonesia. In the Indonesian case it seemed as if the then Minister of Religious Affairs Tamizi would support the Malaysian request. Ultimately however the Malaysia request was not complied with and in fact received strong condemnation not just from the *ulama* and other bodies within Indonesia but from bodies around the region. Most regional observers felt that Darul Arqam represented a reasonably harmless, albeit eccentric, religious movement and that it should be accorded a reasonable amount of freedom to promote its ideas however idiosyncratic or foolish they may appear.

While the organization itself has now effectively been banned and no longer functions openly in Malaysia, many believe that it continues to operate in an underground fashion. Moreover, the critical stance of this organization vis-à-vis the Mahathir government continues to have an enduring impact. If nothing else the harsh and some would say, crass manner in which the organization was crushed opened the eyes of many to the extent to which the Mahathir government was prepared to manipulate and indeed openly confront religious bodies that did not play the game.

ABIM

The racial clash of May 13 1969 sent shock waves throughout Malaysian society. As the community struggled to come to terms with what had happened communal anxiety gave rise to a series of odd phenomena. One such phenomenon was the emergence of millenarian sects offering instruction in Silat, a traditional Malay martial art resembling Kung Fu, as rural communities bunkered down fearing further violence. On the campus of the University of Malaysia, the nation's only university at the time, students began increasingly to question the basis of their Malay identity and the basis of their Islamic belief. As Malay students sought to understand what it was to be Muslim they came to feel that they knew less about their faith than they thought that they really ought to know. This was the beginning of a revival of interest in Islam among Malay youth. The Association of Muslim students at the University of Malaya decided that it was time to launch a Muslim youth organization. The new organization was named Angkatan Belia Islam Malaysia, or ABIM. (Shamsul, 1997) The initial activities to establish this organization occurred in August 1969 but ABIM was not officially registered until 1971. It then grew quickly to a position of dominance and great strength among young Malays by the mid-1970s. The organization took as its raison d'être: "toward building a society that is based on the principles of Islam."

One of most significant things about ABIM and its birth out of the Association of Muslim Students is that at the time in the late 1960s and early 1970s, the majority of Malay students at the University of Malaya were in the arts or social sciences and humanities programs. Only later on, in the mid- to late 70s, did it become common for Malay students to undertake applied science courses such as engineering. The origins of ABIM greatly colored its approach. Because the founding members came from an arts background they were more open to accepting a plurality of ideas and coming to terms with the messy complexities of modern life. In short, they did not habitually think in black-and-white terms, but rather were prepared to grapple with difficult questions for which there were no pat answers. In this respect ABIM contrasts strongly with another organization that came to exert a dominant influence among young Malays. This organization is known as the IRC or the Islamic Representative Council. The IRC, in contrast to ABIM, had its origins among Malay students studying overseas mostly in science, applied science and technical education courses and then later took hold at home as new institutes were founded in Malaysia and large numbers of Malay youth were encouraged to enter science courses. Initially ABIM attracted attention from the government being essentially a student organization although designed to operate outside of the university campuses. But in December 1974 an important rally or demonstration took place in Kuala Lumpur, the national capital where ABIM students gathered to protest over rural hunger and hardship suffered by members of Malay communities who were yet to enjoy the benefits of progress evident in the national capital. The government was caught off guard by this demonstration and arrested 1,200 protesters, treating the rally as a student protest threatening the national order rather than an expression of religious concern. Only later did the government come to realize that in order to address such concerns it needed to respond not just to the presence of student anger nor even just to the issues named, but to the very issue of Islamic resurgence.

One of the key figures in establishing ABIM's credentials was the charismatic young leader Anwar Ibrahim. He led ABIM between 1974 and 1982 and did much to consolidate its standing on the national scene and the degree of creditability it had before the government.

Even before Anwar had joined ABIM however, ABIM had become increasingly influential, particularly after 1973. There are a number of reasons for this. The first was perhaps the decision by PAS to join the Barisan Nasional coalition. This meant that there was a vacuum in regards to significant Islamic criticism of the government and in many respects ABIM and other *dakwah* groups such as Darul Arqam began to fill this void. Unlike Darul Arqam, however, ABIM was studiously professional and non-partisan in its political stance and this enabled it to quickly penetrate the government bureaucracy and national school network. In particular it was able to have an influence in states previously little persuaded by PAS's brand of Islam; in particular the affluent central west coast states of Negeri Sembilan, Selangor, and Perak.

The fact that the Islam so enthusiastically promoted by ABIM was essentially moderate, modern, and open to understanding the complexities facing Malaysians in the late twentieth century meant that it had a power of attraction that went well beyond the youthful enthusiasm of Darul Arqam and other minor *dakwah* groups. In short ABIM had a degree of credibility in urban centers and appealed as a modern organization. This is not to say that some were not worried by the rising success of ABIM. Certainly among the non-Malay, non-Muslim communities many began to feel anxious about what the resurgence of interest in Islam would mean for them.

While ABIM was certainly moderate in comparison to Darul Arqam and the IRC, in comparison with the circle of progressive Islamic intellectuals in Jakarta around Nurcholish Madjid, ABIM was considerably more conservative. This was despite the fact that in its early days ABIM was greatly influenced by Indonesian groups such as HMI. Unlike the Indonesian groups, however, ABIM also looked west to Jamaati Islam in Pakistan and Al Ikwan, or the Muslim brotherhood in Egypt and other parts of the Middle East, organizations well known for their opposition to secularism and secular nationalism. These links not surprisingly, worried many within the UMNO leadership. Interestingly, however, while some within ABIM pushed for the formation of an Islamic state much as some within Masyumi in Indonesia had done, gradually the organization began to develop a stance arguing for the establishment of certain Islamic institutions in order to make the state more Islamic. In other words, recognizing the difficulties inherent in making a plural society like Malaysia into an Islamic state, not to mention the uncertainties as to what that really meant, and the lack of civil models to follow, ABIM proposed that an Islamic bank and Islamic university be established in order to strengthen the Islamicity of Malaysian society.

The emphasis on an Islamic university is particularly important because ABIM itself developed a series of kindergartens which later became private schools and became the power base for ABIM's financial activity and its recruiting of members. This is not simply a matter of convenience either, for ABIM was deeply persuaded even more so than Darul Arqam of the importance of education. Indeed one of the criticisms made by other *dakwah* groups such as Darul Arqam towards ABIM was that it was too modern and too focused on activities such as seminars, discussions, talks, lectures and other educational initiatives.

One of the approaches used by ABIM, however, which is decidedly more traditional in style was the formation of study groups or *usroh*. These study groups began to form the core of ABIM activity and served to strengthen the bond between ABIM leaders and the members and facilitate the development of a deep understanding of ABIM's approach to Islam.

What really transformed ABIM in the eyes of the government from being a curious, but none too threatening, student phenomenon into being a genuinely worrying opposition, or movement, was ABIM's links with PAS. Through the mid-1970s ABIM was generally critical of PAS. This was a time when PAS was a part of the Barisan Nasional coalition government and ABIM's criticism turned on what it saw as a PAS sell out to an insufficiently Islamic UMNO government. There was even a degree of tension between PAS and ABIM to the extent that in PAS-dominated states such as Kedah and Kelantan, the PAS state government moved to hinder or obstruct ABIM activity. To the extent that PAS promoted the deal of an Islamic state, ABIM's more carefully formulated list of demands seemed much more modern and comprehensible.

In 1997 however, events conspired for ABIM to move into a closer relationship with PAS. The political crisis that developed in Kelantan that year resulted in PAS withdrawing from the Barisan Nasional coalition and state elections being held in Kelantan following the dissolution of the PAS government. Though it had been previously critical of PAS, ABIM decided that PAS represented the best alternative to UMNO and was the party with the best Islamic credentials. Consequently ABIM decided to mobilize its members to campaign for PAS in Kelantan. In the end PAS was defeated in Kelantan but the successful collaboration between ABIM and PAS in the Kelantan elections laid the foundation for a new era of close working. This was further reinforced by the fact that for the 1978 general elections several of ABIM's top leaders joined PAS and in due course went on to transform PAS into a more modern and sharply focused organization.

At the same time ABIM was refining its criticism of UMNO. For a period in the late Seventies it focused on UMNO's new economic policy initiatives designed to promote the Malay community over the other communities. ABIM denounced this ethnic chauvinism arguing that it was a narrow nationalism at odds with true Islamic understanding. Anwar, who was somewhat feared in non-Malay communities because of his charisma and his leadership of the pre-eminent Islamic organization began to receive new support among the Chinese and Indian communities. In 1979, 1980, and 1981, ABIM had reached the peak of its powers as the pre-eminent Islamic opposition group particularly in urban areas and particularly to do with issues concerning younger people. So worried was the government by ABIM's growing popularity and influence that it took special steps to curb its influence.

One of the main initiatives was The Societies Act Amendment Bill that many saw as being deliberately aimed at curtailing ABIM activity. The Bill was tabled in 1981 and created a new category of political associations. While ABIM mounted a vigorous campaign against the Bill the campaign eventually failed. Nevertheless it served to cement ABIM's oppositional status. Before very long however, a strange twist of political events would transform the nature of the ABIM-UMNO relationship. In mid-1981 the ailing Prime Minister, Hussein Onn, resigned as Prime Minister, and as party president, because of ill-health. He was immediately succeeded by the Deputy Prime Minister and the deputy UMNO president, Mahathir Mohamad. Replacing Mahathir Mohamad in the second spot was Education Minister Musa Hitam. The result was a breath of fresh air for national politics based on the platform of the so-called 2M leadership, emphasizing clean efficient and trustworthy administration and government. Almost immediately Mahathir as Prime Minister began to respond to the earlier demands of ABIM. He established both an Islamic Bank and an Islamic University and launched his famous North-East policy which included, for a period, "Buy British Last" policy. All of these actions were seen as a sign of decisive new leadership that was going to align itself with the Islamic resurgence and turn away from the West.

At the same time as the new Mahathir Mohamad UMNO leadership was rapidly strengthening its Islamic credentials, the relationship between ABIM and PAS was beginning to sour. In part this was because of the activity of former ABIM leaders who had now become PAS leaders and who alienated some of the older generation of PAS leaders. One of the issues here was the 1979 Iranian revolution that was celebrated within PAS ranks, particularly by the for now ABIM leaders, but was viewed with some caution within ABIM, in part perhaps because of ABIM's links with Saudi Arabia and Kuwait and with Islamic movements in the Arab world. All of this led to ABIM changing its previously pro PAS stance and announcing that for the 1982 elections it would once again be nonpartisan and would no longer be supporting PAS.

The most dramatic development however occurred on March 29, 1982 just as candidates were about to be nominated for the April general elections. Malaysia was rocked by the news that Anwar was resigning as ABIM president and was joining the UMNO campaign team despite the fact that he had not previously been a member of UMNO. While this sudden switch caused some ripples in the ABIM leadership it received tacit support by ABIM as a whole which argued that this was a campaign to Islamize UMNO from within. Mahathir quickly promoted Anwar and he was soon recognized as Mahathir's heir apparent, rising quickly through a succession of ministries before finally settling for a period in the Ministry previously occupied by Musa Hitam, the Ministry of Education.

Nevertheless at village level there were serious repercussions as many village ABIM supporters deserted ABIM to rejoin PAS, disillusioned with ABIM's switch to UMNO. Indeed ABIM's overall level of support quickly waned as it lost its bright star and also its credentials as the leading Islamic opposition force. This further consolidated ABIM thinking about a strategy for Islamizing UMNO from within. Faced with diminished support ABIM leaders became all the more committed to supporting Anwar's initiatives from within the government. By the April 1987 UMNO general assembly Anwar was elected to become one of UMNO's vice presidents and his position was well and truly consolidated. In the years since, ABIM has become less and less an independent pressure group and has passed this mantle effectively to PAS. While PAS' approach to handling issues such as government abuses, injustices and corruption is less sophisticated than ABIM's had been, it is clear that ABIM is no longer able to play the role of being a significant pressure group.

PAS

The Origins of PAS

Just as the nationalists in Indonesia through the 1950s debated what the basis of the Indonesian state should be, so too in Malaysia even before independence, disputes broke out regarding the basis of the new state of Malay. In 1951 in Butterworth, Penang a new party was established, the so-called PAN-Malaysia Islamic Party or Parti Islam seMalaysia, PAS. (Peletz, 1997) Many of its founders were members of UMNO's religious bureau and some had been involved in Hisbul Muslimin, a defunct Islamic organization with left nationalist links. The founders of PAS gave as their reason for founding a new party their disaffection with the overly secular nationalist leanings of UMNO. For PAS it was clear that the new state had to be an Islamic state in which Islam dominated every aspect of life not just the law, but the economy and the government administration. The founders of PAS could not accept an Indonesia style solution where the state was led by a secular government and Islam's link to the state was confined to one bureau or government department. In ways mirroring Nahdlatul Ulama, PAS had its foundations in the so-called *pondok* schools that in some respects were similar to NU's *pesantren*. These *pondok* religious schools were greatest in number in the states regarded as being most traditional and Malay dominated, namely Kedah, Perlis, Perak, Trengganu, and Kelantan, the northern states of the Malaysian peninsula. While in some respects PAS drew upon the *pondok* schools in a manner analogous to the way that NU was shaped in its doctrine and outlook by the *pesantren* network, in most other respects it was much more like Indonesia's Modernist Muslim party Masyumi.

Through the 1950s PAS failed to make much of an impact on the national scene. PAS' fortunes only turned for the better when it appointed a new leader, Dr.. Burhanuddin Al-Helmy, previously a radical nationalist leader who led the Malay Nationalist Party and leftist coalition in the mid-forties. From its early days PAS' ideology was not purely Islamic. The combined emphasis was on the push to achieve an Islamic state much in the manner of Indonesia's Masyumi, with an emphasis on bettering the position of ethnic Malays. In that sense PAS was both an Islamic party and a chauvinist Malay party. Its criticism of UMNO centered on both these axes, namely that UMNO was insufficiently Islamic and that it was too willing to compromise Malay interests. Throughout the sixties UMNO, for its part, exerted considerable pressure on PAS. The UMNO pressure was one of the main factors leading to the downfall of the PAS government in the state of Trengganu in 1961. A number of PAS leaders including Dr. Burhanuddin, were detained under the Internal Security Act. In 1969 UMNO launched a large-scale campaign to gain control of the state of Kelantan also previously a PAS state. The same year the racial riots of May 1969 and the death of Burhanuddin and his replacement by Asri, laid the foundations for rapprochement between PAS and UMNO. Between 1973 and 1977 PAS became part of the Barisan Nasional Coalition government. It justified this rapprochement partly on the basis of the need to overcome the crisis in race relations epitomized by the May 13 riots in 1969.

As has been alluded to above, 1977 saw a new crisis for PAS when it lost control of the state of Kelantan. This crisis also marked the beginning of a new rapprochement between PAS and ABIM that eventually saw PAS completely transformed. Former ABIM leaders entered the PAS leadership and reshaped the party to become a more modern, more sharply focused organization.

The result of this was that Asri felt increasingly disenfranchised and eventually left PAS to join UMNO. Asri was replaced by a former ABIM leader Hadji Abdul Hadi Awang who became leader of PAS in the state of Trengganu and transformed the Trengganu PAS organization into the new center of PAS activity. Later, when Anwar defected from ABIM to UMNO, Hadi was seen as the bright rising star of the Islamic opposition, being referred to as PAS' answer to Anwar. At the same time PAS was being transformed from within by former ABIM leaders to become more and more ABIM-like. Nevertheless PAS remained a rural elite-based organization with its roots among Malay peasants in the northern states. It never became a modern organization along the lines of ABIM. Similarly, Hadi lacked the political instincts and intuition of Anwar as well as his eloquence and public persona, meaning that PAS increasingly ran a poor second to UMNO in the competition to establish itself as the defender of Islam. Then in 1982 the mounting tensions between the old and new guard within PAS reached a crescendo. Asri's rather heavy-handed approach to choosing candidates and directing the party for the April 1982 general election was severely challenged and Asri and many of his key followers resigned, turning over the leadership of the party to the younger guard and to the *ulama*.

PAS in the Mahathir Era of Islamization

In 1982, the rise of Mahathir Muhammad to the leadership of UMNO and the nation marked the beginning of a new phase of Islamization as UMNO under Mahathir sought to out Islam PAS and other opposition groups. Joined by Anwar and later by a leader with a keen understanding of what the public wanted, UMNO was able to completely outflank PAS and the other Islamic opposition groups such as Darul Arqam and ABIM. As has already been noted, Mahathir's policy was to put into practice the key points espoused by ABIM under Anwar, necessary for the transformation of Malaysia into a properly Islamic state. Neither Mahathir nor Anwar was interested in transforming Malaysia formally into an Islamic state but both were keen to transform the nature of the Malaysian state. Mahathir, perhaps, was doing this more out of political opportunism than strong conviction, it was, nevertheless, extremely effective in answering the felt needs of many Malaysian Muslims.

Unfortunately, however, this led to a kind of "arms race" or "Islamicity race" between UMNO and its opponents with each trying to prove themselves more Islamic than the other. Ultimately, PAS was outflanked and could only retreat to a claim for itself the distinction of greater ideological purity and an unparalleled track record of supporting the interests of Islam. In a sense then it became more and more difficult for PAS to increase its support base even if it was able to deepen the ardor of its existing supporters. By 1985 PAS was desperately searching for some new angle to campaign against UMNO and seized upon a policy position previously occupied by ABIM five years earlier, namely a campaign against narrow ethnic chauvinism in favor of broad Islamization intended to benefit all races of peoples. For a period PAS sought to gain the support of the Malaysian Chinese. Nevertheless, while many Chinese welcomed the new openness on the part of PAS and some may have even been persuaded by PAS arguments that its push for an Islamic state was never going to work against the interests of non-Muslims. Understandably however, the very notion of an Islamic state remained simply too threatening for Malaysia's non-Muslims to come to terms with.

The fact that following the Iranian Revolution of 1979 many of PAS' younger supporters became increasingly militant did little to improve its general standing in Malaysian society. In 1984 the Mahathir government moved to jail a number of PAS' youth wing leaders under the Internal Security Act and in November 1985 it took decisive action in the village of Memali in Kedah when PAS extremist, Ustaz Ibrahim led a community of PAS supporters in an armed opposition to the government. Eventually fourteen villagers were to die along with four policemen, and many more were arrested, but UMNO appeared triumphant. Mahathir was successful in turning public attention surrounding the incident away from the fact that it involved ostensibly a government attack on PAS, to an appreciation of UMNO's moderate Islamic position vis-à-vis the extremism which had become evident within PAS. In the late 1980s there was some talk of rapprochement between UMNO and PAS in the form of dialogue. Little resulted from this however, possibly because UMNO saw little to gain from such talks. PAS for its part increasingly concentrated its activities on consolidating its own organizational structure and internal affairs. In 1987, for example, it completed building its national training center and began publishing

Harakah, a weekly newspaper. Despite PAS' failure to extend its membership base it continued to enjoy solid support from a strong committed core. This support extended to considerable financial support and as a result, as an organization, PAS continued to do well.

In the late 1980s internal affairs within PAS saw action on a different front as well. At the 1986 annual national conference, or *muktamar*, of PAS, a young engineer and former leader of the IRC was appointed a deputy of PAS Youth. It was widely anticipated that he would shortly replace the aging incumbent. This was generally seen as marking the beginning of a concerted effort by IRC to infiltrate and control PAS. It was an initiative, however, which was short-lived and destined to failure. One year later at the next PAS Muktamar in April 1987 the IRC push suffered from a spate of bad publicity about the IRC. This effectively blocked further avenues for the IRC to gain control of the organization and meant that the youth wing did not come under IRC leadership. The IRC blamed this bad publicity upon ABIM and there are grounds for believing that they may have been right in this accusation. Other tensions however emerged between the IRC and PAS. In particular the fact that PAS was allegedly Shiite in orientation, as evidenced by the strong support for the Iranian Revolution, whereas the IRC was closely linked to the Muslim brotherhood in the Arab world. As the decade went on PAS increasingly consolidated its position as an opposition group critical of Mahathir as an individual, and of UMNO as a party, for being un-Islamic and unjust.

So successful has UMNO's policy of Islamization been that it has been difficult for PAS to find chinks in the UMNO armor. Instead PAS has increasingly concentrated on criticizing the heavy-handed authoritarian nature of the Mahathir regime and the associated inconsistencies and injustices that go with an authoritarian style of government. In this it has been joined on occasion by former PAS dissidents unhappy with the Mahathir leadership. Through the 1990s there have been periodic alignments between UMNO dissidents and PAS but no formal coalition against UMNO has successfully emerged.

Political Freedom and the State

Islam and the Political Context in Malaysia

It is not possible to understand the role of Islam in modern Malaysian society without an appreciation of the political context. This is because Islam has been so important in the political struggle both between PAS and UMNO, and between UMNO and other oppositional groups in the *dakwah* movement and elsewhere, that much of what happens publicly in Malaysian society with reference to Islam has some political purpose or origin. For just as the resurgence of interest in Islam began earlier in Malaysia than it did in Indonesia so too did the Malaysian government more quickly realize that it would need to embrace the concerns of Islam and Islamicity in order to gain political advantage and outflank its opposition. Whereas Suharto began only in the late 1980s and 1990s to court the interests of conservative Muslims and endeavor to prove himself to be a true defender of their concerns, in Malaysia the process began almost a decade earlier. In fact as soon as Mahathir Mohamad was made Prime Minister he began to court Islamic support. One of the clearest indications of this was the way in which he persuaded Anwar Ibrahim to join UMNO shortly before the 1982 general elections. This move proved to be outstandingly successful for Mahathir, and arguably for Anwar as well, though it was to have a tragic denouement for the latter. Mahathir and UMNO gained more or less the full support of ABIM and the moderates within the *dakwah* movement, and Anwar and the moderate Islamists began to witness the transformation of Malaysian government attitudes towards their concerns.

But in order to understand the forces occurring here we need to take several steps back in order to view Malaysian politics in the wider context. Perhaps the most helpful approach to understanding Malaysian politics comes in the form of the paradigm suggested by Harold Crouch (1992; 1996), in which he argues that the Malaysian government represents a repressive, responsive regime. Earlier the majority of observers of Malaysian politics had argued that government in Malaysia represented a modified form of democracy. In other words, a democracy within limits, a curtailed democracy, but nevertheless a system of governance that had at its core democratic principles and was governed by democratic mechanisms. By the mid-1980s, Crouch argues, it was simply no longer possible to apply the model of modified democracy to the Malaysian scene, instead the model of a modified authoritarianism seemed to offer a better fit. Certainly many aspects of Malaysia governance by this stage were showing signs of authoritarianism and by the end of the decade these trends were fully developed. The ISA Act could be used to imprison people without justifying the basis of imprisonment except to say that they presented a threat to Malaysian security. Other provisions of the state of emergency enacted in 1969 could also be invoked periodically. The Malaysian media was more or less totally controlled either by the government directly or by the governing political parties. The judiciary by the late 1980s at least, was severely emasculated to the point where the separation between the judiciary and executive was almost eliminated. Adding to this, traditional Malay patronage in the form of UMNO money politics and a systemic gerrymander of electoral boundaries meant that the governing UMNO led the Barisan Nasional coalition and had more or less complete control of the political process in Malaysia. And yet, Crouch argues, in many respects the regime has been responsive to public pressure and public concern.

The Mahathir government continues to demonstrate many aspects of repressive authoritarianism. This is most clearly seen recently in the law case against Anwar Ibrahim, which his supporters claim represents trumped up charges, and the gross manipulation of the judicial process in order to eliminate him as a political threat to Mahathir and the Mahathir government. But this is only one of a series of such flagrant abuses of the judiciary and the judicial process even if it is the most widely followed case. One of the reasons why earlier cases have not evoked the same sense of public outrage as the Anwar Ibrahim case is because of the almost total control that the government has over the mass media. In the Anwar case two things conspired to force this case into the center of public attention. Firstly Anwar was an extremely popular political and social figure much admired and respected and Mahathir was widely viewed as coming to the end of a long and successful but nevertheless authoritarian period in power. Secondly, Anwar Ibrahim's trial coincided with the widespread use of the Internet, particularly the World Wide Web, to disseminate information and circumvent the controls on the mainstream press.

On the other hand, the Mahathir government in recent years has made a number of concessions that demonstrate that it has been responsive to public concern. For example, in October 1990 just one month before the 1990 general elections restrictions on Malaysians visiting China were dropped. Previously only Malaysians over the age of sixty and then fifty were allowed to visit China and even then the visits were carefully controlled. This was done in the name of preventing communist influence within Malaysia but was also a point of great grievance to many Malaysian Chinese. More broadly the Mahathir government of course had introduced a large number of concessions and developments aimed at appeasing Islamic interests. Crouch argues that many of the responsive aspects of the Mahathir government have to do with its fear of being threatened politically by any alternative coalition or opposition interests opposing the Barisan Nasional coalition. These opposing interests or at least the new degree of cooperation among oppositional forces has its origins in a major split that occurred in the ranks during the mid-1980s. It is possible that we may be about to witness a similar split in the ranks of UMNO and a parallel emergence of a viable cross-communal oppositional coalition in the late 1990s as we did in the late 1980s. In any case, the UMNO split of the mid-1980s so shaped the political terrain and influenced Mahathir's attitude towards public grievances and oppositional concerns, including the interests of the Islamists, that it warrants closer attention.

The UMNO Split

Mahathir Mohamad was appointed Prime Minister in 1981 following a bout of ill health on the part of the former Prime Minister. His deputy was Musa Hitam. Although, as we have noted above, the Mahathir Mohamad-Musa Hitam team, dubbed the 2M team, initially appeared highly successful, there are reasons to believe that it was troubled almost from the start. In any case the following year, Mahathir persuaded Anwar Ibrahim to join UMNO and immediately began fast tracking his career, while at the same time his relationship with Musa Hitam began to show signs of strain. Finally, Musa Hitam broke with Mahathir after being replaced as Deputy Prime Minister and became increasingly frustrated with Mahathir's dominance of the UMNO machine. He was joined in this by the arrival of Tengku Razaleigh who had long had an axe to grind with Mahathir. When the two joined forces it appeared as if a real split within UMNO might occur such that Mahathir would be toppled and a rival installed to replace him. In the end Musa was persuaded to remain within the ranks, and Razaleigh was left to go it alone. While, with the help of Musa, it was possible that Razaleigh and Musa Hitam may have been able to garner half the votes within the party that

Razaleigh-led, dissidents could not expect the same level of success. In 1988 they were expelled from UMNO and the following year formed the their own party. The Razaleigh-led party was dubbed Semangat 46, or the Spirit of 46. Abdul suggested that it was returning to the original founding vision of UMNO, spelt out in article 6. Even without the backing of most elements, it seemed possible that a viable alternative to the UMNO government could be formed.

In order to do this however it was clear that Semangat 46 would not be able to defeat the Barisan Nasional coalition in its own right. Instead, it had to become part of a viable alternative to the Barisan Nasional coalition and the only way that this could be done was through working with not just the DAP but also with PAS. Razaleigh enjoyed good relations with the leadership of both the DAP and the leadership of PAS but there were natural tensions between the DAP and PAS. Just as PAS was widely viewed, particularly within the Chinese community, as being a chauvinistic Malay party so too the DAP, despite its name, was widely viewed as a chauvinistic Chinese party. Nevertheless if a viable alternative to the Barisan Nasional coalition were to be formed it would have to involve these two elements. To a large extent despite their ostensible differences the DAP and PAS together with Semangat 46 were able to work together. The litmus test of course was the 1990 election.

As was noted above, in the lead up to the 1990 election, the Mahathir government began to show real signs of being responsive to public concern. It was significant, for example, that the dropping of all bans or limits on travel to China occurred just a month before the election. Other concessions targeting different groups in the community must have considerably improved the Barisan Nasional Front's prospects for the 1990 election. It is possible to read the results of the 1990 election in two entirely different ways. From one point of view the 1990 elections are evidence of a strong swing towards an alternative coalition government, from another point of view they demonstrate that even when facing its strongest opposition, the Barisan Nasional coalition was still able to win easily. The parallels here with the November 1999 election are all too obvious.

In the previous elections the Barisan Nasional coalition had previously gained around 80 percent of the seats and between 57 percent and 61 percent of the votes. In the 1990 general election the Barisan Nasional coalition's share of the seats dropped to 71 percent and it was only successful in gaining 53 percent of the votes. In addition to this it lost control of two state governments. These results could be interpreted as evidence of the fact that the Barisan National's position is more or less impregnable, particularly in the light of the 1995 election results in which the Barisan Nasional regained all its lost ground, plus some more, and secured 65.1 percent of the votes. On the other hand, the fact that at the 1990 elections the ruling coalition was able to gain only 53.4 percent of the vote suggests that at least at that election there was the beginning of a viable two-"party" system. Fifty-three point four percent of the total vote is the sort of vote gained commonly within two-party democracies by the winning party. The incumbent government had considerable advantages, and as has been noted above enjoyed considerable control over or domination of the political process in ways that were not at all democratic. Moreover, by the time of the 1995 election the government had enjoyed seven years of strong growth with economic growth regularly in excess of 8 percent per annum. It had also begun to respond to the threat of a real opposition by making a number of compensations. At the same time, it tightened up its control over the political process so it was even more secure.

Clearly by the time of the 1995 election the position of Barisan Nasional was as strong as ever. Nor could it be said that the Semangat 46 plus the DAP plus the PAS coalition any longer represented a viable threat to Barisan National's ruling coalition. Nevertheless, despite the obstacles placed by the incumbent government it is possible to establish an alternative coalition. For this alternative coalition to become strong enough to seriously rival the Barisan Nasional, however, is another matter altogether, as 1999's November 29 elections clearly demonstrated.

The Internal Security Act and Emergency Provisions

The May 13 riots of 1969 so alarmed Malaysians across all communities, particularly the government of the day, that it marked a turning point in Malaysian politics in much the way that the 1965 alleged communist coup in Indonesia was a watershed for Indonesian politics. One of the first things that occurred in 1969 following the inter-communal rioting was the declaration of a state of emergency. The state of emergency provisions in Malaysian law date back to 1960 at the end of the so-called Communist emergency.

One of the reasons that the British had been reluctant to allow the colony of Malaya to move out of colonial control and gain full independence was that in the wake of World War II they were engaged in a struggle with a small but determined number of Communist guerrillas in the peninsula highlands and jungles. By the end of the 1950s the Communist guerrilla movement had been comprehensively quashed and security for the newly independent government was assured. Nevertheless, it was felt the new nation would continue to face similar threats in the coming years. For this reason the British saw to it that a state of emergency law was enshrined in Malaysian national law.

The fact that a state of emergency was declared following the May riots in 1969 is hardly surprising, and indeed is entirely understandable. What is disturbing, however, about the state of emergency is that it was never officially declared to be finished, for while the meeting of Parliament in 1971 effectively marked the return to a state of non-emergency, officially the state of emergency provisions were never switched off. One of the key elements within these provisions is the so-called Internal Security or ISA Act. The ISA was used extensively through the 1960s and 1970s, ostensibly in the face of continued communist threat, to secure dissident voices within Malaysia. Between 1960 and 1981, for example, there were over 3,000 detainees under ISA. Most of these were only held for a relatively short time but some were held for much longer periods. By the 1970s, as the threat of the communist insurgency had tailed off, there were only 900 ISA detainees through the decade. One of Mohamad Mahathir's first acts as Prime Minister in 1981 was to release most of these detainees and by 1986 only forty people detained under the provisions of the Internal Security Act.

Mahathir made much at the time, of his liberality in releasing ISA detainees. But in the wake of the UMNO split in the mid-1980s and the growing tensions both within the party and the broader community Mahathir moved decisively to imprison another series of ISA detainees whom he alleged were threatening the security of the nation through provoking inter-communal tension. In the most famous period of arrests in October-November 1987, 106 ISA detainees were taken into custody including widely respected liberals such Aliran leader, Chandra Muzaffar.

The Media

As has already been noted one of the key ways in which the Mahathir government has controlled the political process and shaped public opinions is through total control of the media. Electronic media, both radio and television are the subject of effectively total government monopolies. The print media, which in many countries such as Indonesia or the Philippines can ordinarily be expected to provide some channels of freedom, is also totally in the hands of either the government, UMNO or the coalition partners the Barisan Nasional. For example, the *New Straits Times* the leading English-language newspaper and its sister publication *Berita Harian*, the Malay language equivalent, are both owned by the Fleet Group, which is itself owned by UMNO.

Consequently, there is very little published in the *New Straits Times* or *Berita Harian* which does not meet with the approval of the government. In practice, editorial control of the Malaysian press is much more direct and tight than is the case in most democratic nations. Whereas in Australia or America, for example, one might see a media magnate subtly manipulate the news content, in Malaysia there is frequently very little such subtlety in control of the news. Outside of the *New Straits Times* and *Berita Harian* other important papers include *Utusan Malaysia* in English and its sister *Utusan Melayu* in Malay, which are both controlled by UMNO and *The Star* which is controlled by the MCA. To some extent *The Star* does air dissenting voices, most famously Tunku Abdul Rahman Malaysia's first Prime Minister and often vocal critic of Mahathir and the new Malaysia. But the MCA's membership of the Barisan Nasional ruling coalition effectively means that really important information that may embarrass the government is seldom allowed, to appear in the pages of *The Star*. In a similar way the Tamil press is effectively controlled by the MIC, the Malaysia Indian Congress. To some extent, the foreign media is also regulated or at least its impact on the Malaysian scene is also controlled. So, for example, the *Far Eastern Economic Review* and the *Asian Wall Street Journal* are often banned outright or at least subject to bans in such a fashion that their release is very much delayed in Malaysia.

Apart from direct political intervention generally through publications, another mechanism for controlling the print media in Malaysia is that unlike Indonesia, the majority of journalists in Malaysia is relatively well remunerated and have comfortable careers particularly in the Kelang Valley region, Kuala Lumpur and Petaling Jaya. They understand very well that if they do not exercise sufficient self-censorship and allow themselves to stray across the line and into territory that brings the displeasure of the government their lucrative careers could either be curtailed or turned along less promising directions. Indeed, it could be argued, the same applies for the Malaysian middle classes in general. Years of rates of growth in excess of 8 percent per annum compounded by a small population in a fertile and resource rich country have meant that life for middle-class Malaysians is pretty good and for the upper middle class exceeds even their wildest earlier expectations. The continued enjoyment of such a lifestyle however, comes at the price of conformity to government expectations. The situation is by no means as extreme as is the case in some other semi authoritarian states, but effectively works in much the same way.

Apart from the fact that control of the press greatly limits the functioning of democracy and mechanisms of accountability in a direct sense, there are rather more subtle and indirect consequences of such a control. For example, in many countries the press, particularly the print media, functions as an avenue for the expansion of civil society not just in terms of content and the airing of debate but in the form of career opportunities for young activists. For example, many young IAIN graduates in Indonesia who combine liberal Islamic thought with strong social convictions begin their careers by working as journalists. And while it might be argued that not infrequently the results of Indonesian journalism tend towards the mediocre, it is important to recognize the extent to which a journalistic career, albeit lowly paid and poorly resourced, provides an important opportunity for student activists to continue activism and learning through their adult careers. Some of the most important civil society activists and public intellectuals in Indonesia such as Gunawan Mohammad, owe their success and prominence in the civil society movement to the opportunity even under Suharto, to engage in such criticism through the media.

More recently the growth of the Internet as has been noted with reference to the Anwar Ibrahim case, suggests that the role of the media in informing Malaysian society and educating them is being supplanted increasingly by the World Wide Web and by e-mail discussion groups.

The Judiciary

Alongside its control of the media one other main mechanism by which the Mahathir government limits the full functioning of democracy and the growth of civil society is by means of its control of the judiciary. The decline of the independent judiciary in Malaysia is one of the sadder aspects of the Mahathir regime. For all of their failings, and they are considerable, for much of the current Malaysia's political mess can in part be sheeted home to them, the British did leave Malaysia with a functioning and robust independent judiciary clearly separated from the executive arm of the government.

This judiciary was never particularly radical or particularly liberal. Like many judiciaries throughout the English-speaking world, the ways in which newcomers to the bench were recruited ensured that it remained a reasonably conservative institution. Most Malay judges tend to come from the conservative Malay elite and can be relied upon to bring down conservative rulings. Nevertheless, occasionally the Malaysian judiciary acts in ways that were completely contrary to the interests of the government of the day. Prior to Mahathir, prime ministers and their governments either took such rulings on the chin, or if they were sufficiently angered by them, changed legislation, sometimes retrospectively, in order to circumvent the ruling of the court. Mahathir, however, was not satisfied with merely making legislative changes. A series of High Court rulings had angered Mahathir in the late 1980s at the time of the UMNO split. In the end his anger intensified to the point where he was determined to bring about permanent changes.

In 1987, for example, a Malaysian judge ruled against the Home Affairs Ministry claiming that it had erred in its disallowing of the journal *Aliran* being published in Malay. Another incident which particularly upset Mahathir was a ruling around the same time in 1987 that a DAP leader should be released from ISA detention because the detention order was "made without proper care, caution and a proper sense of responsibility." Mahathir's ultimate response to such incidents was not simply to change the legislation but to change the constitution itself. In March 1988 Mahathir declared his intention to amend the constitution in order that people had "judges that apply the law made by parliament and not make their own laws as is happening now." In May 1988, the Prime Minister exhorted the Malaysian king, the Yang di-Pertuan Agong, to lay charges of "gross misconduct" against the Malaysian Lord President, or Chief Justice. The Lord President was subject to a judicial inquiry and subsequently dismissed in July that year. Thereafter the Malaysian judiciary remained effectively under the control of the executive arm of government.

The case of the trial against Anwar Ibrahim beginning in September 1998 and resulting with Anwar being sentenced to six years in jail in April 1999 (for allegedly corruptly influencing the police to not follow through on charges of sexual immorality) can be cited. It is perhaps the most dramatic demonstration of the limits of the independence of the Malaysian judiciary. The Anwar trial of 1998-99 had all the elements of a show-trial with only a pretense of an independent traditional process and Mahathir was able to act with impunity and crush his rival in no uncertain manner. It remains to be seen, whether in doing this Mahathir has created a martyr and brought upon himself such public opprobrium as to make the whole exercise ridiculously expensive. Nevertheless, it serves as a clear illustration of the way in which many lesser figures in Malaysian political life have been controlled, intimidated and otherwise constrained in their expression of dissent against the Mahathir government.

Money Politics, Patronage, and Electoral Gerrymanders

The third area in which Malaysian democracy has been severely constrained is in the most direct and extensive of manipulations of the democratic process. That is to say the use of money and patronage to influence political outcomes and the construction of electoral gerrymanders in such a fashion that this political patronage can be most efficiently directed to achieve the desired outcome.

In 1974 new electoral boundaries were drawn up in Malaysia. In general the result of these boundaries was that rural seats had a disproportionate amount of political power vis-à-vis urban constituencies. In this respect, along with some others, Malaysian politics resembles Japanese politics in which the political basis of building the success is built upon electoral gerrymanders and support from rural constituencies for the LDP. In 1970 the largest urban constituency in peninsula Malaysia was three times greater in terms of population numbers than the smallest rural constituency. By 1982 this gap had grown even larger with the largest urban constituency having five times as many people as the smallest rural constituency. This is without even taking into account the forty-eight often very small constituencies in East Malaysia. In 1986 new electoral boundaries were drawn and these boundaries had the effect of giving Malays an absolute majority in 70 percent of peninsula seats, that is to say ninety-two out of the 132 peninsula seats, with a heavy weighting towards rural constituencies.

The effect of this has been twofold. Firstly, it is meant that to the extent to which UMNO can win support of the Malay voters against PAS it can dominate the process. Secondly, it means that patronage and money can be specifically targeted at troublesome constituencies including constituencies in which there is not a Malay majority.

This facilitates the workings of what have come to be called money politics. It has been common throughout the history of UMNO but particularly, as in the Mahathir era, for government assistance to be given to so-called pillars of society that is to say local members of either UMNO, the MCA or the MIC coalition members within the Barisan Nasional government. Similarly, local development programs are often specifically targeted at winning the support of a particular constituency. Unfortunately, this has had the sad effect of leaving many rural Malay constituencies, particularly those strongly supporting PAS relatively undeveloped because the government sees little point in channeling support and resources in their direction.

Under previous governments UMNO strengthened its base through the strategic granting of timber licenses and other concessions. However under Mahathir the process has become somewhat more sophisticated involving a complex network of UMNO-owned businesses and businesses owned by senior political figures benefiting directly from government contracts.

Over time the emphasis has moved away from relatively primitive, low-level local Malay politics at village level to a more sophisticated system of enticement and inducement. This is reflected in the changing nature of the Malay workforce. In 1970 around 62 percent of the Malay workforce was involved in agriculture, by 1985 this percentage had shifted to 41 percent. Similarly, in 1970 around 13 percent of Malaysians were engaged in white-collar professions and by 1985 this figurehead almost doubled to around 24 percent. In the

1970s a large proportion, perhaps as many as 40 percent of UMNO local officials came through the ranks of schoolteachers. By the late 1980s these local community leaders and schoolteachers had lost out in the organization being replaced by urban professionals and businessman mostly residing in Kuala Lumpur, Petaling Jaya Penang or Johor Baharu.

Another means of influence and control under the Mahathir government has been personal loans made to businessmen and business interests affiliated with leading political figures. It is widely speculated for example, that one other factor inhibiting many more UMNO members in joining with Razaleigh's breakaway faction in the mid-eighties was fact that many of these would-be dissidents had large loans which could be called in if they broke with the Mahathir faction.

Complicating the whole scene is the fact that there are very few senior political figures without skeletons in their closets. That is to say, the vast majority of political figures in some way or another have been compromised by the process, with a result that they are reluctant to speak out against it.

Islam, the State, and Attitudes to the West

Malaysian and Indonesian Attitudes to the West

One of the most striking differences between Indonesia and Malaysia, particularly to Western observers, is in the area of attitudes to Western society and Western culture. While both societies maintain a sensible level of critical appraisal of Western current policy initiatives and Western popular culture there is a striking difference between the way the two governments, the two societies and the two different national expressions of Islam situated themselves with respect to the West. In Indonesia, the Sukarno regime positioned itself as being independent of both the West and of the Soviet bloc. It was in Bandung, after all, that the Non-Aligned Movement first began. Towards the end of his regime Sukarno became increasingly anti-Western, at least in his rhetoric. Great displays were made of the government's rejection of Western popular culture and Western imperialism particularly during the 1960s when the American flag was burnt and symbols of popular culture destroyed at public gatherings. Whether in fact Sukarno himself was anti-Western or whether this was merely a ploy to bolster his own domestic situation is difficult to say. Under the Suharto regime the outlook shifted dramatically.

Suharto's new military backed government decided from the outset that it needed the support of the West, in particular America and set out to secure it. Even at the very end of the Suharto regime, the Suharto government remained reasonably positive towards Western economic intervention, Western ideas and certainly Western education. One of the most poignant moments in the last days of Suharto came as he signed the first IMF treaty with Michel Camdessus the IMF head, standing grimly behind him with his arms folded. Photographs depicting this, appeared across the pages of Indonesian press. Clearly at that moment, many Indonesians questioned not just the wisdom of IMF initiatives but of the West's intervention itself. Nevertheless, even then popular feeling was directed towards the ruling regime and exploitation of political circumstances for personal gain rather than against the IMF. Even as the Suharto regime was falling apart on the streets of Jakarta and other Indonesian cities were filled with demonstrating students and activists, there was little reason for Western observers to feel that they were in any way being targeted or that their presence was resented. On the contrary, the demand for democracy and reform that rang out through the streets of Jakarta in May 1998 was based on a clear understanding that what was being sought was Western-style liberal democracy.

This is not say that the Indonesian reform movement was uncritically infatuated with a notion of Western-style liberal democracy or that it was incapable of recognizing the many weaknesses and inconsistencies in the way that it was applied in the West. Rather it was a reflection both of the reform movement and broader still of Indonesian society. This was also true within Islamic institutions and Islamic mass organizations such as Muhammadiyah and Nahdlatul Ulama a similar view predominated.

The premier IAIN state institutes for Islam, for example, as we have seen above, were built up through the 1970s, 1980s, and 1990s on the basis of a deliberate attempt to synthesize classical Islamic scholarship with modern Western learning. Postgraduate students were sent to study in the West specifically so they would learn to think critically and become more open-minded. Not only were charismatic and popular Islamic leaders such as Abdurrahman Wahid

and Nurcholish Madjid known as admirers of many aspects of Western culture and civilization their views were broadly echoed throughout organizations such as Nahdlatul Ulama and Muhammadiyah and
across the country. In this respect, the one-time anti-Western views
of Amien Rais were out of step not just with the views of the broader
community but even with the prevailing views of many within
Muhammadiyah; although, it needs to be acknowledged that to the
extent that there were broadly anti-Western sentiments within Islamic
society in Indonesia, they were most likely to be found on the right
of the Modernist movement. Far more extreme in their views were
the right wing of Dewan Dakwah in particular as they were now to
be found in KISDI. But here they represent a very small minority
not just of all Indonesian Muslims, but also of all Indonesian Islamic
leaders and intellectuals.

In Malaysia, the situation is very different. Not only is the Malaysian government fond of taking a critical stance vis-à-vis the West,
but there is a widespread criticism or oppositional stance to the West
particularly among Islamic leaders. It has to be added however, that
even at its most critical the stance takes the form of a love-hate relationship. Both government leaders such as Mahathir Mohamad and
various Islamic educational institutions and organizations are both
deeply Westernized in terms of the way that they structure themselves and many of their organizations, just as they are often also
deeply critical of the West.

The Dakwah Movements and the West

In studying this critical, or oppositional, stance towards the West
two broad groupings need to be distinguished. On the one hand
there are the Islamic oppositional elements, and on the other hand
members of the government and the administration itself. To this
can also be added Malaysia's nascent civil society. Among the first
grouping a distinction needs to be made between the *dakwah* movements represented by groups such as ABIM, IRC, and Darul Arqam
and PAS as a political party and official oppositional political organization.

Even within the *dakwah* movements, as we have seen above, there
are broad differences of opinion on issues, particularly concerning
attitudes to the West. Within ABIM for example there is, on the whole,
a more moderate and nuanced response to the West. Not surpris-

ingly, some aspects of Western popular culture are rejected or at least criticized, as are some specific current policy initiatives and historical incidents. On the other hand, the soft *dakwah* line represented by groups such as ABIM are very much in favor of modernization and development along Western lines. This soft side of the *dakwah* movement is generally associated with Islamic leaders whose own educational background is in the humanities and social sciences. As we have seen, groups such as Darul Arqam and to an even great extent the ISC, tend to be dominated by science graduates both those trained in Malaysia and those trained abroad.

It is among the IRC and other hard-line or more puritanical *dakwah* groups that anti-Western sentiment is most strongly felt. As Shamsul has noted, (Shamsul, 1997) it is these groups that tend to be most black-and-white in their thinking. Indeed Shamsul argues it is no coincidence that it is those who are trained in Western style positivist sciences or scientific thought who are most given to a kind of positivism in their religious philosophy. Science graduates and applied science graduates such as engineers are trained to think in terms of precise models, equations, formula, and predictable results. The whole educational training of these graduates is geared towards learning what is right and what is wrong, what is true and what is false. This sort of intellectual training serves them poorly when it comes to understanding the application of religious truth to modern society.

The Mahathir regime has tended, not surprisingly, to favor the ideas of the soft *dakwah* strain as opposed to the hard *dakwah* strain. So it was that the ideas of ABIM and ABIM's leader, were deliberately adopted by the Mahathir government in its earlier days. And while the government at times is caught in a race to appear more Islamic than the hard-core *dakwah* opposition, on the whole it is cautious and apprehensive about the hard-line *dakwah* position.

Unfortunately however, while in some respects the Mahathir government has been successful in promoting soft *dakwah* ideas it has done little to change the environmental circumstances that contribute to the formation of new hard-line *dakwah* identities. For it is in the lower science colleges and among Malaysia's engineers and scientists that the hard-line *dakwah* movements have flourished. Ironically, just as the government has tried to open up opportunities to members of the Malay community and promote development through technology and industry it has given rise to educational conditions or social circumstances that greatly favor hard-line *dakwah* recruiting.

So while the government has supported moderate *dakwah* ideas it is the somewhat inflexible and even reactionary hard-line *dakwah* ideas which have proved most popular among Malay youth and integral to these ideas is a critical stance vis-à-vis the West. This is not to say these movements are in every sense anti-Western, for as we have noted they tend to be very modern and in that sense very Western in the ways that they organize and promote themselves. In part because of their international linkages and in part because of their core philosophy, however, the overall tenor of the hard-line *dakwah* position is anti-Western.

These *dakwah* groups have been far more influenced by groups in Pakistan, Iran and the Arab world then have any groups in Indonesia. Whereas Indonesian Islamic groups tend to be proud of their Indonesian identity and critical of what they see to be overly narrow or superficial views from the Middle East or from South Asia, the situation is quite the reverse in Malaysia. The ideas of Jamaati Islam and its founder Mauluna Maududi continue to be popular in Malaysia. As do the ideas of Al Ikwan, or the Islamic Brotherhood, in the Arab world. Similarly, there is widespread support for the PLO and to a lesser extent for Hisbullah and a spirited opposition towards Western engagement in the region. Among many groups there is also continuing admiration for the Iranian thought that came to dominate after the 1979 revolution. On the other hand groups, in Malaysia have also received significant financial support from elements in Saudi Arabia and in the United Arabic Emirates.

To a large extent however, the anti-Western sentiment which seems to prevail among hard-line *dakwah* groups is not so much a critical appraisal of the West as it is a desperate attempt to delineate and separate Muslim and Malay identity for themselves in a complex and rapidly changing world. This is hardly surprising. When one stops to think about it. Malay youth often from rural areas are sent to study at Western institutions and are drawn to campus *dakwah* groups and to the sense of certainty and fellowship that such groups offer in the midst of a confusing and sometimes apparently hostile environment. The fact that many formerly moderate youths return home from studies in America or Great Britain or Australia with a new-found interest in Islam and with a new narrowness of mind is not at all a surprising development given the alternatives open to these youths.

While the government has sought to promote a more moderate kind of *dakwah* thought it has not always been able to control the outcomes of its initiatives. A good example is the International Islamic University in Petaling Jaya just outside Kuala Lumpur. While the initial idea of establishing such a university was to meet the demand of ABIM-style soft *dakwah* activists as well as creating modern Muslim intellectuals, the result has been rather different. In large measures this is because the institution throughout its life has been dependant upon a significant proportion of foreign staff and visiting lecturers. Some of these have been liberal and moderate in their views and others have been quite the opposite. The result has been a very uneven advancement of Islamic thought with little of the synthesis and creative development seen in Indonesia's leading IAIN campus.

PAS and the West

At first glance it would appear that some of the strongest anti-Western sentiment to be found in modern Malaysia society resides within the ranks of PAS. To a significant extent this assessment is not without foundation. PAS continues to push, albeit with increasing weariness and reduced conviction, the nominal ideal of establishing an Islamic state. It has it has made this its platform, in order to set itself against the Barisan Nasional coalition government. It is officially pushing an Islamic state model over and above a Western model for the state. Similarly, the rhetoric of PAS is frequently filled with references to the failure of UMNO to fulfill the demands of Islam and create a properly Islamic society in Malaysia. In criticizing UMNO in this predictable fashion PAS often sets itself up as being opposed to the Western elements of modern Malaysian society and development.

Looked at a deeper level however, it is not at all clear that PAS is any more or less critical of the West than other institutions within Malaysia society. Over the years PAS has been quintessentially a Malay chauvinistic party, founded and run to further the interests of Malays. At times it has been forced to take a different track stressing Islamicity against Malay ethnicity in order to differentiate itself from the government. Nevertheless, it remains that in many respects. PAS appears to been acting out a part in a drama not scripted by itself and in which it has no choice in the role it plays. The sophisticated policy shifts and developments of the UMNO-led coalition have increasingly narrowed the position left for PAS to stand in opposition and left it with few resources. When PAS was forced to consider working with DAP in the late 1980s, many suggested that such an alliance was completely unworkable. And while ultimately the Semangat 46-DAP-PAS alliance did break down its failure had more to do with the overwhelming dominance and control of the Barisan Nasional Coalition than it did with the intrinsic problems within the new alternative coalition. More specifically, it is not inconceivable that a DAP-PAS coalition could be made to work under the auspices of a rainbow coalition opposition charge led by the new People's Justice Party.

In other words, when one disregards the symbolic posturing of PAS vis-à-vis the government and its sometimes superficial use of Islamic symbolism there are real prospects for arguing that given alternative ways of expressing oppositional stance PAS could become a much more moderate organization. Some further grounds for optimism are to be found in the fact that PAS's roots and strength lie in traditional rural Malay society which Coppell claims has always tended towards moderation and tolerance rather than confrontation. In other words given a chance, there is a good reason to expect that PAS may over time be able to reinvent itself though this would require profound change.

Mahathir, the Malaysian State and the West

It is difficult to separate out the extent to which an anti-Western stance to the *dakwah* movement and PAS opposition party is simply a matter of symbolic posturing vis-à-vis the ruling regime and alternately the extent to which it represents a conviction. It is just as difficult to make sense of the government's position.

In reflecting on of the government's position it is difficult not to speak of the personal position of the Prime Minister himself. As is often the case in governments led by strong charismatic leaders it is extremely difficult to distinguish the broad government position from the personal convictions of the leader himself. Prime Minister Mahathir is in many respects a most enigmatic figure. Indeed it would appear that often he enjoys and takes advantage of his enigmatic profile. On the international stage, for example Mahathir often strikes a strongly anti-Western pose. And yet when many incidents are seen in context there is reason for believing that the Prime Minister's posturing has much more to do with domestic politics than it does with deep conviction.

Malaysia's international position means that so long as it can continue to attract international investors, something it generally has little trouble in doing, it does not really matter if occasionally the Prime Minister ruffles a few feathers particularly when those feathers belong to birds as non-threatening, as for example, the Australian state. In other words, for the purposes of domestic political expediency, the Prime Minister can often afford to take a dramatic position on the international stage knowing that such posturing costs him little internationally but can be very beneficial at home. Malaysians as much as any other nation of people can be extremely patriotic, at its worst this patriotism can lead to an uncritical nationalism that reacts sharply and predictably to perceived insults against the state.

A good example of the way in which Prime Minister Mahathir has deliberately tilted against the windmills of the West on the international stage in order to shore up his own domestic position occurred in 1998. One of the reasons why UMNO and the Barisan Nasional Coalition had steamed so easily through the 1995 general elections was that the elections came on the back of seven years of unprecedented growth. By late 1997 however, Malaysia was beginning to feel the full impact of the Asian economic crisis. By 1998 Mahathir was feeling decidedly uncomfortable on a number of fronts.

Firstly, there were signs that his deputy Anwar Ibrahim was not going to continue to be compliant and may even reveal information that would be seriously damaging to the Prime Minister and his government. On other hand there was increasing anxiety in Malaysian society. The anxiety over the economic crisis was only increased as Malaysians watched events next door in Indonesia. Following the May collapse of the Suharto regime Malaysians perhaps for the first time again to mass together in the call for reformation.

Faced with this domestic pressure Mahathir lashed out against the West. He began by picking on the softest targets and at George Soros, implying that there was an international Jewish banking conspiracy behind Asia's current economic woes. Next he turned on the IMF

accusing it of a neo-imperialist mentally. Finally, in what turned out
to be a clever piece of lateral thinking, Mahathir pulled down the
shutters fixed the Ringgat exchange rate and turned his back on IMF
advice.

For a variety of reasons Mahathir's judgement in the latter matter
proved not to be as foolish as first thought. Nevertheless, Mahathir's
performance throughout the first half of the year raised eyebrows
around the world and undoubtedly damaged his international standing. Mahathir has a remarkable track record as a clever and brilliant
strong leader of a country facing numerous challenges. So what
caused this master helmsman to take such an unusual tack?

The answer is clearly Mahathir's action in 1998, just like that of
Sukarno's in the early sixties when his declared confrontation against
Malaysia, was designed to divert attention away from the domestic
crisis. By positioning himself as a champion on the international
stage not just for Malaysia but also for the entire Third World, especially the Muslim world, Mahathir received an enormous boost of
publicity at the domestic level. This is not to say that Mahathir is in
every way anti-Western, but rather that he calculated the cost of taking a stance against the West in the circumstances as being much
less the cost of risking a continued slide in the standing of the domestic economy. Similarly, his anti-Jewish stance and his attack on
George Soros and accusations of the banking piracy can be explained
in terms of searching for the softest targets. Since Malaysia had already position itself under Mahathir as a champion of the Muslim
world and in particular of the Palestinians, from his point of view
there was little to be lost by hurting Jewish feeling.

The question that needs to be asked however is whether Mahathir's
anti-Western stance and his public anti-Semitism are anything more
than a calculated ploy. Or does he harbor deep prejudice towards
the West? The answer to these questions is complex. In all likelihood much of what Mahathir does is a calculated ploy. Nevertheless
there are signs of a genuine anger directed towards the West and a
genuine anti-Semitism. A small but perhaps significant factor which
is occasionally raised by observers in discussions about Dr. Mahathir,
is that his apparent anger towards Australia may, in part, be the result of his failure to procure a place for medical studies in Australia
in the late 1960s. Whether this means anything three decades later,
cannot be confirmed, nevertheless there does appear to be a per-

sonal element to Mahathir's attacks upon the West. Indeed some would argue (as Anwar Ibrahim himself most famously did in the days after being found guilty by Mahathir's court in April 1999) that beneath all of his flamboyant rhetoric, the Prime Minister is genuinely racist in his views.

Civil Society

One of the saddest aspects of Mahathir's anti-Western posturing, and of the consequent general tenor of the Malaysian government, is the way in which this attitude has affected broader Malaysian society. Given the extensive controls over the media and the authoritarian and repressive nature of the Malaysian government under Mahathir it is scarcely surprising that the government position dominates the entire Malaysian scene. This is not to say that everyone agrees with the government position or that no one is critical of the Prime Minister's stance, but rather that in day-to-day operations it becomes natural for people to slip into the language of the regime simply in order to avoid confrontation on lesser issues. Unfortunately, this has, to a certain extent, infected and pervaded Malaysia's nascent civil society.

For a long time, particularly in the latter part of the Mahathir government, through the mid-1980s and onwards during the 1990s, at least up until the arrest of Anwar Ibrahim, a number of formerly dissident voices realized that a less direct strategy would be more effective so long as Mahathir remained in power. Given the level of controls upon Malaysian civil society they came to the conclusion that continued confrontation with the government would achieve little. Instead they decided that it was more efficacious to direct attention towards international concerns which themselves could then be reflected on the Malaysian situation rather than directly confronting the regime.

A good example of this is the veteran civil society activist Chandra Muzaffar. During the 1980s Chandra Muzaffar was active with the NGO Aliran, based in Penang. In the mid 1990s he left Aliran and came to the national capital (or at least the dormitory sister city of Petaling Jaya) and took up a post at the University of Malaya. His chair was as Director the Center for Civilization or Dialogue, itself an initiative of Anwar Ibrahim. Chandra's NGO activities were now focused around Just World Trust, an organization concerned with highlighting North-South issues and broader international issues of social justice. While Chandra came under considerable criticism for having left Aliran and moderated his tone towards the government, in effect he aligned himself with moderates in the government such as Anwar Ibrahim, arguing that it was better to focus efforts where there was the maximum possibility of achieving substantial reform. Indeed up until the arrest of Anwar the strategy appeared to be working very well. Had Anwar gone on to become the next Malaysian Prime Minister there is reason to believe that an evolutionary process of reform would have continued, and indeed accelerated, under the new Prime Minister.

One of the unfortunate aspects of this strategy, however, is that Chandra and the Just World Trust and other related groups occasionally appeared to be endorsing certain aspects of the government's criticism of the West. While as an individual Chandra's liberal credentials are well established, his work under the Mahathir regime in the 1990s gave rise to suggestions that he was endorsing the anti-Semitism evident in Mahathir's attacks on individuals such as George Soros. On the other hand, the very same figures, Chandra especially, have been courageous in the defense of Anwar Ibrahim since his arrest in 1998 and have bravely taken the lead in pushing the reform movement to the next stage. And in opposing the anti-democratic style of Mahathir they, like their Indonesian colleagues, are clearly arguing for the universal applicability of modern Western democratic ideals and institutions, rejecting the cultural relativism of Mahathir's position. Moreover, as they become involved in the process of trying to establish a new national coalition, their long-standing willingness to work with all communities and all ethnic groups in society will be given new emphasis as they try to shape the new political reality.

Prospects for Change

Prospects for Political Change

One of the more tragic aspects about the ways in which the Mahathir government has sought to control and shape opinion in Malaysian society is the way in which it has subverted religion, Islam in particular, for its own political purposes. While it is not completely to blame for this, and some measure of responsibility lies with some sections of the *dakwah* movement, there is a real sense in which the perception of Malaysian Islam being anti-liberal, anti-Western and even intolerant, is the direct product of the Prime Minister's own political manipulations. Ironically, the prospects for social and political change within Malaysia depend very much upon Islam, in particular upon liberal Islamic leaders and a fresh alternative vision of the way in which Islam can contribute to Malaysia society.

There is not space here to go into the details of the Anwar Ibrahim legal case of late 1998 and early 1999. Moreover, the case has been well covered in the media and its details readily available so there is little need to recount this here. The main point to make here is that up until his arrest, or more accurately up until his falling out with Mahathir (presumably because Mahathir felt the need to launch a pre-emptive attack upon Anwar, before Anwar revealed embarrassing details about the Prime Minister and his government) it seemed that Malaysian political life and society might smoothly proceed into a new era under a new Prime Minister. It was widely anticipated that with Anwar as Prime Minister, Malaysian society and Malaysian Islam would become progressively more open and liberal.

Anwar has now been jailed for six years and faces the possibility of other charges and further sentencing resulting from the prosecution. Consequently he cannot be expected to play an active political role for some years to come, however in many ways he remains the focal point of those hoping for change in Malaysian society. The November 1999 elections demonstrated that the National Justice Party currently led by his wife Azizah is not yet a significant threat to UMNO and Barisan Nasional and is not likely to becomes so in the short term either. Nevertheless, there remain grounds for hope that the National Justice Party might be able to continue to bring other dissident elements such as PAS and DAP into a new coalition much as did Semangat 46 in the late eighties.

The irony here is that for such a coalition to emerge as a viable alternative to the Barisan Nasional Coalition there would need to be good co-operation, not just between the New National Justice Party and PAS but between PAS and DAP and other minor opposition parties. In other words, PAS would be required to reinvent itself just as would the DAP. Both would be required to leave aside their ethnic chauvinism and their narrow single-issue character and become genuine allies in a viable alternative coalition. While achieving this will be difficult it is not impossible. Supporting it is the fact that there is greater political conscience and awareness than ever before in Malaysian society, partly as a result of the Anwar trial and partly as a result of the steady maturing political understanding in Malaysian society.

Observers such as Crouch have pointed out that the repressive responsive government of Mahathir was at its best, that is to say its most responsive, when it faced genuine political opposition in the form of the alternative coalition of Semangat 46. In the period shortly after the 1990 election the Mahathir government showed real signs of listening to the needs of Malaysia voters. This suggests that developments that see Malaysia turning towards a more balanced "two-party" style democracy in which the Barisan Nasional Coalition is pitted against a genuine equal in the form of the National Justice Party DAP-PAS coalition could prove very beneficial for Malaysia society. The obvious caveat here is that if PAS continues to be narrowly Islamist and chauvinistic then the sort of gains that it made in November 1999 remain very much a mixed blessing. On the one hand, for Malaysian democracy to function in a meaningful fashion it is necessary for the Barisan Nasional to face real competition. Nevertheless, however, success for PAS without substantial attitudinal change within the party increases the risk of Malaysian politics being dominated by sectarianism.

Is it is obviously foolish to seek to predict what might happen over the next couple of years given the great number of uncertainties currently facing Malaysia. But, Mahathir's advancing years and failing health may well mean that dissent within UMNO may be able to express itself through the appointment of a new leader. It is even possible that a new UMNO leadership may respond to public pressure and reduce Anwar's prison sentence. Another highly significant area of uncertainty is the rate of Malaysia's economic recovery. Past experience suggests that Malaysians are most willing to support the ruling government in large numbers when economic growth is going well and that they become most politically critical when economic growth is stalled or threatened. Another factor is the extent to which new communication technologies, in particular the Internet, are able to contribute to a new level of consciousness among Malaysians by overcoming the government controls over the Malaysian media.

It remains to be seen then, the extent to which political reform is possible in the short-term. Nevertheless, it seems reasonable to expect reform will occur over the medium to long term. Hopefully, as it occurs a more tolerant and inclusive approach to Islam will come together with a more cross-communal approach to Malaysian politics.

Prospects for Social Change

Leaving aside the issues of the potential for political change, it should be noted that there has been a steady ongoing process of social change occurring in Malaysian society for some time now. Firstly, among many ordinary Malays there is a growing disaffection or weariness with a *dakwah*-style Islamic resurgence. Indeed, among rural communities there was from the very beginning a sense of critical response towards resurgent Islam as expressed through the *dakwah* movement. Many ordinary Malays regarded *dakwah* Islam to be superficially hyper-religious and to imply a disregard for the everyday religiosity of conservative Malay Muslims. The superficial emphasis on "Islamic" clothing and on "ultra-*Halal*" foodstuffs went against the grain of traditional Islam in many Malay communities. As a result many people felt upset that their commitment to Islam was being called into question and at the same time responded critically to the overt displays of religiosity on the part of *dakwah* adherents.

Nevertheless many people had no choice but to go along with the new expressions of religiosity even if privately they suspected their worth. Michael Peletz (1997), borrowing from Foucault, speaks of a panopticon effect in which ordinary Malays in rural Malay society feel themselves to be constantly under supervision. He was referring here not so much to a political big brother behind the panopticon, in the form of the Mahathir government, but rather to ordinary everyday local community. The result of this panopticon effect Peletz, suggests is that many Malays erred on the side of caution and went along with outer displays of greater religiosity at the same time as inwardly questioning their worth.

There is reason to suspect however, that as the years have gone on many people have tired of the pressures placed upon them by the *dakwah* movement, and particularly by government organized shows of religiosity, to the extent that they are ready for a more traditional and natural approach to expressing their religious convictions.

At the same time middle-class Malay society in the urban centers has both grown larger in terms of the number of people living in the cities, and number of people now enjoying middle-class lifestyles, and deeper in terms of the way in which modern education has contributed to new levels of awareness among urban middle-class Malaysians. The result of all this, is that there is an increasing willingness to question the manipulation of Islam for government purposes as well as to question some of the more superficial aspects of the *dakwah* movement. Whether this will lead directly to a turn away from highly symbolic usages of Islam of course remains to be seen. There is good reason, however, to believe that in the medium to long run that the kind of Islamicity promoted by the *dakwah* movement, and by the Malaysian government as it sought to harness the Islamic resurgence for its own purposes, will represent a passing fashion.

This is not to say that Islam in the future will be less important in Malaysian society. Indeed, it might be argued the contrary will be true. But rather, ordinary Malaysians, both in rural communities and in urban society will increasingly tire of an overtly symbolic posturing form of religiosity particularly when that form of religiosity is linked to a government whose credibility has been found wanting.

It seems likely then, that social change will be linked closely with political change. Not only is social change likely to support political change, to the extent that it is successful, political reform will create the conditions for ongoing social reform. If this hypothesis is proven true, a new more liberal, more tolerant, cross-communal government will allow Malaysians greater latitude to act and speak according to their consciences rather than according to the contrived expectations of society.

The November 1999 Elections

Dr. Mahathir Decides it is Time

Dr. Mahathir left it until the last minute to declare that Malaysia was going to the polls on November 29 1999. Many had expected that the national elections, which also included elections for eleven state assemblies, would not be held until the following year. This was because late 1999 was unquestionably a bad time for Mahathir. His popularity rating was at an all-time low, especially amongst ethnic Malays, largely as the result of a backlash to the Anwar Ibrahim affair. And whilst the economy was not in a state of decline neither was it enjoying robust growth, having stagnated through the latter half of 1999. At the same time, the opposition movement was rapidly gaining strength and enjoying an unprecedented degree of unity. Particularly worrying for Dr. Mahathir was Keadilan, the new National Justice Party led by Wan Azizah wife of the jailed former Deputy Prime Minister Anwar Ibrahim.

No doubt there were a number of factors that weighed strongly on Mahathir's mind in deciding on the November poll date. Not least of these was a concern that if he delayed going to the polls until after the Muslim fasting month of Ramadan, that began in December 1999, he would find it difficult to clamp down on political dissent. Traditionally during Ramadan many people spend their evenings gathering in mosques and homes listening to religious teachers. The government had been largely successful in regulating large public rallies and in limiting the opposition's access to the national media, but to control every meeting in every mosque during the whole month of Ramadan would have been impossible. Nor could such meetings have simply been banned in the manner of ordinary political rallies.

Another factor that was perhaps even more important in the Prime Minister's calculations was that in January 2000 a new cohort of young voters was to be added to the national election rolls. This cohort was of no mean size as it represented a total of 680,000 new voters. It is safe to assume that given the generational demographics of political sentiment evident in recent years that the vast majority of this almost seven hundred thousand new voters would have voted for the opposition. These two factors were probably decisive in pushing Mahathir and the National Front coalition to opt for a November polling date. They were in ill odor nationally but to have delayed any longer would have seen their already weak position eroded even further.

Barisan Alternatif Emerges

Adding to the National Front's woes were indications of unexpected unity shown amongst opposition forces. Shortly before the

November polls this took concrete form in the shape of the Barisan Alternatif, the Alternative Front (BA). Barisan Alternatif positioned itself very much as an alternative choice to Barisan Nasional, the National Front (BN). The Alternative Front was composed of four opposition parties: the Democratic Action Party (DAP), previously the largest opposition party, the Islamic Party of Malaysia (PAS), the Malaysia Peoples Party (PRM) and the new National Justice Party (Keadilan).

In many ways this was an unlikely union of forces because PAS, as we have seen above, has a long history of being a chauvinistic Islamist party, and is therefore hardly an easy partner for the Chinese dominated DAP or the pluralistic and progressive Keadilan. A particular source of difficulties was the fact that PAS has as one of the core planks of its policy platform, the aim of making Malaysia a more Islamic state, if not actually an Islamic state. Nevertheless, the four parties agreed to overcome their differences and commit to a common platform. What this meant was that PAS pledged itself to moderation and respecting the rights of non-Muslims and the other parties pledged to support PAS in areas where PAS stood the greatest chance of winning.

Indeed the most significant aspect of the arrangements made in this new coalition was the decision to only field one candidate in each seat with each local candidate coming from the party that was considered to have the greatest chance of winning. Consequently, Keadilan provided many of the Alternatif Front's candidates in the electorates in the national capital and the surrounding middle-class environs of Kuala Lumpur and Petaling Jaya. Whereas PAS provided most candidates in the northern Malay States and areas where the Malay vote was strongest. Even so, this arrangements meant that in some cases Chinese voters would be asked to vote for PAS candidates and in other areas Malay voters who had traditionally have voted PAS were being asked to vote for the DAP. The strategy was bold but also risky. Nevertheless, it did provide a clever way of taking the challenge right up to the national front coalition by presenting the people with a viable opposition coalition alternative.

Barisan Nasional's Media Campaign

As we have noted above, the control of the national media, both print and television, is in the hands of the ruling elite and National

Front constituent parties so that it is extremely difficult for opposition parties or dissenting forces to get fair access to the media. Traditionally, Malaysian electoral campaigns are heavy going and no punches are pulled in the national media. The November 1999 campaign, however, was extreme even by traditional measures. The National Front lost no opportunity to attack the Alternative Front and its constituent parties and leading figures at every turn. Newspaper advertisements showed scenes from apparently dangerously out of control Keadilan rallies with headlines urging "don't let anarchy rule" Similar campaigns were run in all the major daily newspapers and magazines. More surreal still, Malaysian television sets were regularly visited by scenes of a harmonious and wealthy Malaysia to the accompaniment of Frank Sinatra singing "My Way."

The Alternative Front had virtually no access to television and only very minimal access to radio time. BA hit back by pushing on regardless with local campaigns, door to door visits and local rallies. In urban areas particularly, this campaign was backed up by a strong Internet presence and the aggressive use of the World Wide Web to voice dissenting concerns that could not be voiced through traditional media. This latter element, the Internet, was a vital element in the campaign but was really only effective in those areas, mostly urban, where considerable numbers of people had access to computers and Internet connections.

What is at Stake?

Also at stake in the November polls were the 193 seats in the parliament or lower house plus control of eleven state assemblies. In the lower house the National Front led by UMNO had enjoyed a ruling majority of 166 seats out of the previous total of 192. It also controlled ten of eleven state assemblies. The state of Kelantan in the North was the exception and had for some time been in the hands of PAS. The real goal for both BN and the BA opposition alliance was the two-thirds of the parliament threshold required to control constitutional change. The opposition knew that it had no realistic chance of winning control of government, at least not in 1999, but it hoped to be able to win sufficient seats to destroy BN's previously unassailable two-thirds plus majority. The National Front saw the target in much the same way and they declared that retaining the two-thirds majority represented their targeted clear victory. Opposition DAP leader Lim declared that the alliance was capable of winning as many as seventy to seventy-four of Parliamentary seats. In addition to this, many analysts expected that the opposition might be able to gain control of one or two extra state assemblies, probably in the strongly Malay states in the north of the peninsula.

A Swing to PAS

When the election results were known in early December there were sighs of relief in the National front camp. Once again BN had easily succeeded in controlling its two-thirds majority. It had lost a number of seats. Its share of the now 193 seats dropped back from 166 to 148 seats. But this was still well in excess of the 129 it required to clear the two-thirds threshold. This meant that the alternative front had managed to gain just forty-two seats, a good deal short of the sixty-five they had been aiming at to break the two-thirds majority. And so on the face of it the results of the November 29 poll seem to represent a remarkable victory for the national front coalition. Despite all of the bad publicity and ill will towards Mahathir and towards UMNO over the Anwar Ibrahim case, despite rising concerns about corruption, and anxiety about the flagging economy, BN had managed to retain unquestionable control of the parliament.

Nevertheless, a closer examination of the results, reveals that in many respects they were as bad or worse than BN might reasonably have expected. In particular the results were bad for UMNO. UMNO's share of parliamentary seats fell from ninety-four to seventy-two. This meant that for the first time ever there were more seats held by the BN coalition members than by UMNO itself. UMNO may still have out-polled any other single party but after dominating Malaysian politics for half a century the supremacy of UMNO was finally in question. What was clear from the voting pattern was that Chinese voters had swung strongly towards BN. The bad news for UMNO however, was that Malay voters had swung strongly towards the opposition, in particular to PAS. This was seen very clearly in the north of the peninsula where PAS was able to pick up a further state assembly and gain control over the resource rich state of Trengganu.

The MCA Saves the Day for Barisan Nasional

It was ironic that the political fortune of the man who had become famous for writing the provocative *The Malay Dilemma* and championing a radical affirmative action policy to defend and promote ethnic Malays was saved by the Chinese vote. The Malaysian Chinese association (MCA) won twenty-seven out of the thirty-five seats contested. Further seats were added by the much smaller Gerakan, also largely Chinese in its support base. At the same time, BN was helped out enormously by support from the East Malaysian States of Sabah and Sarawak on the island of Borneo where it gained victories in forty-five out of forty-eight seats contested.

It appeared that for Dr. Mahathir, his recent efforts in courting the Chinese vote had paid off. Earlier in the year he had lead a 205 strong delegation of business leaders to Beijing, 193 of whom were ethnic Chinese. Despite the fact that the Chinese make up only 26 percent of the Malaysian population he was only too aware that a swing in the Chinese vote could make or break his political fortune.

It seems more likely, however, but it was not so much Mahathir's campaigning for the Chinese vote as it was a fear of PAS and Islamist ethno-nationalism that drove the Chinese back to supporting BN. Specifically, the business orientated Chinese were afraid that a surge towards PAS would undermine national unity and stability and spook investor confidence. Given a choice of supporting a Prime Minister they were weary of and an opposition party they feared, the choice was easy. Historically, around a third or so of Chinese votes have reliably been available to BN and a third or so to the opposition with the remaining third representing swinging voters. In 1995, for example, as many as 55 percent of Chinese voted for the BN coalition. But five years earlier, in the 1990 election, only 35 to 40 percent of Chinese had voted for BN. The difference was that in 1990 the government's image had been badly tarnished following harsh repression of dissidents and economic recession. The upshot of this was that in 1995 the government tried hard to placate Chinese concerns. At the same time the nation was enjoying renewed economic growth and prosperity.

PAS Leads the Opposition

The surprise result from the November polls was the surge of Malay support for PAS, and to a lesser extent for Keadilan. The fact that Malay voters should have swung over to PAS and Keadilan was in itself no great surprise. What was surprising was the enthusiasm with which they did this. This was seen very clearly in the number

of seats gained by PAS. In the previous parliament, PAS had con-
trolled a mere seven seats. Following the November 29 elections
PAS now controlled twenty-seven seats, an almost four fold increase.
This means that for the first time ever the Prime Minister now stares
across the parliament and faces a Malay leader of the opposition.
Malays are now evenly divided between UMNO and the BN government and PAS and Keadilan and the BA opposition. Previously,
National Front supremacy was based on control of the Malay vote.
UMNO had always had to be careful about popular support in rural
areas for PAS but had largely countered this by strengthening its
Islamic credentials, at the same time ensuring that major works funding went to sensitive regions. Now, it appears for the first time that
the BN government has lost control of the Malay vote. Were it not
for the fact that Chinese voters, voting perhaps largely out of fear,
backed the BN together with voters in the Eastern States of Sabah
and Sarawak, then the government would have well and truly been
sunk, at the very least losing its two-thirds majority and probably
dropping well below the psychologically important barrier of 50
percent of the total vote even if it managed to retain control of the
majority of parliamentary seats.

In East Malaysia BN supremacy came relatively cheaply. The
government's control over infrastructure spending proved irresist-
ible. Further reinforcing the strategy was a clever division of electoral boundaries that ensured it was not difficult for the ruling coalition to tweak its campaign in ways necessary to ensure success. In
the past, the same strategy had worked reasonably well in the northern Malay-dominated peninsula states. To have voted against the
BN coalition in the past would have meant that constituencies were
guaranteed to lose out on funding for new roads, bridges, schools,
hospitals and so forth. The risk of doing so was in most cases sufficient to maintain voter discipline. In 1999, however, Malay voters
effectively declared that this was no longer sufficient incentive to
hold them back from expressing their anger towards UMNO and the
Prime Minister.

PAS' major defining feature had always been its commitment to
Islam. But in entering into the Alternative Front coalition it made a
deliberate point of downplaying this element and stressing instead
its commitment to moderation. It can be reasonably assumed that
the majority of Malay voters newly voting for PAS did not do so on

the basis of PAS' commitment to Islamist political policies. In fact, in the past, this was probably a strong disincentive for many moderate Malay voters. Instead, it seems likely that the vote for PAS was a protest vote by Malay voters who had become fed up with UMNO and the BN government.

After the Event—The Malaysian Economy Surges

The leaders of the National Front, particularly the leaders of UMNO, were privately shattered by the results of the November polls whilst trying to maintain a brave face in public. Nevertheless, they soon received good news in the form of resurgent economic growth. In the early part of 2000 the economy surged forward rapidly making up for previous losses. In 1998 the economy had shrunk by 7.5 percent but in 1999 had grown by 4.3 percent and it seems likely to exceed 5 percent growth in 2000. Even more significantly, the trade surplus is set to continue growing strongly over the course of 2000. In part the reasons for this are simple. Malaysia has enjoyed a rapidly rising trade surplus as a result of strong export growth fuelled by its strengths in the vital semiconductor market and a devalued ringgit. At the same time, controls over foreign investment have insured that the foreign currency flowing into the country has not been able to quickly leave. New confidence in the economy is seen in Standard and Poor's change of Malaysia's credit rating from BBB minus to be BBB. In the longer term, however there are concerns that the plentiful availability of cheap credit may lead to a repeat of the problems that contributed to the earlier economic crisis, namely unwise investment in real estate and stock market speculation at the expense of productive investment. All the same, the signs of strengthening economic growth gave the beleaguered government fresh confidence.

Opposition Figures Jailed

This fresh confidence was quickly demonstrated in a variety of ways not least in the government's harsh reaction to political dissent. The BN coalition and particularly UMNO had received a rude awakening in the November elections. Nevertheless, in the months following the elections the Malaysian economy continued to improve and indeed began the New Year by surging ahead at a rate not seen since the beginning of the Asian economic crisis. Mahathir's confidence, if it were shattered by the election, quickly appeared to recover and by the first months of 2000 the government and the Prime Minister were taking the upper hand. Evidentially, one of the first actions taken by the government in the New Year was to initiate the arrests of leading opposition figures. The police who carried out the arrests claimed that these arrests were due to straightforward criminal prosecutions and had nothing to do with politics. In fact at the time of the arrests the Prime Minister was overseas enjoying a vacation in South America. Few in Malaysia, however, see these arrests in any other context other than a political one.

Three of the four arrested are leading figures leading figures in the BA opposition. The first was Marina Yusoff, Vice President of Keadilan. Her sin occurred during the lead up to the November poll when she allegedly said that UMNO was the source of the May 1969 race riots. Following her was Karpal Singh, Deputy Chairman of DAP and also defense lawyer for Anwar Ibrahim in his recent trials. He was arrested because of a claim he made in court in September 1999 that Anwar had been poisoned and that "I suspect that people in high places are responsible." The remaining two figures, Zulkifli Sulong and Chea Lim Thye, were arrested because of an article in the biweekly PAS newspaper Harakah. The article quoted Keadilan deputy president Chandra Muzaffar as alleging that there was a major conspiracy by the Prime Minister and his cohorts. Zulkifli Sulong is the editor of Harakah and Chea Lim Thye is the printer of the newspaper. The charge against all four was sedition and all four were granted bail after pleading not guilty.

A fifth person was arrested in mid-January. He was Mohamed Ezam Mohamed Noor, youth chief of Keadilan and also Political Secretary of Anwar Ibrahim when he was in office. His crime was that he had allegedly revealed to the media anti-corruption agency reports on two senior UMNO politicians. He was charged under the Official Secrets Act.

The charges rocked Malaysian society. They were interpreted as a clear sign, that the government was strongly on the comeback and did not intend to brook any dissent. This impression was reinforced when the government moved later in the year to ban all large public rallies. The March banning of public rallies followed in the wake of a series of protests against curbs on PAS paper Harakah as well as protests following the early arrests of leading opposition figures.

Mahathir and Badawi Confirmed in UMNO

Mahathir's confident reassertion of his political authority was also evident within the ranks of UMNO. Since late 1999 there had been considerable speculation that maverick UMNO politician and Malay Prince Tunku Razaleigh Hamzah might challenge Mahathir for the leadership of the party. Ten years earlier Razaleigh had very nearly been successful in snatching away the Prime Ministership from Mahathir and although the relationship between the two men had since improved and Razaleigh had at one stage been made Finance Minister, he was widely regarded as being one of a few figures capable of taking on Mahathir. As it happened Razaleigh was forced to declare his intention not to run against Mahathir. By April he had received only one nomination for his candidacy and under UMNO party rules, a candidate requires at least fifty. A total of 133 of 165 divisions had already indicated that they were nominating Mahathir. It was clear that Razaleigh faced a mathematical impossibility of garnering enough votes.

No one was really surprised by Razaleigh's defeat. In December 1999, after waiting eleven days after the polls the Prime Minister had announced his new cabinet line-up. Despite the considerable help given to the National Front by the Chinese, the Chinese share of portfolios had not increased at all. The East Malaysians States of Sabah and Sarawak, however, which had also played a vital important role in returning BN to power were well rewarded. Former Sabah Chief Minister, Bernard Dompok for example, was rewarded for his efforts by being moved into the Prime Minister's Department as a full cabinet member. In fact the new National Front cabinet was stacked with familiar faces, all of them Mahathir loyalists. Consequently, when it came ready for nominations of UMNO President and Deputy President, important positions because they historically determined the position of Prime Minister and Deputy Prime Minister, Mahathir very much had the upper hand.

The Way Forward—Prospects for Reform

UMNO now faces a dilemma. In the short-term its position is strong as is the position of Mohamad Mahathir and his deputy Badawi. In the longer term, however they will have to contend with a political opposition which is more united than it has been ever before and now has a real claim to Malay support. Short-term tactics such as banning public rallies or opposition newspapers could seriously back-fire on the government in such a climate. It is more likely that both UMNO and the government will respond to their humiliation in November 1999 in much the same way that they did ten years ear-lier when they faced near defeat in the 1990 election. In other words, it is likely that they will try to actively court the very people who turned against them. But this time around there is a new twist and that is that PAS has taken the votes that flowed from UMNO whilst Sabah, Sarawak and the Malaysians Chinese Association have kept it from going under completely. Consequently, efforts to try and lure back voters from PAS may have the effect of annoying those who came over to support the government in its hour of need.

Specifically, if UMNO responds to PAS' recent success by trying, as they have done in the past to prove themselves more Islamic than PAS then they risk losing the very voters who saved their political fortunes in November 1999. It is likely then, that UMNO will resist the temptation to respond to PAS simply in the terms of greater Is-lamization, and instead will concentrate on trying to prove that is not simply in government for the big end of town.

Nevertheless there is a real risk that if PAS responds to attempts by UMNO to redeem itself by challenging UMNO's Islamic creden-tials then a repeat of earlier rounds of competition in which each party attempted to out-Islam the other may occur. This would be disastrous for both UMNO and for PAS, and arguably for the nation as a whole. There are grounds for believing that both parties recog-nize this and instead will be trying to prove themselves responsive to the demands of the people for a more just and equitable style of government.

Even in this, however, there exists the danger that UMNO efforts to appeal to Malay farmers and small businesspeople may result in it backing an extension of the affirmative action policy which has for so long annoyed non-Malay voters in Malaysia. If this were to be the case then the Chinese voters who backed the MCA may in future direct support to the DAP.

The best result for everyone, with the exception of certain UMNO politicians, would be if the new BA coalition is able to develop in itself such that it becomes a true alternative to the present ruling coalition. In order to do this several things would have to happen.

PAS would have to decide to become a modern pluralist party and move away from its previous narrow stance. It would need to work hard to prove that it is neither chauvinist in ethnic terms nor in religious terms. Similarly, the DAP would need to demonstrate that it can represent interests of Malay voters as well as Chinese voters. On top of all this Keadilan needs to develop as a party to strengthen its national network and build up its leadership ranks.

If all this happens then UMNO and the BN coalition face genuine competition and real pressure to reform themselves. In such circumstances the government, will be forced to become more accountable and the Malaysia political system would for the first time in decades make a genuine shift towards democracy.

This sounds like a pipe dream and it is easy to see the many ways in which it could all go wrong. Nevertheless, there are grounds for hope. There are signs that PAS is trying hard to reinvent itself. Or at least some within PAS are working to the reform of the party and desirous of making PAS into a genuinely modern and plural party. But perhaps the greatest hope comes from Keadilan. Keadilan is from the outset a modern, democratic, pluralist party. At the moment its resources are limited and its leaders face ongoing harassment from the authorities. Nevertheless it has made considerable advances. For example, in the November 1990 election it contested a number of seats around the national capital. The fact that it won only five of the fifty-nine seats that it contested is not quite the disaster that it first appears to be. Keadilan may have won only five seats but polled just over 11 percent of the total vote and it came very close to defeating the National Front coalition in a number of the seats that it contested. In many of the seats the margin by which the Keadilan lost to the National Front was less than 5 percent suggesting that at the next election it may well be possible to win those seats. This seems even more likely when the 680,000 young voters whose names were added to the electoral roll in January 2000 are taken into account. All of this suggests that at the next election BN and BA may be much more evenly matched. Such evenly matched competition is the only reliable mechanism by which governments can be made accountable and so this development augurs well for democracy in Malaysia.

It is easy to look at the situation in Malaysia and to despair both of the prospects of democracy fully maturing and of race and religious community relations ever each enjoying significant improvement. But further reflection on these matters reveals that there are grounds for optimism about future political and social developments in Malaysia. For the first time in the decades during the run-up to the 1999 election many young Malaysians, and some older Malaysians, talked as if race and religion were no longer the barriers that they had always been assumed to be in Malaysian politics. The chauvinistic nature of PAS, and to a lesser extent DAP, and the amateurish nature of Keadilan and PRM are grounds for despair but there is reason to believe that these parties can mature over the current term of government.

At the same time, there is good reason to believe that UMNO will not respond to its humiliation in November 1999 by attempting to lure back Malay voters back simply by cheaply exploiting chauvinistic ethno-nationalism and the political manipulation of Islam. Indeed, it seems likely that just as UMNO was at its best after its 1990 electoral humiliation so too in this new term the government may be forced to become more "reformist." Even so, much depends on the person of the Prime Minister. Some commentators have speculated that Mahathir, although safely into his final term, is a bitter and angry man determined to restore his good name by whatever means. Even within the person of Dr. Mahathir, however, there are good grounds for hoping for something better.

Postscript

With Anwar Ibrahim sidelined in dubious circumstances, the main opposition party, the Islamist PAS, continues to surge in its support, most significantly in its campus following where it is now the most popular party among the newest generation of voters. Under pressure from its opposition coalition partners in the Barisan Alternatif (Alternative Front), PAS has softened its line on implementing Shar'iah law and has generally sought to reassure non-Muslims. In August 2001 the opposition parties, including PAS, protested against a government order banning all political rallies and meetings — a move seen as part of an effort to counter the sharp decline in support for the ruling UMNO party since the jailing of Anwar.

At the grassroots level, small ultra-fundamentalist Islamic sects continue to cause disturbance, with the most notable being the Al-Ma'unah (Brotherhood of Inner Power) group which seized military supplies and hostages during a four-day stand-off with government troops in July 2000. Nineteen of the twenty-nine group members brought before the court are currently facing treason charges and could face the death penalty if convicted. In June 2001, nine members of another small group were arrested under suspicion of planning to wage holy war to bring fundamentalist Islam to Malaysia — several members admitted to having fought in Afghanistan and on Indonesia's Ambon island in the name of "jihad." Having watched Islamic extremism spiral in neighbouring Indonesia and the Philippines, Malaysian authorities have been particularly wary of groups that have had contact with religious extremists in the Middle East.

Malaysian Prime Minister Mahathir Mohamad continues to show little inclination to relinquish the reins of power, despite murmurings of discontent within the UMNO rank-and-file membership. Over the decades of Mahathir's long rule Malaysian politics has evolved a system of interlocking dependencies in which the pull to return to equilibrium is far more powerful than any of the countervailing forces that Malaysia's enfeebled civil society or disunited opposition movement are able to produce. The dominance of Barisan Nasional (the ruling National Front coalition) over Barisan Alternatif has yet to be seriously challenged just as UMNO's dominance over the other parties in the coalition is unquestioned. Not entirely unquestioned, but nevertheless without effective challenge, is Mahathir's domination over it all – party, coalition and civil society, the press included. In many other countries this degree of political stability would be very welcome. Certainly, it has reaped considerable benefits for Malaysia

Bibliography

Ahmad, Aziz Zariza, (1990), *Mahathir: Triumph after Trials* (Kuala Lumpur: S. Abdul Majeed and Co.).

Ahmad, Kassim, (1986), *Hadis: satu penilaian semula* (Selangor: Media Intelek Sdn. Bhd.).

Ahmed, Akbar S. and Hastings, Donnan, (1994), *Islam, Globalization and Postmodernity* (London: Routledge), xi-xiv, 190-212.

Alagappa, Muthiah, (1995), *Political Legitimacy in Southeast Asia: The Quest for Moral Authority* (Stanford: Stanford University Press).

Ali, S. Husin, (1996), *Two Faces: Detention without Trial* (Kuala Lumpur: Insan, 1996).

Anwar, Zainah, (1987), *Islamic Revivalism in Malaysia: Dakwah among the Students* (Selangor Darul Ehsan: Pelanduk Publications [M] Sdn. Bhd.), 1-95, 97-122.

Ariffin, Jamilah, (1992), *Women and Development in Malaysia* (Selangor Darul Ehsan: Pelanduk Publications (M) Sdn Bhd.).

Bartley, Robert, Chan Heng Chee, Samuel P. Huntington and Shijuro Ogata, (1994), *Democracy and Capitalism: Asian and American Perspectives* (Singapore: Institute of Southeast Asian Studies).

Barton, Greg, (1997a), "Indonesia's Nurcholish Madjid and Abdurrahman Wahid as intellectual *ulama*: the meeting of Islamic traditionalism and Modernism in neo-Modernist," *Islam and Christian-Muslim Relations*, vol. 8, no. 3, October 1997, pp. 323-50.

———, (1997b), "The Origins of Islamic Liberalism in Indonesia and its Contribution to Democratisation," *Democracy in Asia* (New York: St. Martins Press).

Berger, Peter L., (1992), *A Far Glory: The Quest for Faith in an Age of Credulity* (New York: The Free Press), 25-46, 191-211.

Brookfield, Harold, ed. with the assistance of Loene Doube and Barbara Banks, (1994), *Transformation with Industrialisation in Peninsular Malaysia* (New York: Oxford University Press), 14-35, 290-307.

CARPA (Committee against repression in the Pacific and Asia), *Tangled Web: Dissent, Deterrence and the 27ᵗʰ October 1987 Crackdown*, 1-88 (Kuala Lumpur).

Case, William, (1993), "Semi-democracy in Malaysia: withstanding the pressures for regime change." *Pacific Affairs* 66, vol. 2.

Crouch, Harold, (1996), *Government and Society in Malaysia* (Sydney: Allen and Unwin).

———, (1992), "Authoritarian Trends, the UMNO Split and the Limits to State Power," in Joel S. Kahn and Francis Loh Kok Wah (eds.), *Fragmented Vision: Culture and Politics in Contemporary Malaysia* (Sydney: Allen & Unwin), pp. 21-43.

Douglas, Mary and Steven Tipton, eds., (1983), *Religion and America: Spiritual Life in a Secular Age* (Boston: Beacon Press, 1983).

Eickleman, Dale F., (1976), *Moroccan Islam: Tradition and Society in a Pilgrimage Center* (Austin: University of Texas Press), pp. 1-13, 211-237, 286-297.

Esposito, John L., ed., (1987), *Islam in Asia: Religion, Politics, and Society* (New York: Oxford University Press), pp. 10-27, 177-270.

———, ed., (1980), *Islam and Development: Religion and Sociopolitical Change* (New York: Syracuse University Press), pp. 163-181, 246-249.

Esposito, John L. and John O. Voll, (1996), *Islam and Democracy* (New York: Oxford University Press).

Gill, Ranjit, (1997), *Black September* (Singapore: Epic Management Services Pte Ltd.).

Gilsenan, Michael, (n.d.), *Recognising Islam: An Anthropologist's Introduction* (London: Croom Helm), pp. 251-281.

Gomez, Edmund Terence, (1990), *Politics in Business: UMNO's Corporate Investments* (Kuala Lumpur: Forum Enterprise), pp. 166-183.

———, (1996), "Electoral funding of general, State and party elections in Malaysia." *Journal of Contemporary Asia*, 26, no. 1, pp. 81-99.

———, (1996), *The Malaysian general elections: a report and commentary* (Singapore: Institute of Southeast Asian studies, occasional paper no 93), pp.1-61.

Gomez, Edmund Terence, and K.S. Jomo, (1997), *Malaysia's Political Economy: Politics, Patronage and Profits* (Cambridge: Cambridge University Press).

Haddad, Yvonne Yazbeck, John Obert Voll and John L. Esposito with Kathleen Moore and David Sawan, (1991), *The Contemporary Islamic Revival: A Critical Survey and Bibliography* (Westport: Greenwood Press), pp. 3-56, 200-210.

Hefner, Robert W., (1998), "Civil society: Cultural possibility of a modern ideal," *Society*, 35, no. 3 (March-April), pp. 1-15.

Hunter, Shireen T., ed., (1988), *The Politics of Islamic Revivalism: Diversity and Unity* (Bloomington: Indiana University Press), pp. 247-261.

Huntington, Samuel P., (1993), "The Clash of Civilizations?" *Foreign Affairs* 72 (Summer), pp. 22-49.

——, (1996), *The Clash of Civilizations and the Remaking of the World Order* (New York: Simon and Schuster).

Ibrahim, Ahmad, Sharon Siddique, and Yasmin Hussain, (1985), *Readings on Islam in Southeast Asia* (Singapore: Institute of Southeast Asian Studies).

Ibrahim, Anwar, (1997), *The Asian Renaissance* (Singapore: Times Books International).

Ismail, Yusof and Khayati Ibrahim, (1996), *Politik melayu dan demokrasi* (Kuala Lumpur: A.S. Noordeen).

James, Wendy, ed., (1995), *The Pursuit of Certainty: Religious and Cultural Formulations* (London: Routledge), pp. 112-133, 285-308.

Jesudasan, James V., (1989), *Ethnicity and the Economy: The State, Chinese Business, and Multinationals in Malaysia* (New York: Oxford University Press), pp. 76-127.

Johns, Anthony H., (1993), "Islamization in Southeast Asia: reflections and reconsiderations with special reference to the role of Sufism," *Southeast Asian Studies* 31, no. 1 (June), pp. 43-61.

Jomo, K.S., (1989), *Beyond 1990: Considerations for a New National Development Strategy* (Kuala Lumpur: Institute of Advanced Studies), pp. 1-19, 100-113.

——, (1994), *U-Turn? Malaysian Economic Development Policies after 1990* (Townsville: James Cook University), pp. 1-28, 51-56, 96-109.

——, (1990), *Growth and Structural Change in the Malaysian Economy* (Basingstoke: The Macmillan Press), pp. 201-254.

——, ed., (1995), *Privatising Malaysia: Rents, Rhetoric, Realities* (Boulder: Westview Press, 1995), pp. 1-60, 250-261.

——, (1991), "Whither Malaysia's new economic policy?" *Pacific Affairs* 63, no. 4, pp. 469-99.

——, (1986), *Development Policies and Income Inequality in Peninsular Malaysia* (Kuala Lumpur: Institute of Advanced Studies), pp. 3-17, 91-115.

Jomo, K.S. and Cheek, Ahmad Shabery, (1992), "Malaysia's Islamic Movements," in Joel S. Kahnand Francis Loh Kok Wah (eds.), *Fragmented Vision: Culture and Politics in Contemporary Malaysia* (Sydney: Allen & Unwin), pp. 79-106.

Jomo, K.S., ed. (1988), *Mahathir's Economic Policies, 87-89* (Kuala Lumpur: INSAN [Institute of Social Analysis]).

Kessler, Clive S. (1978), *Islam and Politics in a Malay State: Kelantan 1838-1969* (London: Cornell University Press), pp. 22-35, 208-235, 256-265.

——, (1980), "Malaysia: Islamic revivalism and political disaffection in a divided society," *Southeast Asia Chronicle*, no. 75, pp. 3-11.

Keyes, Charles F., Laurel Kendall and Helen Hardacre, eds., (1994), *Asian Visions of Authority: Religion and the Modern States of East and Southeast Asia* (University of Hawaii Press), pp. 99-139.

Kim, Khoo Kay, (1995), *Malay Society: Transformation and Democratisation* (Selangor Darul Ehsan: Pelanduk Publications).

Laothamatas, Anek. *Democratization in Southeast and East Asia. Thailand and Singapore* (Silkworm Books [trademark of Trasvin Publications L.P., Thailand, and Institute of Southeast Asian Studies, Singapore]).

Lee, H.P., (1995), *Constitutional Conflicts in Contemporary Malaysia* (New York: Oxford University Press).

Lee, Raymond L.M. (1988), "Patterns of religious tension in Malaysia," *Asian Survey*, 4, no. 10, pp. 400-418.

Lee, Raymond L.M., (1986), "The ethnic implications of contemporary religious movements and organizations in Malaysia," *Contemporary Southeast Asia* 8, no. 1, pp. 70-87.

McVey, Ruth, ed., (1992), *Southeast Asian Capitalists*, Southeast Asia Program (New York: Cornell University Press), pp. 65-144.

Mauzy, Diane K. and Milne, R.S., (1983), "The Mahathir administration in Malaysia: discipline through Islam." *Pacific Affairs*, pp. 617- 648.

Maidin, Zainuddin, (1994), *The Other Side of Mahathir* (Kuala Lumpur: Utusan Publications and Distributors Sdn. Bhd.).

Mead, Richard, (1988), "Malaysia's national language and the legal system." *Journal of Asian Studies* 48, no. 1, pp. 227-8.

Means, Gordon P. (1991), *Malaysian Politics: The Second Generation* (New York: Oxford University Press), pp. 82-151, 274, 347.

Milne, R.S., and Diane K. Mauzy, (1986), *Malaysia: tradition, modernity, and Islam* (Boulder: Westview Press), pp. 65-184.

Milne, R.S., and Diane K. Mauzy, (1978), *Politics and Government in Malaysia* (issued under the auspices of the Institute of Southeast Asian studies, Singapore. Singapore: Federal Publications), pp. 320-393.

Mohamad, Mahathir, (1996), *Islam: Agama Yang Disalahertikan* (Selangor Darul Ihsan: Afro-Arab Centre Sdn. Bhd.).

——, (1995), *The Challenge* (Selangor Darul Ehsan: Pelanduk Publications (M) Sdn. Bhd.).

——, (1994) *Dilema Melayu* (Kuala Lumpur and Singapore: Times Books International).

Mutalib, Hussin and Taj ul-Islam Hashmi, eds., (1996), *Islam, Muslims and the modern State: case studies of Muslims in thirteen countries* (Hampshire: The Macmillan Press), 152-196.

Muzaffar Chandra, (1979), *Protector?: An Analysis of the Concept and Practice of Loyalty in Leader-Led Relationships within Malay Society* (Pulau Pinang: Aliran), 114-154.

Muzaffar Chandra, (1982), "The 1982 Malaysian General Election: an analysis," *Contemporary Southeast Asia,* 4, no. 1, pp. 86-106.

——, (1987), *Islamic Resurgence in Malaysia* (Petaling Jaya: Penerbit Fajar Bakti Sdn. Bhd.).

Nagata, J., (1997), "Ethnonationalism versus religious transnationalism: nation-building and Islam in Malaysia," *The Muslim World,* 85, no. 2, pp. 129-150.

Norton, Augustus Richard, ed., (1995), *Civil Society in the Middle East,* vol. 1 (Leiden: E.J. Brill), 27-119, 269-313.

Omar, Ariffin, (1993), *Bangsa Melayu: Malay Concepts of Democracy and Community, 1945-50.* (New York: Oxford University Press), pp. 212-241.

Peletz, Michael G., (1997), " 'Ordinary Muslims' and Muslim Resurgents in Contemporary Malaysia: Notes on an Ambivalent Relationship," in Robert W. Hefner and Patricia Horvatich, Islam in an Era of Nation-States: *Politics and Religious Renewal in Muslim Southeast Asia* (Honolulu: University of Hawaii Press), pp. 231-73.

Rachagan, Sothi S., (1993), *Law and the Electoral Process in Malaysia* (Kuala Lumpur: University of Malaya Press), pp. 218-286.

Rashid, Rehman, (1996), *A Malaysian Journey* (Selangor: Rehman Rashid).

Raslan, Karim, (1996), *Ceritalah: Malaysia in Transition* (Singapore: Times Books International).

——, (1996), *Heroes and Other Stories* (Singapore: Times Books International).

Robinson, Richard, Kevin Hewison and Richard Higgott, eds., (1987), *Southeast Asia in the 1980s: The Politics of Economic Crisis.* A publication of the Asian Studies Association of Australia: Southeast Asia Publication series (North Sydney: Allen and Unwin), pp. 112-149, 220-237.

Roff, William R, ed., (1987), *Islam and the Political Economy of Meaning: Comparative Studies of Muslim Discourse* (Sydney: Croom Helm, 1987), pp. 13-287.

Said, Muhammad Ikmal and Zahid Emby, eds., (1996), *Malaysia: Critical Perspectives. Essays in Honour of Syed Husin Ali* (Selangor Darul Ehsan: Vinlin Press Sdn Bhd.).

Sheridan, Greg, (1997), *Tigers: Leaders of the New Asia-Pacific* (St Leonards: Allen and Unwin).

Siang, Lim Kit, (1987), *The $62 Billion North-South Highway Scandal* (Petaling Jaya: Democratic Action Party), pp. iii-vii, 1-31.

Sik, Ling Liong, (1995), *The Malaysian Chinese: Towards Vision 2020* (Selangor Darul Ehsan: Pelanduk Publications [M] Sdn. Bhd.).

Soong, Kua Kia, (1990), *Malaysian Cultural Policy and Democracy* (Kuala Lumpur: The Resource and Research Centre of the Selangor Chinese Assembly Hall).

——, (1987), *Polarisation in Malaysia: The Root Causes* (Selangor: K. Das Ink).

Syamsul, A.B., (1997), "Identity Construction, Nation Formation, and Islamic Revivalism in Malaysia," in Robert W. Hefner and Patricia Horvatich, eds.,

Islam in an Era of Nation-States: Politics and Religious Renewal in Muslim Southeast Asia (Honolulu: University of Hawaii Press), pp. 207-27.

Teik, Goh Cheng, (1996), *Malaysia: Beyond Communal Politics* (Selangor Darul Ehsan: Pelanduk Publications).

Teik, Khoo Boo, (1996), *Paradoxes of Mahathirism: An Intellectual Biography of Mahathir Mohamad* (New York: Oxford University Press).

Tonnesson, Stein and Hans Antlov, eds., (1998), *Asian Forms of the Nation* (The Nordic Institute of Asian Studies, studies in Asian topics, no. 23. Surrey: Curzon Press), pp. 270-352.

Wong, Loong, (1993), "The State and organised labour in West Malaysia, 1967-1980," *Journal of Contemporary Asia* 23, no. 2, pp. 214-237.

3

Militant Islamic Separatism in Southern Thailand

Peter Chalk

Introduction

Islamic fundamentalist violence in Thailand centres on the separatist activities of the Malay-Muslim population in the three southern provinces of Pattani, Yala, and Narathiwat.[1] Historically constituted as part of the former Kingdom of Patani, three main pillars underscore Malay separatist identity in this region: a belief in the traditional virtues and "greatness" of the Kingdom of Patani (Patani Darussalam); an identification with the Malay race; and a religious orientation based on Islam.[2] These three ingredients are woven together in the principle of *hijra* (literally translated, means "emigration in the cause of God"). This asserts that all Islamic communities have both a religious right and duty to "withdraw" from any form of persecution or discrimination that is serving to place their survival in jeopardy.[3] It is on the basis of this religious edict that Malay-Muslim instigated civil disobedience and political violence in southern Thailand has been justified over the past three decades.

Malay Muslims originally settled Patani[4] in the fourteenth century. The region evolved as a distinct socio-political religious entity, enjoying an identity completely separate from the Buddhist T'ai kingdoms that had been established to the north. By the seventeenth century, the Kingdom had emerged as the main centre of Islamic scholarship in the Malay world, regarded by many as the equivalent of the prestigious Sultanate of Aceh itself.[5]

Following the establishment of the modern Thai/Siamese state by the Chakkri Dynasty in the eighteenth century, a vigorous attempt was made to extend control over Patani. Although the indigenous Muslim-Malay population was able to initially resist external penetration, by the late 1700s the entire Kingdom had been brought under effective Siamese rule.[6] During the nineteenth century increasingly uniform and centralized administrative structures were introduced throughout the region to forestall the steady expansion of British colonial influence throughout the Malay peninsula. As part of this process, chieftains in the Patani rajadoms were absorbed into the salaried administration, effectively becoming Siamese civil servants. In addition, a conscious effort was made to reduce the range of issues that Islamic law could independently deal with by extending the jurisdiction and ambit of the Siamese legal system.[7]

The British take-over of the four Malay states of Kelantan, Trengganu, Kedah, and Perlis in 1909 encouraged further centralization, with taxation, education and, eventually, language being brought under varying degrees of Siamese control. Although these moves stirred Malay-Muslim irredentist aspirations, it was not until the turbulent years of the early 1930s that they were fully awoken. Following the military's overthrow of the Thai monarchy in 1932, a modified concept of popular sovereignty emerged which increasingly came to define citizenship not so much in terms of political obedience but on the basis of national unity. Stressing ever more state centralization and the need to rapidly assimilate outlying ethnic groups, the new integrationist push was to have a decisive impact on the local administrative level in Patani.[8]

Several key changes were introduced. The old local government structure, which had, at least, allowed some autonomous Malay political representation, was replaced by a simpler and more centralized system. Three provincial units were carved from the original Patani region—Pattani, Yala, and Narathiwat - all of which were placed under the direct control of the Ministry of the Interior. In 1939 a modernization program was also initiated to eliminate "backward" Islamic customs and dialects and enforce uniformity in language and social behavior.[9] Western cultural and customary habits were stressed, the Muslim Friday holiday was banned and steps were taken to phase out, altogether, the use of Islamic law.[10]

Although these accelerated integrationist designs were not solely directed at the Malay Muslims of southern Thailand (they were also brought to bear against the Hmong hill tribes in the north of the country), they clearly did constitute a direct threat to the region's particular ethno-religious identity. As Christie observes: "In Islamic terms, there could be no clearer justification for *jihad*; and, although there had always been [opposition] to Siamese rule, it is from this time that the modern Pattani separatist and irredentist movements began."[11]

The outbreak of a full scale Islamic insurgency in the 1940s was forestalled by the British assumption of post-war surrender tasks in Thailand, Malaya, southern Indochina, Sumatra, and Java following the defeat of Japan in the Pacific War. In particular, the period of interim British rule from mid-1945 gave the Pattani-Malay leadership the opportunity they needed to press their irredentist demands.[12] This they duly did, sending a petition to the British Secretary of State for Colonies in November. This outlined Patani grievances against the Thai Government, requesting the British "to release [the] country...from the pressure of Siam."[13]

Although the British were sympathetic to the Pattani plight and despite Thailand's complicity with Japan during the Second World War, no moves were taken to realise the southern Malays' irredentist ambitions.[14] However, although there was no change in Pattani's status at this time, the threat that London *might* annex the region (on the pretext of Thai misrule) did serve to mollify Bangkok's policy toward Pattani, Yala and Narathiwat between 1945 and 1946. In particular:

- The Friday holiday was restored for Muslim areas.

- New regulations were passed which permitted the application of Islamic law in the areas of marriage, the family and inheritance.

- A state-sanctioned Islamic hierarchy was established for Muslim provinces consisting of a crown-appointed national head of Islam (*chularajmontri*), a National Council for Islamic Affairs and Local Councils for Islamic Affairs.[15]

These concessions represented a clear shift in previous Thai policy towards its southern Muslim provinces and did, at least temporarily, serve to satisfy the region's irredentist aspirations. Somewhat ironically, however, they also encouraged the Pattani Malay leadership to press for greater local autonomy. Accordingly in April 1947, Haji Sulong, head of the Islamic Council for Pattani Province, presented Bangkok with a petition calling for the creation of a self-governing

Patani Malay and Satun region, with direct control over its language, culture and religion.[16]

These demands went far beyond anything that the Thai government was prepared (or able) to accept. This, together with a (military-manoeuvred) shift in the balance of political power towards overtly conservative and authoritarian elements in late 1947, resulted in a return to the assimilation policies of the 1930s and early 1940s, a re-orientation which has remained ever since. Integral to this integrationist effort has been a concurrent policy aimed at severing the link between the southern Malays and Islam while simultaneously attempting to "Thai-ize" local culture, language, and religion.[17]

Save for the special case of Satun,[18] however, these efforts to draw the Malay Muslim into the national Thai family have largely been unsuccessful. Indeed for the past three decades, Pattani, Yala, and Narathiwat have essentially remained "zones of dissidence" with intermittent outbreaks of insurgent activity and, if anything, only sullen submission to Thai rule. The reason for this failure has undoubtedly been the determination of the southern population to maintain their Malay ethnic identity and Islamic religious beliefs, a resolve that has been strengthened through repeated cross-border contacts with northern Malaysia. In addition, the underdeveloped nature of southern Thailand compared to the rest of the country,[19] corruption, arbitrary repression and often brutal internal security measures have all contributed to a general sense of social dissatisfaction, frustration and alienation—all of which have further fuelled separatist designs and aspirations.[20]

Islamic Separatist Activity in Southern Thailand Since the 1960s

Since the 1960s, a variety of militant separatist movements have operated in the southern Thai provinces. While these groups have been characterized by different ideological outlooks, all have been motivated by the common desire to carve out an independent Muslim state with Pattani as the center.[21] Violent action in pursuit of this objective has fallen into the classic pattern of low intensity conflict and terrorism, typically involving ambushes, assassinations, kidnapping, extortion, sabotage, and bomb attacks. The main aim has been to present the southern provinces to the outside world as a lawless and volatile region; to create a sense of insecurity among the ethnic Thai living in this region; and to burden Bangkok with the responsibility of having to counter yet another insurgency.[22] The main targets of aggression have been those symbols of the Thai state that are considered to pose the greatest threat to Malay-Muslim culture and identity. These have included, most particularly, schools, teachers, local government officials and administrators, and Buddhist settlers.[23]

During the 1960s, 1970s, and 1980s, stability in the south was undermined by repeated outbreaks of unrest and civil disturbances associated with the southern secessionist struggle.[24] Inept and, often, brutal government responses, typically based on inadequate intelligence, merely stimulated and justified intensified resistance, some of which manifested in serious acts of violence.[25] Notable in this regard were:

- A bomb attack during the 1977 royal visit to Yala. Although the King and Queen escaped unhurt, five others were killed and forty-seven were injured.

- Strikes against Don Muang Airport and Hualampong Railway Station, Bangkok's two main communication centres.

- The ambush of a truck full of *nikhom* self-help settlers who had migrated from northeastern Thailand as part of a government-sponsored transmigration program, resulting in eight deaths and more than a dozen injuries.

- The massacre of several monks during a rampage against a remote Buddhist meditation center.

- The hijacking of two buses in Pattani, both of which resulted in the systematic "execution" of all Buddhist passengers aboard.[26]

Despite government moves towards greater regional autonomy, socio-economic development and religious tolerance, political violence, and terrorism associated with the Malay-Islamic secessionist struggle in southern Thailand has continued into the 1990s. Most of this unrest has been linked to three main militant groups: the Barisan Revolusi Nasionale (BRN); the Pattani United Liberation Organization (PULO); and New PULO.[27]

The Barisan Revolusi Nasionale (BRN)

The BRN was established in 1960 by progressive Pattani elements drawn largely from the *pondoks*, a network of independent, traditional institutions dedicated to Islamic learning and Malay identity. Ideologically opposed to the Barisan Nasional Pembebasan (BNPP, see note 27) and retaining strong ties to the Communist Party of

Malaya (CPM), the BRN harbored avowedly pan-Malay religio-nationalist aspirations which were essentially based on three main principles:

- Anti-colonialism and anti-capitalism.

- Islamic socialism aimed at the promotion of a just and prosperous society sanctioned by God.

- Malay nationalism defined in terms of the oneness of God and humanitarianism.[28]

From its inception, the BRN was fully committed to armed struggle, vigorously rejecting the Thai Constitution and political system as irrelevant. The group saw its objectives in two distinct phases. First to bring about the complete secession of the Muslim provinces of southern Siam in order to reconstruct the sovereign Malay-Muslim state of Pattani, completely independent of Thailand. Second, to incorporate this state within a wider Malay socialist nation, stretching from Pattani to Singapore, governed by one head of state and united under one common flag.[29]

Benefiting from clear ideological objectives and with a solid operational apparatus at its disposal, the BRN gradually emerged as a reasonably prominent threat to law and order during the Cold War years. Indeed by the 1980s, individual fighting cells had demonstrated a proven ability to conduct operations throughout the southern provinces as well as in Bangkok itself.[30] Despite this, two important weaknesses prevented the BRN's campaign of political violence attaining the type of "critical mass" needed to seriously challenge Thai central authority. First was the fact that the organization was essentially local in nature, lacking the international support structure that other groups such as PULO were able to draw on (see below). Second, the BRN's strong left-wing platform did not sit well with the basically conservative sentiments of the Malay-Muslim population in southern Thailand, particularly as socialism began to lose its broader appeal during the latter years of the Cold War.[31]

These two basic weaknesses have continued to afflict the activities of the BRN into the 1990s. While the organization continues to engage in sporadic acts of violence, it has been increasingly sidelined by PULO and New PULO. Despite making a brief re-appearance in 1997 as part of "Operation Falling Leaves" (see below), it appears that the group currently operates more as a local crime syndicate, engaging mostly in fear-extortion strategies against southern business interests which it views as exploitative or "contrary to the interests of the people." Most commentators agree that, given its (now) very small support base and a lack of real issues suitable for mass mobilization, the BRN is unlikely to re-emerge as a prominent threat to Thai national security, at least in terms of a sustained campaign political violence.[32]

The Pattani United Liberation Organization (PULO)

PULO is the largest and most prominent of the various Malay Muslim groups that have been active in southern Thailand. The organization was formed in 1968 by Kabir Abdul Rahman, an Islamic scholar who had become disillusioned with what he saw as the "limited" and "ineffectual" nature of the established Malay opposition in Pattani. PULO grouped together a younger, more militant generation of Thai Muslims—many of whom had been radicalized while studying overseas—becoming an active insurgency with the politicization of Malay students in the early 1970s.[33]

PULO's ideology is based on the *UBANGTAPEKEMA*, an acronym derived from Ugama, Bangsa, Tanach Air and Perikemanusiaan (Religion, Race/Nationalism, Homeland and Humanitarianism). Integral to the *UBANGTAPEKEMA* is recognition of the need for a long-term strategy to prepare for the goals of secession. To this end, PULO has placed priority on improving the standard of education among the southern Malay population as well as fostering and nurturing their political consciousness and national sentiments. The group sanctions violence as part of its secessionist struggle and recognizes the need to intensify international publicity on the plight of Pattani's Malay-Muslims. Militant insurgent actions are carried out by a separate armed wing known as the Pattani United Liberation Army (PULA), which has claimed responsibility for several bomb and arson attacks against government establishments in the south. Perceived symbols of Thai cultural dominance have also been periodically targeted, including schools and Buddhist temples.[34]

During the Cold War years, PULO constituted the principal vehicle for the violent expression of Malay-Muslim secessionist sentiments. One of the main strengths of the organization was the political support it enjoyed from the Middle East[35] and co-religionists in

Malaysia—particularly the Islamic opposition Parti Islam Se-Malaysia (PAS, which currently rules the staunchly Muslim northern Malay state of Kelantan). Such external backing not only helped to legitimize (at least in the eyes of the Muslim world) the group's cause; it also proved vital in terms of providing PULO activists with military training in the Middle East and safe haven in northern Malaysia. Taking advantage of these tactical and logistical advantages, the group carried out numerous attacks in the south throughout the 1970 and 1980s, as well as sporadic bombings in Bangkok. [36]

PULO is currently thought to be composed of approximately 350 hard-core members. Thailand has repeatedly alleged that many of these cadres have benefited from the provision of safe haven in the Malaysian State of Kelantan and that this support has come with the sanction of PAS (as well as the official indifference of the central Kuala Lumpur government). Somewhat more seriously have been periodic charges of radicals in northern Malaysia facilitating with the trans-shipment of weapons from Cambodia to avail terrorist operations in southern Thailand. These allegations (which have yet to be proved) have typically been made in the context of a possible Islamic insurgent ring operating in Southeast Asia, linking Pattani radicals with extremists in Aceh and Mindanao.[37]

In 1993, PULO made regional and international headlines after it carried out a series of co-ordinated operations in less than a month. These included:

- Arson attacks against thirty-four schools in Yala, Pattani, and Narathiwat.

- The ambush of a military/civilian development unit in Yala Province.

- An assault on a rapid train in the Rengae district of Narathiwat Province.

- A grenade attack on a Buddhist temple, also in Narathiwat Province.[38]

The following year international attention on PULO was again raised after allegations that the group had played a significant role in the attempted Iranian-sponsored Hizbollah truck bombing of the Israeli embassy in Bangkok. According to Thai security sources, the group assisted with the local logistics of the operation, including supplying the one ton vehicle which military intelligence believe was to have been used for the attack.[39] The bombing was aborted after the truck had an accident with a taxi motorcyclist at the Chidlom-

Lang Suan intersection, causing the terrorist-driver to flee on foot. Thai police subsequently arrested an Iranian, Hossein Shahriarifar, on charges of robbery, murder, possession of explosives and intent to blow up the US embassy. Although Sharhriarifar was found guilty on all charges and sentenced to death, in 1998 the Supreme Court overturned the verdict on the grounds that the prosecution's evidence was inconsistent.[40] The release has helped to improve relations between Thailand and Iran, with both governments now seeking to consolidate closer bilateral economic ties (see below).

Fears of a possible Pattani-international Islamic tie-in were further heightened in 1995 after Thai police claimed to have discovered evidence that PULO were co-ordinating their operations with radical Shi'ite Muslims trained in the Middle East. Supposedly designed to create widespread tension in the south of the country, the alleged link was discovered during investigations into a bomb blast in Hat Yai in January 1995. According to Thai intelligence, the incendiary device had exploded prematurely and was actually meant to have been used in a joint PULO-Shi'ite sabotage mission.[41] Since then, repeated accusations have been made by intelligence sources that PULO (and New PULO) operatives have facilitated the entry of foreign nationals into Thailand, both for operational and logistical purposes.

Although definitive evidence linking Pattani radicals to foreign, non-Southeast Asian extremists has yet to materialize, regional and Western governments evidently consider it to be a realistic possibility. The U.S. has held several meetings with Thai officials specifically in relation to this question, going to the extent of closing its Bangkok embassy in November 1998 after the Central Intelligence Agency (CIA) warned Pakistani terrorists had entered the country to stage sabotage attacks against American targets.[42] Australia, too, has shown some concern, initiating high level talks with Thailand's National Intelligence Agency (NIA) in November 1999 to upgrade "barrier defenses" in the run up to the 2000 Olympic Games.[43]

Notwithstanding this potential international dimension (which does remain a matter for concern), the immediate threat emanating from PULO has declined markedly in recent years, largely as a result of improved cross-border co-operation between Thailand and Malaysia since January 1998 (see below). Arrests of some of its principal members, including Hayi Sama-ae Thanam, the group's military leader, have already had a decisive impact on the overall threat potential of PULO and could well mark the beginning of the end for the organization.[44]

The New Pattani United Liberation Organization (New PULO)

New PULO emerged as a dissident faction of the original PULO in 1995. Established by Ar-rong Moo-reng and Hayi Abdul Rohman Bazo (who, up until 1998, acted as the Chairman of New PULO's political/*Kasdan* wing),[45] the group has pursued the goal of Pattani self-autonomy through less dramatic but more consistent actions than its parent organization. To this end, the focus has been on carrying out minor attacks that are intended to constantly harass and pester police, local authorities and other symbols of Thai socio-political suppression, particularly schools.[46] Choice of this particular modus operandi probably reflects a desire on the part of the New PULO leadership to conserve limited operational resources as well as enhance the perceived legitimacy of the separatist Islamic struggle in the south.

Up until his arrest in January 1998, it was Haji Da-oh Thanam who led the operational wing of New PULO. Acting as the Supreme Commander of an Armed Force Council, Thanam co-ordinated, directed and controlled three separate sabotage wings, each with a specific area of geographic concentration:

- The Sali Ta-loh Bueyor Group, responsibility for Narathiwat's Ja-nae and Sri Sakhon districts.

- The Maso Dayeh Group, responsibility for Yala's Betong district.

- The Ma-ae Tohpien Group, responsibility for all districts throughout Narathiwat and Yala provinces.[47]

According to the Thai Interior Minister, Major General Sanan, New PULO relies on young drug addicts to carry out many of its more rudimentary sabotage missions. Again, this almost certainly reflects a desire on the part of the group's leadership to conserve limited operational human resources. In addition, it presumably helps to minimize the possibility of the group's security being compromised in the event that a saboteur is captured and made to confess. Thai military intelligence believe that New PULO is currently prepared to pay up to 500 baht to drug addicts who agree to carry out basic attacks such as torching bus depots or bombing bridges.[48]

Since its establishment in 1995, New PULO has been instrumental in the perpetration of several small-scale bomb, incendiary and shooting attacks throughout the southern Thai provinces.[49] In common with PULO, it is alleged that the group's ability to carry out these assaults has been considerably availed by passive Malaysian support, not least because its leaders are believed to have had the benefit of operating out of secure safe havens in the jungles of Kelantan state.[50] Following improved border relations between Bangkok and Kuala Lumpur since January 1998, however, it is likely that any external assistance of this kind that might have existed will now be curtailed. Indeed a number of New PULO's leading figures have already been arrested in a series of combined Thai-Malaysian police operations, including Thanam, the group's military leader, and Rohman Bazo, the group's chairman.[51] As with PULO, this is likely to have a decisive impact on the organization's immediate and long-term future.

Linkages between the BRN, PULO, and New PULO

According to Thai intelligence officials, the BRN, PULO, and New PULO have been largely unwilling to co-ordinate their operational activities, essentially due to their different ideological outlooks and external affiliations.[52] Nevertheless, it does appear that the three organizations did agree to form a tactical alliance in mid 1997 in an attempt to refocus national and regional attention on the "southern question."[53] Operating under the name of "Bersatu," or "Solidarity," the three groups allegedly carried out a series of co-ordinated attacks aimed at killing off state workers, law enforcement personnel, local government officials, schoolteachers and other perceived symbols of Thai Buddhist repression. Code-named "Falling Leaves,"[54] the combined operations included bomb explosions, grenade assaults, drive-by shootings, assassinations of government officials and incendiary attacks.[55]

Between August 1997 and January 1998, no less than thirty-three separate attacks were carried out as part of Operation Falling Leaves, resulting in nine deaths, several dozen injuries and considerable economic damage. According to Tony Davis, specialist Asia correspondent with *Jane's Intelligence Review*, this campaign of violence marked the most serious upsurge of Muslim separatist activity since the early 1980s.[56] One of the worst attacks occurred on 29 December when a group of unidentified individuals, who later claimed to belong to PULO's operational wing, planted a bomb in front of the Veerarajprasarn School in Yala's Betong district. The subsequent explosion killed three, seriously injuring fifteen others.[57]

Although the 1997 campaign of violence did engender increased attention on the "Southern question," it also dramatically increased pressure on the Kuala Lumpur government to step up cross-border co-operation with Thailand. Following the attacks, a string of high-level arrests were carried out against secessionist leaders in northern Malaysia. Prominent amongst these were:

- The Chairman of New PULO's *kasdan* wing, Abdul Rohman Bazo.

- Haji Maer Yala, senior assistant to Bazo.

- The Supreme Commander of New PULO's Operational Wing, Haji Da-oh Thanam.

- PULO's military leader, Hayi Sama Ae Thanam.[58]

These detentions signalled a major shift in policy by Malaysia, away from the "hands-off" stance to what Kuala Lumpur had traditionally referred to as a purely domestic Thai problem. The change came with the specific approval of Mohamad Mathathir, almost certainly to protect the much-publicized Malaysia-Indonesia-Thailand Growth Triangle (MITGT). Indeed the arrests came on the heels of earlier visits by the Thai Interior Minister, Sana Kachornprasart, the Foreign Minister, Surin Pitsuwan, the Deputy Foreign Minister, Sukhumbhand Paribatra and the Chief of Police, General Pracha Promnok. During these meetings, all four officials specifically warned Mahathir that unless Malaysia stepped up efforts to control violence in the south, closer cross border economic co-operation, which is critical to the success of the MITGT, would be curtailed.[59]

Quite apart from the immediate impact that the arrests had on the leadership of the southern separatist cause, they additionally galvanized a major tactical re-assessment on the part of other members of PULO and New PULO. Indeed since February 1998, both groups have suffered from major internal haemorrhaging, with many activists either surrendering directly to the authorities or fleeing abroad.[60] While scattered pockets of separatist resistance do remain, there can be little question of the significance that the loss of Malaysian safe haven represents to the overall integrity and longevity of the Malay independence movement in southern Thailand. As one intelligence official recently remarked: "If Malaysia has shifted its policy and [is genuinely denying] the separatists sanctuary, it will undoubtedly cause them more trouble....The movements simply cannot survive militarily [without the benefit of external] Malaysian...support."[61]

Conclusion

At the time of writing, the long-term future of the BRN, PULO, and New PULO appears highly questionable. The BRN's ideological platform is at odds with the conservative sentiments of most of the southern Thai population, a factor that has increasingly marginalized the group during the 1990s. The operational activities of PULO and New PULO have been severely disrupted by the arrests and surrenders of some of its leading members, not to mention the ramifications of heightened cross-border co-operation between Malaysia and Thailand. Added to this, the Thai government is beginning to show greater sensitivity to the lack of economic and administrative development in the Yala, Narithiwat, and Pattani provinces. Moves in his direction are starting to ameliorate (though not eliminate) memories of past discrimination, which is, in turn, helping to reduce popular support for armed separatism. Bangkok's provision of 15 million baht to finance occupational training for Malays in the south, including former militants, as well as its commitment to ensure the success of the planned MITGIT by developing Pattani's natural resources and rubber plantations, should help to consolidate this process even further.[62]

Facilitating moves in this direction, Iran has expressed an interest in developing closer economic ties with Thailand, particularly since the release from prison in February 1998 of Shahriarifar, the man held in connection with the attempted 1994 bombing of the Israeli embassy. The two countries have already agreed to enter into a multi-million-dollar joint venture to produce fertilizer and refine oil and are seeking to cooperate in tourism, industry and telecommunication projects, several of which are planned for the southern Muslim regions.[63] Moreover, Iran, Morocco, and Egypt have all agreed to offer scholarships for overseas study to Thai Islamic students from Yala, Pattani, and Narithiwat as part of a cooperation drive in human resource development. Oman, Kuwait, and the United Arab Emirates (UAE) are also thinking of offering similar schemes following requests from Foreign Minister Surin Pitsuwan.[64]

Despite this, it is still too early to conclude definitively that political violence in southern Thailand is at a complete end. The Muslim population in this part of the country has become increasingly politicized since late 1998, reacting particularly forcefully both to the arrest of Anwar Ibrahim in Malaysia[65] as well as the U.S. air strikes against Sudan, Afghanistan, and Iraq between August and December.[66] The latter factor has especially engendered a more militant, anti-Western attitude, with private Islamic organizations and Muslim student groups calling for a boycott of all American products and reprisals against Washington.[67] In addition, a new political party has emerged in the south, calling for greater unity among Muslim communities and adherence to the traditional Islamic values as a way of dealing with political, economic, labor, and environmental problems.[68] The party, known as the Santiparb (Peace) Party, has been specifically inaugurated to woo southern Muslim voters and, arguably, reflects a more assertive and active religious undertone in the region.

Compounding this is the fact that, for at least two reasons, the Malay districts of Pattani, Yala, and Narathiwat continue to be characterized by a certain degree of discontent and frustration. First, although absolute growth rates are increasing, the region remains underdeveloped relative to other parts of Thailand, "enjoying" an average per capita income of at least 7,000 baht less than neighboring provinces. Second, the south still exists against a backdrop of perceived linguistic and religious discrimination, while Muslim participation in local business is minimal. Both of these factors continue to feed at least residual feelings of discontent and frustration—hindering the prospects for true national reconciliation to occur. [69]

Operationally, PULO and New PULO are also proving to be somewhat resilient, even without the benefit of Malaysian safe haven and in spite of the surrender of many of their cadres. Between October 1, 1998 and August 1, 1999, for instance, fifty, albeit sporadic, attacks were carried out by the two groups, including thirteen in July alone.[70] Such persistence is almost certainly a function of the lingering feelings of deprivation and alienation that continue to underscore Malay perceptions in the south, providing militant groups with a social context that is passive, or at least not actively opposed, to their activities. Conceivably, it could also reflect the working relationships PULO radicals are alleged to have established with external groups in the Middle East and Southeast Asia, although as previously alluded, there is no evidence to definitively support this.

Overall, however, the possibilities for peace in Pattani, Yala, and Narathiwat remain good. Future stability will depend on the Thai government remaining conscious of the need to foster continued economic development and education in the south and moving to address those perceived inequities that continue to persist. It will also rely on Kuala Lumpur maintaining a positive border relationship with Bangkok and ensuring that extremist groups are not allowed to exploit its territory as a safe haven. Provided economic difficulties in Thailand and current leadership instability in Malaysia do not unduly impinge on either of these factors—and so long as external forces do not move to "hijack" the Malay cause for their own purposes—genuine ethno-religious reconciliation is something that may yet occur in southern Thailand.

Postscript

The election of tycoon Thaksin Shinawatra as Prime Minister in March 2001 has not prompted any significant changes in national policy towards Islamic separatism. While the terrorist groups in the south lack organisation and financial support, the Thai government has maintained its policy of suppression. In some instances, terrorists who had earlier considered giving themselves up have banded together with their former colleagues to recommence terrorist activities, and have sought outside support from the Middle East.

The most notable example of this occurred when remnants of PULO and Barisan Revolusi Nasional (BRN) merged in April 2001 under the name Bersatu, which means "united" in Malay and claim between 60 and 80 members trained in the Middle East, according to officials. Intelligence officials in the South blamed the group for two explosions in one day in April 2001 that killed one boy and injured 40 others. Prime Minister Thaksin criticised intelligence agencies for failing to prevent the attack despite receiving a warning that a bomb would be planted.

Army sources have said Bersatu wanted to show the separatists in the deep south that the movement was still active, in a bid to impress the Organisation of the Islamic Conference (OIC) meeting in Malaysia last May and gain covert financial support. However, some security watchers in the region have expressed doubts over the government's claim and doubt the movement has the potential to conduct such acts of terrorism, saying the organisation had weakened much since they were denied support and refuge in Malaysia in 1998.

Isolated, low-level incidents have continued to occur. While the region remains underdeveloped, growth has slowly been increasing as the national economy recovers, helping to ameliorate past inequity and discrimination, thereby limiting the appeal of the separatists.

Notes

1.   Muslims constitute approximately 80 percent of the population in these three provinces.
2.   Connor Bailey and John Miksic, "The Country of Patani in the Period of Re-Awakening: A Chapter from Ibrahim Syukri's Sejarah Kerajaan Melayu Patani," in Andrew Forbes ed., *The Muslims of Thailand, Volume II: Politics of the Malay-Speaking South* (Bihar: Centre for Southeast Asian Studies, 1989), 151.
3.   Clive Christie, *A Modern History of Southeast Asia: Decolonization, Nationalism and Separatism* (London: Tauris Academic Studies, 1996), 133. See also Truong Buu Lam, *Patterns of Vietnamese Response to Foreign Intervention, 1858-1900* (New Haven, CT: Yale University Press, 1967), 116-20.
4.   This is the Malay spelling of Pattani. In Thai, the province is spelt with two "t's." Patani will be used when referring to the region as an independent entity; Pattani when referring to the region as a province of Thailand.
5.   Christie, *A Modern History of Southeast Asia*, 174; Virginia Matheson and M.B Hooker, "Jawli Literature in Patani: The Maintenance of the Islamic Tradition," *Journal of the Malaysian Branch of the Royal Asiatic Society* 61/1 (1985): 10-13.
6.   Michael Leifer, *Dictionary of the Modern Politics of Southeast Asia* (London: Routledge, 1996), 35; R. J. May, "The Religious Factor in Three Minority Movements," *Contemporary Southeast Asia* 13/4 (1992): 403.
7.   Donald Tugby and Elise Tugby, "Malay-Muslim and Thai-Buddhist Relations to the Patani Region: An Interpretation," in Forbes ed., *The Muslims of Thailand*, 73-7; Christie, *A Modern History of Southeast Asia*, 174-175; Muthiah Alagappa, *The National Security of Developing States: Lessons from Thailand* (Massachusetts: Acorn House, 1987), 200; Seni Mudmarn, "Social Science Research in Thailand: The Case of the Muslim Minority," in Omar Farouk, ed., *Muslim Social Science in ASEAN* (Kuala Lumpur: Yayasan Penataran Ilmu, 1994), 24; Omar Farouk, "The Historical and Transnational Dimensions of Malay-Muslim Separatism in Southern Thailand," in Lim Joo Jock and S. Vani, eds., *Armed Separatism in Southern Thailand* (Singapore: ISEAS, 1984), 235-36. For a detailed discussion of these changes see Tej Bunnay, *The Provincial Administration of Siam, 1892-1915* (Kuala Lumpur: Oxford University Press, 1978).
8.   Leifer, *Dictionary of the Modern Politics of Southeast Asia*, 35; Christie, *A Modern History of Southeast Asia*, 175-76; A. Stockwell, *British Policy and Malay Politics During the Malayan Union Experiment, 1942-48* (Kuala Lumpur, Royal Asiatic Society, 1979), 142-3; Surin Pitsuwan, *Islam and Malay Nationalism: A Case*

Study of the Malay-Muslims of Southern Thailand (Bangkok: Thai Khadi Research Institute, 1985), 37-44; Farouk "The Historical and Transnational Dimensions of Malay-Muslim Separatism in Southern Thailand," 236; Alagappa, *National Security of Developing States*, 200-204; and Ruth McVey, "Identity and Rebellion Among Southern Thai Muslims," in Forbes ed., *The Muslims of Thailand*, 38-9.

9.   In 1939, Siam was also renamed Thailand. This change was very much part and parcel of Bangkok's new integrationist push, essentially being designed to emphasize the "oneness" of Thai ethnic and national identity.

10.   See Christie, *A Modern History of Southeast Asia*, 176-7; May, "The Religious Factor in Three Minority Movements," 403; Nantawan Haemindra, "The Problem of the Thai-Muslims in the Four Southern Provinces of Thailand, Part I," *Journal of Southeast Asian Studies* 7/2 (1976): 205; M. Ladd Thomas, "The Thai Muslims," in Raphael Israeli ed., *The Crescent in the East: Islam in Asia Major* (London: Curzon Press, 1982), 160; Pitsuwan, *Islam and Malay Nationalism*, 87-93; and H. E. Wilson, "Imperialism and Islam: The Impact of 'Modernization' on the Malay Muslims of South Thailand," in Forbes ed., *The Muslims of Thailand*, 59-60.

11.   Christie, *A Modern History of Southeast Asia*, 177.

12.   Mudmarn, "Social Science Research in Thailand: The Case of the Muslim Minority," 25-6; Farouk, "The Historical and Transnational Dimensions of Malay-Muslim Separatism in Southern Thailand," 236-37; and Christie, *A Modern History of Southeast Asia*, 179.

13.   Quoted from "Petition to the Right Honourable the Secretary of State for the Colonies, Through the Commander-in-Chief, British Forces, Malaya," 1 November 1954, sourced in Barbara Whittingham-Jones Collection, School of Oriental and Asian Studies (SOAS) Library, London, MS 145 982.

14.   The British reluctance to endorse and support Pattani separatist designs was essentially a function of London's desire to promote and ensure stability on the Malay peninsula. Following the end of the Second World War, Britain was adamant that all independent states should be viable political entities. As far as possible, the creation of small states (such as Pattani) was to be avoided as these, Britain believed, would have neither the resources to defend themselves or sustain economic development. This, it was further concluded, would necessarily invite aggressive, expansionist policies - a perception that was largely shaped by the European Balkan experience during the two world wars.

15.   Ministry of Foreign Affairs, *Thai Muslims* (Bangkok: Ministry of Foreign Affairs, 1979), 5-6; Mudmarn, "Social Science Research in Thailand: The Case of the Muslim Minority," 26; Farouk, "The Historical and Transnational Dimensions of Malay-Muslim Separatism in Southern Thailand," 23-7.

16.   Christie, *A Modern History of Southeast Asia*, 183; Haemindra, "The Problem of the Thai-Muslims in the Four Southern Provinces of Thailand," 208; and Alagappa, *The National Security of Developing States*, 204. The petition contained the following specific demands with regard to the four provinces of Pattani, Yala, Narathiwat, and Satun:

- The appointment of a single individual with full powers of governance.
- Provision that 80 percent of the government officials be Malay Muslims.
- The institutionalization of Malay and Siamese as official languages.
- The institutionalization of Malay as the official medium of instruction in primary schools.
- The establishment of a separate Islamic court.
- The formation of an Islamic Board having full powers to direct all Muslim affairs, including taxation.

17. Christie, *A Modern History of Southeast Asia*, 185-87; Ministry of Foreign Affairs, *Thai Muslims*, 3; Forbes, "Thailand's Muslim Minorities," 189; Alagappa, *The National Security of Developing States*, 204-07.
18. The success of integrationist policies in Satun was essentially a product of two main factors. First, despite being overwhelmingly Malay in terms of ethnic origin, most people in Satun speak Thai in their everyday lives. Second is the fact that the province's main links of communication are northwards to Thailand while road and rail access to Malaysia is minimal. This has engendered a greater affinity with Thai culture and customs than has been the case in Pattani, Yala, and Narathiwat, all of whom maintain very close cross-border contacts with northern Malaysia.
19. The average per capita income in the southern Thai provinces is currently at least 7,000 baht less than neighboring regions. See Peter Chalk, *Grey Area Phenomena in Southeast Asia: Piracy, Drug Trafficking and Political Terrorism* (Canberra: SDSC, 1997), 62.
20. May, "The Religious Factor in Three Minority Movements," 403; Liefer, *Dictionary of the Modern Politics of Southeast Asia*, 35; Christie, *A Modern History of Southeast Asia*, 187-88; and David Brown, *State and Ethnic Politics in Southeast Asia* (London: Routledge, 1994), 166-170.
21. Uthai Dulyakasem, "Muslim-Malay Separatism in Southern Thailand: Factors Underlying Political Revolt," in Joo-Jock and Vani eds., *Armed Separatism in Southeast Asia*, 231; A. Suhrke, "Loyalists and Separatists: The Muslim in Southern Thailand," *Asian Survey* 17/3 (1977): 245.
22. Alagappa, *The National Security of Developing States*, 212.
23. Christie, *A Modern History of Southeast Asia*, 188; McVey, "Identity and Rebellion Among Southern Thai Muslims; and May, "The Religious Factor in Three Minority Movements," 403-4.
24. One of the worst years for violence during this period was 1981, a twelve-month period which Muthiah Alagappa terms as a "vintage year for secessionist activities." One source has documented no less than eighty-six separate fire-fights that took place at this time, with the government suffering twenty-two dead and sixty-four wounded. During the same period, thirty-nine civilians were killed, 129 were injured and seven abducted. See Alagappa, *The National Security of Developing States*, 212. See also Tony Davis, "Coming to Grips with Muslim Separatism," *Business in Thailand* (July 1982): 34. For a detailed account of the evolution of Malay Muslim political violence in southern Thailand during the 1970s and early 1980s see Pitsuwan, *Islam and Malay Nationalism*, 216-44.
25. See Arong Suthasan, "Thai Society and the Muslim Majority," in Forbes, ed., *The Muslims of Thailand,* 104-11.
26. See Mudmarn, "Social Science Research in Thailand: The Case of the Muslim Minority," 29-30; and Alagappa, *The National Security of Developing States*, 212.
27. Other groups which have operated in southern Thailand since the late 1960s include:
     - The Barisan Nasional Pembebasan (BNPP). This organization was formed in 1971 among traditional religious southern Thai leaders, with strong support from Malay students in Saudi Arabia, Egypt and Pakistan. The BNPP aimed to establish an independent and sovereign Islamic state of Patani through a multi-pronged program in the political, psychological, diplomatic, and military spheres (the latter through its armed wing, the National Liberation Army of the Patani People). By the end of 1982, the BNPP had essentially ceased to exist as a coherent insurgent group in southern Thailand, with most of its leaders living

abroad in exile.
- The Sabil-illah (literally, "The Way/Path of God"). This organization briefly emerged between 1975-1976 as an urban-based movement opposed to the more moderate stances that the BNPP, BRN, and PULO were then adopting.
- Black December 1902. This is the least known of all the groups to have operated in southern Thailand. The organization's name is derived from the date of the final incorporation of Greater Patani into the Thai Kingdom.
- The Gerakan Mujahidin Pattani (GMIP). This organization was established in 1986 under the leadership of Vae-hama Vae-Yuso. It was set up as an alien faction of the Bersudu, a militant group of Malaysian origin. By 1993, internal feuds over the earnings and expenses had effectively dissolved the group as an effective insurgent force. Although the organization continues to exist in name, it operates more as a straight crime syndicate, relying primarily on fear-extortion tactics aimed against companies located in the south. There is some speculation that the GMIP continues to retain certain residual links with PULO and participated in Operation Falling Leaves during 1997.
- The Barisan Nationale Baru (BNB). The BNB is an organization that was established in 1995 by a group of young Malays formerly of PULO. Ostensibly the BNB claimed it was a socio-economic organization dedicated to the welfare and interests of Thai Muslims. The organization was able to build up a solid support base between 1996 and 1997 largely by offering four-year membership cards that guaranteed access to jobs and security in Malaysia. According to intelligence officials in Bangkok, however, a select number of BNB members were also sent abroad (most notably to Syria) for insurgent training to carry out armed attacks in the southern Thai provinces. Although these claims have never been verified, the Thai government nevertheless proscribed the BNB as a threat to national security in 1995.
- In 1995, another small radical group emerged known as the Tantra Jihad Islam (TIJ). Thai intelligence sources claim that this organization is a small loose coalition of disgruntled PULO and BRN members whose main aim is simply to destabilize the entire southern Thai region through extortion, arson, sabotage and other acts of violence. The group is believed to be responsible for several minor arson and shooting attacks that have taken place since 1995.

Personal correspondence between the author and Thai military intelligence, Bangkok, July 1997.

For further details of these groups see Hans Indorf, *Impediments to Regionalism in Southeast Asia* (Singapore: ISEAS, 1984), 40-1; Farouk, "The Historical and Transnational Dimensions of Malay-Muslim Separatism in Southern Thailand," 241; May, "The Religious Factor in Three Minority Movements," 403-4; "The Story Behind *Gerakan Mujahidin Islam Pattani*," *The Bangkok Post*, 18/01/98; and "New Muslim Terrorist Movement Claims 100,000 Members," *Nation*, 19/01/95.

28. *Undang-Undang Dasar, Barisan Revolusi Nasional, Pattani (4 Wilayah) Selatan Thai*, Clause 1. See also Farouk, "The Historical and Transnational Dimensions of Malay-Muslim Separatism in Southern Thailand," 239; May, "The Religious Factor in Three Minority Movements," 404-405; and Mudmarn, "Social Science Research in Thailand: The Case of the Muslim Minority," 30.

29. *Undang-Undang Dasar*, Clause 3, para. 2. See also Farouk, "The Historical and Transnational Dimensions of Malay-Muslim Separatism in Southern Thailand," 239-40.

30. Mizan Khan, "Muslims in Thailand," unpublished paper prepared for the Thai Military Forces (1995), 1; Indorf, *Impediments to Regionalism in Southeast Asia*, 40-41.
31. Farouk, "The Historical and Transnational Dimensions of Malay-Muslim Separatism in Southern Thailand," 24-41.
32. Personal correspondence between the author and Thai Military Intelligence, Bangkok, July 1997.
33. Liefer, *Dictionary of the Modern Politics of Southeast Asia*, 199-200.
34. See Farouk, "The Historical and Transnational Dimensions of Malay-Muslim Separatism in Southern Thailand," 242; and Ramli Ahmad, "Pergerakan Pembebebasan Pattani," unpublished report prepared for Jabatan Sejarah Universiti Malaysia, Kuala Lumpur, 1975/76, 116-117.
35. In particular, PULO received considerable political, and a certain amount of economic and logistical support from Syria Libya, the Palestine Liberation Organization (PLO) and the Organization of Islamic Conference (OIC). For further details see Praisal Sricharatchanya, "PULO and the Middle East Connection," *Far Eastern Economic Review*, 09/10/81; and Alagappa, *The National Security of Developing States*, 215.
36. Christie, *A Modern History of Southeast Asia*, 188-89; Surin Pitsuwan, *Issues Affecting Border Security Between Malaysia and Thailand* (Bangkok: Thammasarat University Series No. 4, 1982), 33; Farouk, "The Historical and Transnational Dimensions of Malay-Muslim Separatism in Southern Thailand," 243-251; "Border Pact Under Scrutiny," *Far Eastern Economic Review*, 21/05/76; and "A Frontier of Fear and Factions," *Far Eastern Economic Review*, 20/06/80.
37. See, for instance, "Worse to Come," *Far Eastern Economic Review*, NEED DATE, 1999; "Minister: 'Southern Separatists Receive Foreign Training,'" *Nation*, 06/01/95; "Malaysia Denies Thai Terrorist Claims," *Australian*, 06/01/98; and "Malaysia 'Not Training Ground for Thai Rebels,'" *Straits Times*, 05/01/98.
38. See "Malaysia Warns Muslim Separatists to End Terrorism," *Bangkok Post*, 13/01/95; "Train Ambush Kills 1, Wounds 8," Bangkok Radio Thailand Network transcript, 22/08/93; "Southern Discomfort," *Far Eastern Economic Review*, 02/09/93; "PULO Claims Responsibility," Bangkok Army Television Channel 5 transcript, 22/08/93; and "Officials Comment: 'Attack Context Given,'" *Bangkok Post*, 23/08/93.
39. The chief suspect in the attempted bombing is Hussein Shahriari Far, an Iranian who was caught in possession of a one ton truck bomb near the embassy. Personal correspondence between the author and Thai Military Intelligence, Bangkok, July 1997. See also "Security Council Prepared to Counter Terrorist Activities," *Thailand Times*, 05/11/95; and "Witness Identifies Iranian Suspect in Botched Truck Bombing," *Nation*, 10/02/95.
40. See "Thailand: International Efforts Urged to Halt Terrorism," *Bangkok Post* (Internet version), 15/08/98; and "Iranian Man Acquitted and Released," *Bangkok Post* (Internet version), 19/02/98.
41. See "*Shi'ite*-PULO Link Seen in New Hat Yai Blast Theory," *Bangkok Post*, 13/01/95.
42. See "Terrorist Report Prompted Closure," *Bangkok Post*, 21/11/99; and "US Embassy Closes Amid Security Alert," *Bangkok Post*, 20/11/98.
43. Personal correspondence between author and Office of National Assessments (ONA) officials, Canberra, November 1999. See also "ASIO Briefs Thailand on Olympic Fears," *Sydney Morning Herald*, 15/11/99. ADD RECENT ARTICLE.

44. See, for instance, "Mystery Shrouds Sama-ae's Arrest," *Nation*, 11/02/98; "Separatists Arrested in Malaysia," *The Bangkok Post*, 20/01/98; "Secrets of the South," *Bangkok Post*, 22/01/98; "Arrests in South Boost Malaysian Ties, Security," *Nation*, 24/01/98; and "Terrorist Suspects Arrested in South," *Nation*, 23/01/98.

45. Rohman Bazo also periodically used the name Haji Buedo.

46. Personal correspondence between the author and Thai Military Intelligence, Bangkok, July 1997. See also "Terrorist Suspect Has Violent Past," *Sunday Nation*, 25/01/98.

47. See "Terrorist Suspect Has Violent Past," *Sunday Nation*, 25/01/98; "Secrets of the South," *Bangkok Post*, 22/01/98; and "New PULO's Organizational Structure," *Bangkok Post*, 25/01/98.

48. Personal correspondence between the author and Thai Military Intelligence, Bangkok, July 1997. See also "Terrorist Suspect Has Violent Past," *Sunday Nation*, 25/01/98; "Plague of Terrorism Ruins Thai Economic Growth," *Bangkok Post*, 18/01/98; "Violence in South Seen as Drugs-Related," *Nation*, 29/01/98; and "Motives Behind Violence in the South," *Bangkok Post*, 18/01/98.

49. See, for instance, "New PULO Faction Suspected in Grenade Attack in South," *Bangkok Post*, 04/03/95; "Chronology of Southern Violence," *Bangkok Post*, 01/02/98; and "Is It So Hard to be a Good Neighbour?" *Bangkok Post*, 21/01/98.

50. Personal correspondence between the author and Thai Military Intelligence, Bangkok, July 1997. See also "Malaysia 'Not Training Ground for Thai Rebels,'" *Straits Times*, 05/01/98; "Is It So Hard to be a Good Neighbour?" *Bangkok Post*, 21/08/98; "Mutual Distrust Hampers a Solution in the South," *Nation*, 05/01/98; "Separatists in Malaysia Flee Abroad," *Bangkok Post*, 22/02/98; "Surin Set to Seek Malaysian Help in Curbing Terrorists," *Nation*, 03/01/97; "Malaysia Denies Thai Terrorist Claims," *Australian*, 06/01/98; "Separatists Flee 'Haven,'" *Bangkok Post*, 26/02/98; and "Plague of Terrorism Ruins Thai Economic Growth," *Bangkok Post*, 18/01/98.

51. See "Terrorist Suspects Arrested in the South," *Nation*, 23/01/98; "Terrorist Suspect Has Violent Path," *Sunday Nation*, 25/01/98; "Malaysians Hand Over Separatists," *Bangkok Post*, 23/01/98; "KL Decides It Is Time to Help," *Bangkok Post*, 05/02/98; "Net Closing in On Rebels in Malaysia, *Bangkok Post*, 12/02/98; "Malaysia's Policy Shift to Benefit South," *Bangkok Post*, 25/01/98; "Arrests in South Boost Malaysian Ties, Security," *Nation*, 24/01/98; and "Separatists Arrested in Malaysia," *Bangkok Post*, 20/01/98.

52. Personal correspondence between author and Thai Military Intelligence, Bangkok, July 1997. See also Alagappa, *National Security of Developing States*, 213; and "The Story Behind the Gerakan Mujahidin Islam Pattani," *Bangkok Post*, 18/01/98.

53. There is some indication to suggest that the GMIP also participated in the attacks.

54. The operation was code-named "Falling Leaves," as it initially aimed to kill off state workers one by one in the same way that leaves fall off trees.

55. See, for instance, Peter Chalk, "The Evolving Dynamic of Terrorism in Southeast Asia," *Terrorism and Political Violence* 10/2 (1998); "Chronology of Southern Violence," *Bangkok Post*, 01/02/98; "Plague of Terrorism Ruins Thai Economic Growth," *Bangkok Post*, 18/01/98; "Teachers Rush to Find Passage Out of Troubled South," *Nation*, 29/01/98; and "Tourism Damaged by Bomb Attacks," *Bangkok Post*, 19/01/98.

56. Personal correspondence between the author and Tony Davis, Canberra, September 1998.

57. See "Chronology of Southern Violence," *Bangkok Post*, 01/02/98.

58. See "Separatists Hold Urgent Talks," *Bangkok Post*, 24/01/98; "Net Closing in Rebels in Malaysia," *Bangkok Post*, 12/02/98; "Malaysians Hand Over Separatists,"

Bangkok Post, 23/01/98; "KL Decides it is Time to Help," *Bangkok Post*, 05/02/98; "Separatists Arrested in Malaysia," *Bangkok Post*, 20/01/98; "Arrests in South Boost Malaysian Ties, Security," *Nation*, 24/01/98; "Wanted PULO Man Nabbed," *Nation*, 10/02/98; and "Terrorist Suspect Has Violent Past," *Sunday Nation*, 25/01/98.

59.　Personal correspondence between the author and Tony Davis, Canberra, September 1998. See also "Border Breakthrough," *Politics and Policy*, 23/03/98; "PM: Peace in South Vital to Growth Triangle," *Bangkok Post*, 21/01/98; "Is it so Hard to be a Good Neighbour?" *Bangkok Post*, 21/01/98; "Malaysia's Policy Shift to Benefit South," *Bangkok Post*, 25/01/98; and "Surin Set to Seek Malaysian Help in Curbing Terrorists," *Nation*, 03/01/98.

60.　Key separatist figures who are believed to have fled abroad include PULO leader, Tunku Bilor Kortor Nilor, former New PULO leader, Ar-rong Mooreng and former New PULO deputy leader, Haji Abdul Hadi bin Rozaali.

61.　"Quoted in "Separatists Hold Urgent Talks," *Bangkok Post*, 24/01/98.

62.　See Syed Serajul Islam, "The Islamic Independence Movements in Patani of Thailand and Mindano of the Philippines, *Asian Survey* XXXVIII/5 (1998): 452; "50 Southern Separatists Surrender," *Bangkok Post*, 12/03/98.

63.　See, for instance, "Iran and Thailand Agree to Joint Ventures," *Straits Times*, 03/12/98; "Nateq-Nuri, Thai Foreign Minister Favor Improved Ties," *Tehran IRNA* (in English), 23/11/98; "Thailand-Iran Visit," *Tehran IRNA* (in English), 23/11/98; and "Iran Radio: Iran-Thailand Ties Benefit from Official Visits," *Tehran Voice of the Islamic Republic of Iran*, 21/11/98.

64.　"Scholarships for Thai Muslims," *Bangkok Post*, 04/07/98.

65.　See, for instance, "Thai Muslims Seek Justice for Anwar," *Philippine Daily Inquirer*, 09/10/98; "Muslim Lawyers Prepare to Back Anwar," *Bangkok Post*, 09/10/98; "Thai Muslims Hold Prayers for Anwar," *Bangkok Post*, 26/09/98; and "Muslims Demand Justice for Anwar," *Bangkok Post*, 25/09/98.

66.　See, for instance, "Thai Daily Criticizes US Bombing of Iraq," *Nation* (Internet Version), 24/12/98; "Thai Column Condemns Strikes Against Iraq, *Bangkok Siam Rat*, 22/12/98; "Muslims in Southern Thailand Collect Donations for Iraq," *Nation* (Internet Version), 21/12/98; "Muslims Denounce US," *Bangkok Post*, 19/12/98; and "Terror Alert Shuts US Embassy," *Australian*, 21/11/98.

67.　"Muslims in Southern Thailand Collect Donations for Iraq," *Nation* (Internet Version), 21/12/98; "Muslims Denounce US," *Bangkok Post*, 19/12/98.

68.　"New Party Focuses on Muslims," *Bangkok Post*, 19/10/98.

69.　Chalk, *Grey Area Phenomena in Southeast Asia*, 62; "Ties of Faith," *Far Eastern Economic Review*, 11/04/96; and Ladd Thomas, "Thailand," in Carpenter and Wiencek, eds., *Asian Security Handbook*, 242-3.

70.　Michael Shannon, "Asia Watch," *Review* 24/9 (1999): 7.

4

Militant Islamic Extremism in the Southern Philippines

Peter Chalk

The Historical Context of the Islamic Insurgency in the Southern Philippines

The island of Mindanao constitutes the traditional heartland of Islam in the southern Philippines. For several reasons, this particular region existed in more or less isolation from the rest of what is presently known as the Philippines. By the sixteenth century, the island had developed as a major international link in what was rapidly becoming an expansive maritime trade network between Southeast Asia, India, China, and the Middle East. Largely as a result of the influence of Arab merchants, Islam quickly developed as Mindanao's dominant religious creed with the territory's various indigenous communities forming themselves into sultanates and principalities based on distinct Muslim cultural, social, and political institutions.[1]

Following the Spanish colonization of the Philippines in the mid-1500s, a vigorous attempt was made to impose Catholicism throughout the archipelago as part of the overall attempt to forestall the spread of Islam in Southeast Asia. Coming with a deep-seated hatred of Muslims as a result of their own epic struggle for independence from Moorish rule on the Iberian peninsula, the Spaniards were not prepared to show any respect for, or tolerance of the separate Islamic communities that have begun to emerge in the region.[2]

The Christianization of the northern and central Philippine districts proceeded relatively quickly, largely on account of the fragmented and unconsolidated nature of the tribes in the Luzon and Visayas areas. In Mindanao, however, the Spaniards found highly

187

organized Muslim societies with built-in cultural and religious defenses against foreign intrusion. These communities were able to effectively mobilize themselves against the Spanish, successfully resisting Christian religious coercion for the next three centuries. Indeed, except for a few settlements in the northern and eastern parts of the island, the Spaniards were essentially unable to gain a significant foothold—religious or political—anywhere on Mindanao.[3]

Despite the failure to Christianize and fully colonize Mindanao, the island was nevertheless included in the Treaty of Paris (1898) which transferred Spanish sovereignty over the Philippines to the United States. The Muslims strenuously objected to this, violently rejecting any idea of being involuntarily incorporated into a predominantly Christian Philippine Republic. The Americans responded by initiating a concerted military pacification campaign to forcibly integrate Mindanao with the rest of the Philippines; by 1913 this had succeeded in effectively eliminating all Muslim armed resistance on the island.[4]

Following the neutralization of armed resistance, the U.S. began a massive re-settlement of Mindanao—encouraging Christian migration from the more crowded parts of Luzon to the less developed island in the south. The overall purpose of this transmigration program was to alter regional demographic balances in such a way that a majority of Mindanao's population would support voluntary integration with the rest of the Philippines. Encouraged by lucrative land and financial incentives, Christians quickly began to re-locate to the south. Starting with a handful of settlements in 1913, migration from the north grew during the 1920s and 1930s, accelerating after the Philippines gained its independence in 1946. By the time of the 1975 census, it is estimated that 6 million of Mindanao's 9.7 million had their origins in the Christian dominated Luzon and Visays regions.[5]

The re-settlement of Mindanao caused deep resentment among the local Muslim population. Christian agricultural communities, created by the Philippine government in the heart of indigenous Muslim territories, precipitated bitter conflicts in land distribution and ownership. In particular, the Muslims complained that they were not only being displaced from their traditional areas but were also being dispossessed of their ancestral and communal property rights by the Christian newcomers. These disputes periodically escalated into armed confrontation as both the Christians and Muslims organized themselves into self-defense militias—respectively known as the *Ilagas* (rats) and "Blackshirts" or "Barracudas."[6]

The overall situation on Mindanao took a turn for the worse in March 1968 following the Jabidah massacre. This incident related to the summary execution of twenty Muslim recruits (who were being trained by the Philippine Army for infiltration into Northern Malaysia, ostensibly to facilitate the Philippine claim on Sabah) by their Christian officers, allegedly for mutiny. For many Muslims the episode symbolized their persecution at the hands of the predominantly Christian Philippine Republic. A local resistance organization, the Muslim (later Mindanao) Independence Movement (MIM), was subsequently formed in May by Udtog Matalam with the objective of creating an independent Islamic Republic out of Mindanao, Sulu, and Palawan. MIM also served as the focus for the Muslim "Blackshirt" militia in its escalating campaign against the Christian *Ilagas.*[7]

At this stage, no move was taken to extend armed resistance against the Philippine State with the objective of secession firmly rooted in the context of non-violence. However, two subsequent developments served to radically alter the course of this strategic choice.

First, was a complete unwillingness on the part of the Marcos regime to consider the creation of a separate Islamic republic in the south. Second, was the increasingly explicit support given by the Philippine Army to the Christian *Ilaga* campaign aimed at purging Islam from Mindanao.[8]

Growing exasperation and frustration as a result of these factors culminated in 1971 with a decision to replace the ostensibly peaceful MIM with a violent alternate group, the Moro National Liberation Front (MNLF). The aim of the new organization (which was formed and led by Nur Misuari) was to achieve independence for (an Islamic) Mindanao through armed struggle against the (predominantly Christian) Philippine State.[9]

The Socio-Political Context of the Mindanao Conflict Since 1971

Since 1971, the Islamic insurgency in Mindanao has been sustained by four main socio-political factors. First is resentment of Catholic transmigration from the north. This has not only dispossessed many Muslims of what are considered to be ancient and communal property rights; it has also reduced the Moro population to a minority in their own homeland. Second is an unwillingness to subscribe to Manila's secular civil, political, judicial, and penal constitutional system. Third is frustration borne of Mindanao's lack of economic and infrastructural development. Fourth is fear of having religious, cultural and political traditions weakened (or possibly destroyed) by forced assimilation into a Catholic-dominated Philippine Republic. Fifth is the fact that a lack of consensus has emerged within the Muslim population on how best to secure its long-term future. In essence, a two-way split has emerged between those who are prepared to accept a moderate autonomous Islamic entity located within the context of the Philippine Republic; and those who will not settle for anything short of a fully separate, fundamentalist Islamic state.[10]

It is against this socio-political context that the Islamic insurgency in the southern Philippines is currently being fought. Since 1971, this struggle has come to involve three main protagonists—the MNLF and two MNLF "rejectionist" organizations: the Moro Islamic Liberation Front (MILF) and the Abu Sayyaf Group (ASG).

Before looking at each of these groups, however, it is necessary to briefly examine the concept of Islamic fundamentalism and how it has manifested itself in the southern Philippines.

Militant Islamic Fundamentalism

The popular perception of Islamic fundamentalism being intrinsically violent and synonymous with violence and terrorism is far from accurate. Islam is neither a single, unified religion, nor is it necessarily fundamental in nature. Furthermore, just because one is an Islamic fundamentalist it does not inevitably mean that one is also a holy warrior and prepared to die, if necessary, as a martyr to the faith.

At the risk of gross over simplification, both the Sunni and Shi'a traditions of Islam[11] can be found in one of two forms in the modern world. More moderate, accomodationist versions do not seek the total rejection of modernization and development, but rather seek to transform these influences to make them more compatible with traditional Muslim values and beliefs. The more radical, fundamental approach, however, completely rejects modernization as a force responsible for the wholesale and systematic corruption of the Islamic ideal. It calls for a revolutionary transformation of society and a return to the traditional classical Islamic community as being the only way to achieve true moral virtue and enlightenment.[12]

Islamic extremism is associated with this second, anti-accommodative branch of the Muslim religion which advocates a *jihad* (literally meaning "striving in the path of God") against the corrupt orthodox establishment, the main purpose of which is to achieve the cleansing and purification of the Islamic religion.13 However, whilst it would be correct to state that virtually all Islamic fundamentalists have a major pre-occupation with the *jihad*, it would be incorrect to argue that this necessarily means that they also have a penchant for violence and "holy war."

Islamic extremism identifies a variety of ways by which the *jihad* can be pursued through peaceful means. These include:

- The *jihad al-lisan* (literally "striving of the tongue");

- The *jihad al-qalam* (literally "striving with the pen");

- The *jihad al-da'wa* (literally "striving by propagating the faith").[14]

These peaceful ways of pursuing the *jihad* are distinguished from the *jihad al-saghir*, regarded as the lesser *jihad*, which advocates legitimate forms of strife with other human beings through war and violence.15 It is thus only possible to equate Islamic fundamentalism with a form of religious teaching that rationalizes the use of violence as a legitimate and sacred means to an end within the context of the second, more narrow interpretation of the *jihad al-saghir* (hereafter simply referred to as the *jihad*).

It is the latter category, which is the focus of this chapter.

Militant Islamic Fundamentalism: A Philippine Perspective

The Moro National Liberation Front (MNLF)

The Philippines' contemporary experience with militant Islamic fundamentalism can essentially be traced back to the formation of the MNLF. This organization was founded by Nur Misuari in 1971 as a violent successor to the MIM. Since its creation, the MNLF has served as the main (though not only) focus for armed Islamic resistance in the southern Philippines. Its main ideological tract is based on three main ideas. First, that the Moro people constitute a distinct *bangsa* (nation) which has a specific Islamic historical and cultural identity. Second, that the *Bangsamoro* have a legitimate right to determine their own socio-political future. Third, that the MNLF has both a duty and obligation to wage a *jihad* against the Philippine State on behalf of the *Bangsamoro* and in pursuit of their objectives.[16]

During the 1970s, the MNLF forged links with a number of conservative Middle Eastern Islamic states, developing especially strong connections with Libya. These ties proved instrumental in allowing the organization to participate as an observer in various Islamic international fora as well as benefit from the provision of external financial, political and logistical support. By the mid-1970s, the MNLF had been accepted by the Organization of the Islamic Conference (OIC) as the main representative of a displaced Islamic minority engaged in a deserving and legitimate *jihad* against a colonial and repressive Philippine government.[17]

Although originally instituted as a fully-fledged fundamentalist independence movement, the MNLF has, for most of its existence, pragmatically oriented its aims towards political autonomy and accommodation. Such a stance has been encouraged largely by the realization that the Manila government (given the Christian majority) will never countenance independence for the southern Philippines and that limited local autonomy is, perhaps, the best that can be hoped for. While this more moderate approach has complicated the MNLF's (and Misuari's) relations with more uncompromising, radical elements within the Muslim Moro population (see below), it has allowed the organization greater latitude in considering formal peace proposals. To a certain extent, it has also served to distance the MNLF in the eyes of Manila policy-makers from the aims and methods of Islamic extremism in the southern Philippines.

In 1994, largely as a result of the aforementioned factors, the MNLF and (the then) President Ramos agreed to enact a cease-fire and enter into formal peace negotiations. These discussions culminated in September 1996 with the signing of the Davao Consensus. This accord aims to establish the basis for a full and lasting peace in the southern Philippines by introducing a limited autonomous Muslim enclave in the region over three years. Substantively, the agreement provides for the following key points:

- A permanent cessation of MNLF hostilities.

- The creation of a Southern Philippines Council for Peace and Development (SPCPD) to implement and coordinate peace and development projects throughout the fourteen provinces of the southern Philippines. The Council is led by Nur Misuari and consists of 81 members, 44 of whom are directly nominated by the MNLF.

- Provision for elections, to be held in 1999, for the establishment of a final Autonomous Region of Muslim Mindanao (ARMM) in the southern Philippines. This will have local powers of governance in the following key areas:

    ❖ The administration of justice;

    ❖ Taxation;

    ❖ The protection of the domain and ancestral lands of all indigenous communities living within the autonomous enclave;

    ❖ Law and order; and

    ❖ Education.

- The integration of the MNLF guerrilla army into the Philippine security forces. It is thought that these armed cadres will eventually form the backbone of an autonomous ARMM police service.[18]

Misuari insists that as leader of the largest and most influential of the Islamic resistance groups in the southern Philippines, he has the moral authority to represent the interests of the Moro people. He also maintains that he has the right to settle for a solution that he feels is acceptable to the fulfillment of their long-term aspirations. However the issue of who and what Misuari actually represents remains a matter of serious dispute for the MILF and ASG. Each of these organizations exhibit a far more radical, fundamentalist ideological identity than does the MNLF. Moreover, both have categorically refused to accept the 1996 peace deal on the grounds that it represents a "sell out" of fundamental Muslim interests in the southern Philippines.

The Jamia-atul Al Islamic Tabligh

A second major milestone in the contemporary history of radical Islamic fundamentalism in the Philippines occurred with the formation of the Jamia-atul Al Islamic Tabligh. Originally stimulated by the Iranian Revolution of 1979, and further encouraged by return-ing Muslim scholars from the Middle East, the organization was founded by Amilhussin Jumaani and Abe Dalogan in the early 1980s. Upholding the infallibility of the Qur'an, the Tabligh essentially aims to counter Westernizing influences; calls for solidarity, unity and peace among Filipino Muslims; and espouses a return to strict Is-lamic practices. The Tabligh receives financial support from a num-ber of Islamic countries, including Pakistan and Saudi Arabia. Preach-ers from these two countries are frequent visitors to the southern Philippines, actively participating in Tabligh affairs.[19]

Although the Tabligh is, itself, a legal, largely apolitical organiza-tion, the Islamicization process it espouses has provided a fertile environment for the growth and development of both the ASG and MILF. It is around these two groups that Islamic extremist violence in the southern Philippines currently revolves.[20]

The Moro Islamic Liberation Front (MILF)

Background and Objectives

The MILF is the largest Islamic rebel group currently operating in the southern Philippines. Although it was officially formed in 1980, the organization's roots can be traced back to a major schism that occurred within the MNLF leadership during the latter part of the 1970s. In 1976, Nur Misauri took the alleged autocratic decision to scale back the MNLF's demands from independence to autonomy, signing the Tripoli Agreement with the Marcos government in 1976.[21] Hard-liners within the MNLF, however, refused to endorse the agree-ment on the grounds that it did not provide for full secession. These "rejectionists" petitioned for the resignation of Misauri in favor of the then MNLF Vice Chairman, Hashim Salamat. Misauri ignored the petition and, instead, expelled Salamat from the group's leader-ship. Growing inner-party tension and rivalry finally resulted in the formation of a rival MNLF Central Committee (MNLF-CC) under the chairmanship of Salamat in 1977. It was this group which be-came the core of the MILF when it was formally established in 1980.[22]

The MILF espouses a far more fundamentalist ideology than does the MNLF. The present leadership comes mainly from aristocratic and religious elites who are more concerned with the promotion of Islam than the pursuit of *Bangsamoro* nationalist objectives. Indeed, the incorporation of "Islamic" in the group's name was a deliberate move designed to set the organization apart from the more secular orientation of the MNLF. Hashim Salamat, MILF's present Chairman, hails from a theocratic academic background developed at Cairo's Al Azhar University, the world's most prestigious seat of Islamic learning. Philosophically, his strongest influences are said to be Syed Quth of Egypt's Muslim Brotherhood and Syed Abul Ala Mau'dudi of Pakistan's Jamaat I Islami party—the teachings of whom (although both now deceased) have a substantial following among Islamic militants worldwide.[23] Salamat defines the ideology of the MILF as one that recognizes, obeys and submits to no other laws but those handed down by the "supreme being—Allah." Islam is seen to be a complete way of life and as the ultimate solution to all human problems.[24]

The avowed political objective of the MILF, which is anchored on the Qur'an and the Sunni interpretation of Islam, is the creation of a separate Islamic state in all areas where Muslims exist in a majority in the southern Philippines.[25] The essential purpose of this polity, to be known as the Mindanao Islamic Republic (MIR), is to establish a system of government which upholds and applies *shari'ah* law in all aspects of daily life. The Front is committed to achieving this goal through a combined strategy of *dakwah* (Islamic preaching) and *jihad* (holy war/armed struggle).[26]

Strength, Weapons, and Financing

According to Philippine National Police (PNP) and military intelligence estimates, MILF's current strength is around 10,800.27 The bulk of the organization's membership come from the 1.6 million Maguindanaoan tribe (who are scattered throughout central Mindanao), the 1.9 million Maranaos (a trading community from Lanao del Sur) and the Iranos from North Cotabato and Basilan. The MILF's fighters are organized into a military wing, known as the Bangsamoro Islamic Armed Forces (BIAF), which is composed of at least six separate divisions. These troops are trained (mostly by instructors who fought in the Afghan War) and systematically rotated through the organization's thirteen major camps. All of these are linked to the MILF's central headquarters—Camp Abubakar As-Siddique, which located in the jungled foothills to the northeast of Cotabato City.[28]

The Manila government's National Intelligence Coordinating Agency (NICA) has admitted that the MILF's armory is extensive, including hundreds of Russian-made rocket-propelled grenades (RPGs), Stinger surface to air missiles (SAMs), AK 47, and M-16 assault rifles and explosives. In addition, the organization is believed to have stocks of high-powered weaponry such as 75mm anti-aircraft guns, American-made B40 anti-tank rockets, and 81mm mortars.29 Overall, the MILF arsenal was thought to number at least 8,466 firearms by the end of 1998, an increase of 4.07 percent from 1997's total of 8,115.30 While some of these armaments have either been indigenously made31 or have been covertly purchased from the Philippine Armed Forces (AFP), a significant proportion are also thought to have been procured from abroad. Afghanistan, Pakistan, and Cambodia appear to be the main external sources, with most munitions being trafficked to the MILF either directly or via regionally organized shipments that link Mindanao with southern Thailand and Aceh.[32]

In terms of finance, the MILF is known to raise a fair amount of its money "indigenously," either in the form of voluntary contributions made to the organization or from "revolutionary taxes" imposed on companies operating in MILF dominated areas. According to Salamat, this is where the vast majority of the Front's funds come from. He cautiously rejects the idea that his organization needs foreign financial assistance, stressing the viability of the group's self-sufficient status: "We don't need [foreign backing]. The Front has devised a sustained self-reliance program....If only one million [of the Muslims on the island] contribute a peso each month, we have [a monthly income] of P1 million."[33]

Most analysts believe, however, that the group *does* enjoys substantial external backing—generally from the Organization of Islamic Conference (OIC) and specifically from Libya, Iraq, Afghanistan, and "private groups and individuals" living in Saudi Arabia.[34] Tom Oldham, who at the time of writing headed the political desk at the Australian Embassy in Manila, considers one of the biggest problems in this regard is the difficulty of effectively monitoring nongovernmental organization (NGO) funding for Muslim development and educational projects. While he concedes some is undoubtedly being used for legitimate socio-economic purposes, he also argues a significant proportion is obviously being diverted to pay for such things as weapons procurement and military training.35 Certainly Salamat's figure of P1 million a month (approx. A$45,450, quoted above) would not appear to be enough to run a civil-guerrilla infrastructure of the size that even the most conservative estimates of the PNP attest to.

Violent Activities

Traditionally, most of the MILF's violent activities have taken the form of orthodox guerrilla warfare with hit-and-run attacks directed against members of the military. Generally speaking, the group has not emphasized indiscriminate violence against civilian and noncombatant targets. Such "self-restraint" has been used to distance the Front from the activities of the ASG (see below) and is very much in line with the group's own image of itself as a revolutionary military (as opposed to terrorist) force.[36]

Nevertheless, terrorist-type tactics have been periodically used. Characteristically, this type of violence has been directed against either Christian-populated communities, employees of companies who have refused to pay their revolutionary taxes, or local government and police officials. According to the PNP Directorate for Intelligence, the MILF retains a highly secretive terrorist "sub-division" known as the Special Operations Group (SOG) specifically for this purpose, composed mostly of young, unmarried cadres whose identity is known only to the highest echelons of the group's leadership.[37]

Foreign Linkages

There is no doubt that foreign Muslim extremists have established links with the MILF. Intelligence sources within the Philippines believe that Salamat maintains close relations with *ullamas* heading fundamentalist Islamic organizations in a number of other countries, most notably Pakistan, Afghanistan, Iraq, and Egypt, many of whom were his classmates at Cairo's Al-Azhar University.[38] Indeed, the MILF's Vice Chairman for Political Affairs, Ghazali Jaafar, has admitted to journalists on a number of occasions that the Front receives foreign help from external Islamic organizations.[39] Ustadz Shariff Julabbi, the MILF Chairman for western Mindanao, has similarly hinted that the group's insurgency benefits from external Arab aid, though he has refused to specify either the groups themselves or the precise form that this support takes. In an interview with *Deutsche Presse* in January 1999, Julabbi affirmed: "We don't ask from them, but they are extending support because they know the cause of our struggle. I'm not at liberty to divulge the specific Arab countries. But a revolutionary group like ours needs help from foreigners."[40]

Apart from financial assistance (see above), external backing is thought to take the form of religious instruction and military training. The NICA maintains that it has concrete proof to show that foreign nationals are currently residing in MILF camps, providing a variety of "educational" services ranging from theology classes to basic weapon handling seminars.[41] Moreover, both the PNP and AFP claim to have evidence that extremists and mercenaries from the Middle East and South Asia have traveled to Mindanao to train MILF cadres on the fundamentals of assassination, bombing, sabotage and, possibly, suicide attacks. A 1997 raid against the AFP headquarters in central Mindanao, for instance, is alleged by intelligence sources to have been a foreign sponsored operation, carried out by Pakistani and Saudi Arabian nationals who were in the country as part of a six-man overseas MILF suicide-assault training team. [42]

MILF cadres are additionally alleged to have benefited from military training abroad, particularly in camps run by ex-Mujahideen fighters located along the Pakistani-Afghan border. Recruits are believed to travel to South Asia on the grounds that they are taking theological courses at the University of Pakistan. Once there, however, it is alleged they are diverted to regional camps where they receive intensive instruction in techniques of unconventional warfare.[43] Of particular importance in this regard is a group known as Al-Afghani, a "freelance" organization that is thought to have been providing external training for MILF (and ASG) cadres since 1994. According to U.S. intelligence sources, Al-Afghani runs a major "military academy," which recruits mainly from the University of Dawhat and Jihad in the Pakistani province of Peshwar. The school is thought to have literally transformed the tactics of Philippine and other Islamic groups around the world, with an estimated 1,000 Arab and Asian Muslims passing through this and other similar camps each year.[44]

The MILF's uncompromising and hard-line reaction to the 1998 air strikes initiated by the U.S. against Afghanistan[45] and Iraq[46] would certainly appear to suggest some sort of residual connection between the group and overseas extremists. Following Washington's attack on Baghdad in December 1998, the group's Western Mindanao Chairman, Julabbi, declared a *jihad (al-saghir)* against the U.S. imperialist in defense of the innocent Muslims slaughtered by the "great Satan" and its Western allies. Repeating an earlier call for Muslims worldwide to forcibly unite against the U.S., Julabbi expressed the Front's deep concern about the atrocities against its "brothers in Iraq and Afghanistan, stating: "Muslims are like a human body, once you are hurt, you feel the pain all over."[47]

MILF-Government of the Republic of the Philippines (GRP) Negotiations

Following the signing of the 1996 Davao Consensus and the integration of the MNLF into mainstream society, the MILF emerged as the main rallying secessionist group in the southern Philippines. The group rejected the 1996 agreement on the grounds that it neither satisfied fundamental Muslim aspirations (especially in relation to religious freedom) nor provided for the creation of an independent Islamic state in Mindanao.[48] Since then, the MILF has declared itself as the only legitimate organization that upholds the revolutionary aspirations of Muslims on Mindanao.[49]

Rhetorically at least, the MILF has continued to assert that it is not willing to compromise on the fundamental issue of Islamic independence. Behind this hard-line sloganeering, however, the group has been talking with the Philippine government, engaging Manila through a specially enacted "bi-lateral technical committee." More importantly, it appears that the Front is, in fact, prepared to negotiate on certain issues, including the geographical scope of an Islamic territorial entity and, critically, the question of secession. According to Salamat: "The so called Autonomous Region of Muslim Mindanao does not represent real autonomy. So we're sticking to our idea that we can't accept anything less than independence. [However], if some real, practical, attractive alternative were to come up [in negotiations], then its possible we could change our minds." Al-Haj Murad, MILF's Military Chief, echoes this pragmatism: "If we could find some alternative whereby the [Moro] people could enjoy their own system of life and government, we'd look at it."[50]

The fundamental question, therefore, concerns the feasibility of reaching such a formula. During the second half of 1997, the MILF and Manila government took part in a series of phased negotiations. These culminated in November with the signing of an agreement which outlines the specific rules for a "general cessation of hostilities" between the two sides.[51] According to Bil Hansen, senior lecturer in Politics at the University of Atheneo in Manila, this was part of a concerted effort by the Ramos to conclude a comprehensive peace settlement for Mindanao before the expiry of his presidential term. Hansen believes that the truce was the first stage in negotiations (which were being conducted through Ramos' chief negotiator, Jose de Venecia) for a final agreement, possibly involving the creation of some sort of Islamic enclave based wholly on *shar'iah* law.[52]

However, the cease-fire agreement has already been broken several times by both sides (see above). Moreover, it is not yet apparent that the successor government of Joseph "Erap" Estrada has the ability to maintain the peace momentum built up under the previous Ramos administration. Indeed, several independent political analysts have already concurred that he lacks the political acumen and experience to manage an effective conflict resolution process in the south. In particular, reservations have been expressed over his ability to:

- Ensure that any new-MILF agreement will not have a negative impact on the present 1996 Davao Consensus and the political credibility of Misuari.

- Gain the support of the majority Christian population in the southern Philippines who is opposed to devolving more power to the Muslims in Mindanao.

- Marginalize MILF hard-liners who will not compromise on the issue of independence.

- Overcome the deeply held reservations felt throughout the rest of the Philippines concerning the wisdom of enacting a *Shar'iah* legal system that is completely at odds with the jurisprudence principles practiced in the rest of the country (something that has already been especially controversial with regard to criminal matters).[53]

- Integrate political reconciliation with a comprehensive program of socio-economic development and infrastructure creation.[54]

It remains to be seen whether or not Estrada will demonstrate the fortitude and leadership necessary to overcome these obstacles and succeed where so many of his predecessors have failed. The signs, however, are not encouraging. Although the peace process initiated under Ramos continues (at least in theory), relations with the MILF are currently at a major "low." The Front has categorically ruled out accepting an MNLF-like autonomy deal, which, thus far, is all that Manila has been prepared to offer. Further straining what is already a tense standoff have been repeated threats by Estrada to unleash the full force of the AFP in the south if the MILF does not adopt a more conciliatory approach to peace talks.[55] Such blunt negotiating tactics are extremely unlikely to bear dividends and could well scuttle even the tenuous progress made under Ramos. As the *Economist* observed back in 1998 when assessing the future prospects for peace in Mindanao, the Philippines may well come to regret voting for the blustering and posturing of an Estrada-type Presidency.[56] Certainly "Erap's" somewhat unsophisticated, "tough man" image has yet to show results in the government's current dealings with the MILF.

The Abu Sayyaf Group (ASG)

Background and Objectives

The birth of the ASG can be traced back to 1989 when a small group of Islamic militants broke away from the Tabligh and formed an organization known as the Mujahideen Commando Freedom Fighters (MCFF). Its initial leaders were Abdurajak Abubakar Janjalini, Amilhusin Jumaani and Wahab Akbar[57] who oversaw a core group of ex-Muslim volunteers that had fought with the International Islamic Brigade (IIB) against the Soviet Union in Afghanistan during the 1980s. The MCFF renamed itself first the Jundullah (literally, "Servants of Allah") in 1992 and then the ASG in 1993. The group is loosely organized along a cell structure and is governed by an Executive Committee headed by a Caliph and eight other religious leaders. Together these constitute the so-called Minsupala Islamic Theocratic State Shadow government (MIT-SG).[58] Up until late 1998, Janjalani represented the supreme power within the ASG. However, in December he was killed during a shoot-out with PNP forces in the Barangay Tumakid district of Lamitan town in Basilan. Since then the group has been effectively leaderless, although its members have stated their determination to re-group under a new Caliph as soon as a suitable successor has been found.[59]

The overall objective of the ASG is the establishment of an independent and exclusive Islamic Theocratic State in Mindanao (MIS).

It differs from the MILF in that whereas the former merely aims for independence, the latter additionally espouses no co-existence with other religious groups—advocating the deliberate targeting of all southern Filipino Christians (including then beheading of women, children, and the elderly) to this effect. The ASG also sees its objectives in Mindanao as intimately tied to an integrated effort aimed at asserting the global dominance of Islam through armed struggle (see below)—an extreme religious fervor not generally shared (at least overtly) by the MILF.[60]

Strength, Weapons, and Financing

In 1999, the AFP Southern Command estimated the ASG's overall support base at 1,148, with a regular armed component consisting of approximately 330. The majority of the group's members are Muslim youths aged between sixteen and their early thirties, with many of the older cadres reportedly ex-volunteers of the IIB that fought in Afghanistan. Most of the organization's active backing is concentrated in Zamboanga, Basilan, and Sulu (where the ASG's main training camp is situated). However, pockets of residual support are also thought to exist throughout the southern Philippines, notably in the poverty stricken regions of Western Mindanao where 52 percent of the population falls below the poverty line.[61]

As of the end of 1998, the AFP Southern Command put the total number of weapons in the group's possession at 387 firearms, down from 392 in 1997.[62] The majority of these arms are of the basic combat variety, including assault rifles, grenade launchers, and mortars, mostly procured from stocks left over from the Afghan War. The group is also thought to have developed a limited ability to produce home made bombs composed of nitrates and fertilizers used for agricultural purposes.[63]

The ASG raises most of its money "indigenously" from criminal activities such as kidnap-for ransom, extortion, and marijuana cultivation. Hostage-taking has been an especially favored finance-generator. The practice has been encouraged by the general willingness of victims' families to pay ransoms as well as the fact that no abductee has ever sued in court. In one recently highlighted case, two Hong Kong hostages were released for a "board and lodging fee" of P2 million (KK$400,000), 106 days after their original capture.[64] According to the AFP, this is typical of most ransom demands, which generally run between a minimum of P500, 000 and a maximum of P2 million.[65]

In addition to criminal activity, the organization is also believed to benefit from a certain amount of overseas financial support. According to the NICA, most of this funding is coordinated by Osama Bin Laden, the alleged financial backer of the U.S. embassy bombings in Kenya and Tanzania in 1998 who was stripped of his Saudi citizenship in 1991 for aiding militant groups worldwide.[66] Government sources believe Bin Laden channels funds to the ASG through a network of legal companies and non-governmental groups created by Mohammad Jamal Khalifa - the Saudi renegade's brother-in-law. Prior to his arrest in San Francisco in December 1994,[67] Khalifa doubled as the President of the Philippine Chapter of the International Islamic Relief Organization (IIRO) and Director of the World Muslim League (WML), using both positions to create an array of business and charitable interests throughout the country. In 1997, the ASG allegedly received P20 million via this institutional conduit, most of which was used to cover the travel and accommodation costs of ASG recruits attending overseas training courses (see below) as well as to purchase arms.[68]

Violent Activities

In terms of revolutionary political violence, virtually all of the ASG's activities are terroristic in nature. These acts are carried out by special urban units, composed of so-called *Mollah* and *Mujaheedat* forces that are trained in demolition and weapons handling. The group's terrorist capacity was first demonstrated in August 1991 by the bombing in Zamboanga City of the *M/V Doulos*, an international vessel used by a global Christian missionary movement. Since then, the ASG has claimed responsibility for successive violent acts against Christian targets throughout Mindanao, including bombings, kidnappings, "liquidations," raids and other various acts of sabotage. Some attacks have been particularly violent in nature. In 1993, the group bombed the San Pedro Cathedral in Davao City, which resulted in seven deaths and 130 injuries. In 1994 ASG members ambushed a bus in Basilan, massacring forty-five Christian passengers. The following year, an ASG-orchestrated raid on the coastal settlement of Ipil led to the deaths of fifty-three civilians, while in January 1999 a bomb attack in Jolo killed eleven, injuring another seventy.[69] Most recently, two explosions on buses being transported on an inter-island ferry killed forty-five civilians, making it the most deadly assault carried out by the ASG since the Ipil massacre.[70]

In addition to terrorism, the ASG has also perpetrated numerous acts of criminal violence to funds its activities (see above). Indeed, violent these activities have become so rife that certain members of the Philippine intelligence community are now arguing it is more accurate to describe the ASG as a straight crime syndicate as opposed to an organization exhibiting a specific religious/political ideology. Although it is true that much of the ASG's activity during 1997 and 1998 has been in the form of extortion and armed robbery, it is too early to conclude that the notion of the Islamic *jihad* and the goal of Mindanaon independence no longer forms the central defining characteristic of the group.[71] As Professor Aprodicio "Prod" Laquian, Joseph Estrada's ex-National Campaign Officer for Political Affairs, observes, there has certainly been no let up in the rhetoric justifying the ASG's actions in the name of establishing a theocratic state where Muslims can follow Islam in its purest and strictest form.[72] Moreover, there are indications to suggest that the ASG continues to maintain extensive international links with Islamic extremist groups overseas, most notably in the Middle East and North Africa (see below). At least at this stage, therefore, it would probably be fair to suggest that the ASG's illicit acts are integral to, rather than independent of, a higher political-religious Islamic cause.

Foreign Linkages

One factor that has consistently been stressed as exacerbating the threat posed by the ASG is the group's tie-ins with international Islamic extremist organizations. Both military and police intelligence maintain that ASG members have undergone training overseas, primarily in camps located in Pakistan and Afghanistan. As with the MILF, it is believed that the ex-Mujahideen free-lance group Al-Afghani plays a critical role in this regard.[73] Indeed, according to the PNP Directorate for Intelligence, the Afghan influence is one of the strongest external forces currently being exerted on the ASG, perhaps even stronger than that found in the MILF. It is argued that this is essentially a legacy of the intensive role played by the ASG leadership in the Afghan War during the 1980s - an association which, at least in relative terms, tended to be far more intimate than that which characterized MILF commanders.[74]

Apart from overseas training, there is also evidence to suggest that the ASG has established formal operational links with international terrorist groups. Military and intelligence officials now firmly believe that the ASG, possibly in conjunction with renegade elements of the MILF, has facilitated with the creation of local logistics for transnational Islamic organizations wishing to operate out of the Philippines, something that fits well with the group's overall international self-identity (see above).[75] Military and intelligence sources believe that the Republic has assumed significance to foreign militant Islamists as a base or gateway for overseas operations due to a number of reasons:

- The state's strategic location in the heart of Southeast Asia.

- The broad latitude of democratic space that exists within the Philippines, which, together with memories of the Marcos dictatorship, has served to effectively tie the government's hands in trying to initiate far-reaching law and order and internal security provisions.[76]

- The fact that the country is highly vulnerable to foreign intrusions due to its extremely porous borders and vast coastline.

- The strong ties that the Philippines has with the U.S. (a product of its colonial past), making the Republic a good alternative for groups wanting to take revenge for counter-terrorist drives initiated either by Washington or its allies.[77]

Concrete evidence of an international connection between the ASG and other Islamic organizations first began to surface in January 1995. This followed the raid of a flat rented in Malate, Manila, to Ramzi Ahmed Yousef—the "free-lance" terrorist convicted of the 1993 World Trade Center bombing in New York with known links to the radical Egyptian cleric Sheik Omar Abd Al Rahman, Al-Jamma'at al-Islamiyya,[78] and Osama bin Laden. Material seized from the one bedroom apartment revealed details of a sophisticated plan by Yousef to carry out a series of high-profile international operations during 1995 and 1996, in conjunction with the ASG. As part of the overall objective of "turning the democratic Republic of the Philippines into a major center of international terrorism," the attacks were to have included:

- The assassination of the Pope during his visit to Manila in 1995.

- Synchronized bombings of the U.S. and Israeli embassies in Manila and other Asian capitals, most notably Bangkok.

- The mid-air destruction of two trans-Pacific United Airlines 747 jumbo jets over Hong Kong's Kai Tek airport by exploding nitroglycerin bombs hidden in the upper-deck washrooms of each plane.[79] The scheme was apparently "trial-tested" in December 1994 when Yousef, traveling under the alias of Armaldo Forlani, planted a liquid explosive bomb aboard a Philippines Airlines jet bound for Tokyo. The device exploded 220 miles east of Okinawa (Yousef had already left the plane in the Philippine city of Cebu), killing one passenger (a Japanese engineer), injuring ten others, and blowing a hole in the floor of the aircraft.

- The assassination of President Clinton during his attendance at the Philippine Asia Pacific Economic Cooperation (APEC) Summit in 1996.

- Suicide assaults on the headquarters of both the Federal Bureau of Investigation (FBI) and Central Intelligence Agency (CIA).[80]

Three months after the raid in Malate, six members of the so-called Islamic Saturday Meeting Group (ISMG), or Likah Asept Al Islamiyya, were detained in a follow-up police operation against two apartments in Kalookan City.[81] In addition to the individual arrests, various Islamic literatures, travel documents, a computer notebook, diskettes, taped Islamic lectures, two .45 caliber pistols, two M16 assault rifles, explosives, and assorted ammunition were also seized. The ISMG has since been identified by Philippine intelligence as spiritually affiliated with the Islamic teachings of Sheik Rahman and as closely involved with Ramzi Yousef's own plans for terror attacks in the Philippines during 1995.[82]

Although the Malate and Kalookan raids successfully aborted Yousef's planned terrorist strikes, it does appear that the ASG has, nevertheless, been plugged into a burgeoning Islamic international terrorist network. This has caused particular concern in the U.S. and Australia, with both governments increasingly conscious of the need to ensure that transnational groups are not allowed to use Mindanao as a springboard for carrying out attacks either in the run up to or during the 2000 Sydney Olympic Games. As with the Thai government in the context of mitigating the threat from Pattani, Yala, and Narathiwat, efforts in this direction are currently focusing on bilateral intelligence exchanges and cooperative measures designed to upgrade barrier defenses.[83]

Apart from these international links, a residual concern also exists that the ASG has been in the process of developing a regional terrorist network, connecting the group's cadres with militants in Malaysia and Islamic separatists operating out of Aceh and southern Thailand. Concerns about possible Southeast Asian connections were first aroused in August 1996 when, acting on a tip-off by U.S. sources, the AFP successfully intercepted a major arms cache that was being shipped through the central Philippine city of Cebu. According to security sources, the weapons were part of an armory that was being prepared for a regionally organized attack on the 1996 Philippine Asia Pacific Economic Cooperation (APEC) Summit meeting.[84]

Fears of mutually supportive arms links have been further heightened in the wake of increased instability in Aceh, with regional threat assessments now focusing on the possibility of Cambodian weapons shipments being trafficked to northern Sumatra, Pattani, and Mindanao.[85] Although there is, as yet, no concrete proof linking the ASG with other radical Islamic elements in Southeast Asia, Philippine security sources continue to view such a tactical union as a distinct possibility. As Concepcion Clamor, Assistant Director of the NICA, explains:

> Asia is ripe for militant Islamism for the following reasons: it is a new frontier with plenty of playing fields; it has enormous political and economic power; and it has a restive Islamic population. The possibility that…[extreme] Islamic groups could band together and challenge secular governments cannot be discounted. Islam serves as a strong rallying point for these organizations. It is [possible]…that the presence of foreign radical Islamist groups in the country [is] part of an effort to make the Southern Philippines a part of a reported international terrorist plot to create an "Islamic state" that will include Malaysia, Indonesia and [southern Thailand].[86]

Linkages with the MNLF and MILF

A further factor serving to compound the perceived threat of the ASG is the suspected links that the group has established with hardliners in both the MNLF and MILF. Although both Misauri and Salamat have officially denied that their organizations have any dealings with Janjalini's group, security forces in Mindanao do believe that certain "lost commands" within the MNLF and MILF have been actively involved with the ASG. The AFP allege, for instance, that in addition to tactical alliances, instruction has been provided in guerrilla and terrorist tactics, sabotage techniques and demolition procedures. Suspicions of a possible MNLF/MILF - ASG tie-in were first raised following the 1995 raid against Ipil. Although it is accepted that the massacre was essentially orchestrated by the ASG, military sources believe the fact that it was claimed in the name of the Islamic Command Council of the MNLF (ICC-MNLF) points to some sort of MILF and MNLF involvement. Backing for this idea was further heightened when security forces over-ran one of the ASG's main camps in Basilan. According to eye witness accounts, members of the group fled to Sulu aboard MNLF pump boats and took refuge at Patikul, a Muslim base then under the control of the MNLF.[87]

If verified, the formation of strategic alliances between the ASG and MNLF/MILF lost commands would substantially enhance the potential threat of the latter organization. Not only would it give the ASG a greater capacity to carry out more concerted large-scale attacks (such as the Ipil massacre); it would, additionally, serve to increase the group's tactical reserve base and, thereby, its ability to recover from government-inflicted losses and setbacks. It is also worth pointing out that linkages between the three organizations would provide hard-liners in both the MNLF and MILF with a perfect conduit for maintaining military pressure on Manila without sacrificing the ostensible political gains that their respective groups have otherwise achieved.[88]

ASG-GRP Negotiation

At present, no contacts have been made between the Philippine government and the ASG. The previous Ramos administration consistently refused to open even exploratory talks with the group, officially denouncing the organization as terroristic and lacking any legitimate religious or political basis. For its own part, the ASG has been equally reticent about talking with Manila, seeing the predominately Christian and largely pro-U.S. Philippine state as a threat to Islamic aspirations not only locally, but regionally as well as internationally.[89]

In the run up to the 1998 presidential elections, however, the ASG made an unprecedented peace overture, with the former leader, Janjalini, for the first time stating that the group would be prepared to enter into peace negotiations should an Estrada-based central government emerge. Exactly what accounts for this about-turn remains unclear. Janjalini justified his change of tack on the grounds that

Estrada was both "more pro-people and pro-poor" than Ramos and, therefore, more in tune with fundamental Islamic principles.[90] Certain security sources, on the other hand, maintain that the decision had more to do with the growing weakness of the group and the inability of the governing Executive Committee to maintain unity. According to sources within the PNP, the ASG is riven by internal tribalism and clanism, tending to function less as a structured political grouping and more as a loose collection of private "lost commands" motivated purely by greed. The PNP maintains this necessarily forced Janjalini to adopt a more pragmatic line over negotiation with the government in the hope that some sort of beneficial agreement can be worked out while the group continues to exist, at least notionally, as a single entity.[91]

At this point, it is certainly too early to conclude that the ASG is on the verge of internal collapse and that it is this which is driving the group to seek a compromise with the government. In its traditional strongholds of Zamboanga and Basilan, the ASG continues to exert an extremely destabilizing influence with some sort of violent activity occurring almost on a daily basis.[92] Moreover, military and central intelligence sources within Manila tend to reject the PNP's view of the ASG, arguing that the organization has actually evolved into a *more* structured group which, thanks to its extensive international connections, is now capable of carrying out better planned and orchestrated acts of violence and terrorism.[93]

The most likely reason for Janjalini's sudden willingness to negotiate was to ensure that his group would not be completely marginalized should some sort of compromise emerge in talks between Estrada and the MILF. In this way, the ASG was probably merely striving to keep its options open by having one "foot in the political door." Such an approach is a classic "bullet and ballot box" tactic shared by many other terrorist groups around the world, including the Tamil Tigers, Hamas, the Provisional Irish Republican Army (PIRA), Hizbollah, and even the GIA.

With the virtual collapse of the MILF-Manila peace process (see above), prospects for a more conciliatory ASG have been severely dashed, largely because the group no longer has any need to fear marginalization. Although official sources in Manila have remained optimistic that the death of Janjalini in December 1998 would give the organization no other option but to negotiate, no such re-orientation has yet materialized. The group has expressed its determination to re-group under a new leader and has vowed to increase its level of activity in revenge for Janjalini's death.[94] Moreover, heightened anti-U.S. sentiments among the southern Philippine population in the wake of Washington's 1998 missile strikes against Sudan, Afghanistan, and Iraq will almost certainly work to the ASG's advantage, as will continued economic difficulties and perceived social injustices on Mindanao—possibly driving the group to even greater violence. Certainly the December 1998 assault on the Zamboanga shopping complex and the February 2000 inter-island ferry would suggest any suggestion that the ASG is on the verge of collapse is entirely pre-mature.

Conclusion: The Future

Militant Islamic fundamentalism has posed a serious challenge to the stability and security of the southern Philippines for the past two and a half decades. Perceived Christian discrimination and oppression, dispossession of land rights, a lack of local governance, and economic deprivation have been the major forces driving the Moro Islamic insurgency since the early 1970s. Although the MNLF signed a peace deal with the Manila government in 1996, both the MILF and ASG have continued to exert a highly destabilizing influence, keeping the military, in the words of Tom Oldham, "on a virtual war footing."[95]

In many ways, the threat posed by these two groups is far greater than that which ever eventuated from the MNLF. This is essentially because both:

- Exhibit a radical fundamentalist Islamic identity that is largely unwilling to compromise on its basic beliefs and demands.

- Appear to have tapped into an intensive international extremist network, itself the product of the resurgence of Islamic fundamentalism since the end of the Cold War.

- Have benefited from the huge outflow of weapons, militant indoctrination and guerrilla experience that is the legacy of the U.S.-supported Afghan campaign against the Soviet Union in the 1980s.

- Are able to draw on a personnel resource base that is far from insignificant—especially if allegations of possible MILF/MNLF and ASG tie-ins prove to be correct.[96]

Given the present political context in the Philippines, any notion of granting independence to the south is completely out of the question. The existence of an in-built Christian majority which firmly upholds the vision of a fully unified and integrated Philippine Republic ensures that no government would receive an electoral mandate to accede to the secessionist demands of a largely isolated (in terms of the country as a whole) Islamic minority.[97] This necessarily means that any *permanent* negotiated settlement to the insurgency in Mindanao will have to involve compromise on the part of both the MILF and ASG.

Most analysts concur that the best hope for effecting such an outcome lies with implementing a sustained program of socio-economic growth and development. Achieving this would not only undermine the civilian support-base of the MILF and ASG; in doing so, it would also remove both groups' raison d'être, necessarily forcing each to adopt a more pragmatic and conciliatory negotiating line with Manila. Critical to this overall process has been the MNLF-led peace and development council. In creating the body as part of the 1996 Davao Consensus, (then) President Ramos and Nur Misauri were calculating that increased prosperity would help to eliminate memories of past inequities and discrimination and, thereby, provide the stability and confidence necessary to marginalize rejectionist group sentiments.[98]

Little progress has been made in this direction, however, Mindanao's enormous economic potential notwithstanding.[99] The Manila government has been preoccupied with the fall-out of the Asian economic malaise, which has undercut its own plans for macroeconomic reform and infrastructural development. ASEAN and APEC states have been more concerned with the implications of their expanding memberships and dealing with their own immediate economic problems than investing in Mindanao as part of the proposed East ASEAN Growth Area (EAEG). [100] Other international fora such as the United Nations (U.N.) have neither the budget, mandate nor inclination for the type of economic intervention that would be required in Mindanao, particularly given the financial commitment that is now required in East Timor.[101] And while foreign companies and corporations would no doubt be attracted by the southern Philippines' abundant supply of natural resources, the continuing lack of law and order in the region continues to detract from its reputation as a safe, long-term investment opportunity. It should be noted that, at least in terms of the current rate of corporate kidnappings, Mindanao ranks as one of the most dangerous places in the world in which to conduct business.[102]

Unless something truly phenomenal unfolds over the next few years, prospects for peace and stability in the southern Philippines appear bleak. Any negotiated settlement in the region will have to involve compromise on the part of the MILF and ASG. This is only likely to occur if the legitimacy and support structure of both groups are undermined by a widespread perception that the MNLF/ARMM peace process is paying dividends in terms of promoting socio-economic growth and development. At present, it is difficult to see where the money to finance this task is going to come from, at least in the short term. Indeed elements of the MNLF are reportedly already beginning to defect to the side of the MILF and ASG as a result of dissatisfaction with the 1996 Davao Consensus, particularly over the lack of viable infrastructural and employment opportunities that have so far been created.[103]

Years of what Muslim minorities living in Mindanao, Sulu, and Palawan[104] regard as unjustified neglect - perceived deprivation which has been further fueled by the unabated influence and support of foreign militants - are the main factors accounting for the ascendancy of Islamic extremism in the southern Philippines. This particular ideological force owes its strength and legitimacy to a portion of the indigenous Muslim minority, which views itself as the discriminated victim of a Christian-dominated Christian republic. Socially disillusioned and economically discontented, these people have become vulnerable to the agitational thrusts and international Islamist appeal of groups such as the MILF and ASG. So long as these basic underlying conditions continue to exist, there may be little hope of successfully resolving the present insurgency in the southern Philippines.

Postscript

Recent months have seen a prolonged period of confrontation between Government and the Moro Islamic Liberation Front eventually subside into a ceasefire and resumed negotiations under a new administration.

The cease-fire agreement negotiated in 1997 between the Government and the MILF was repeatedly broken during the tenure of Ramos' successor, Joseph "Erap" Estrada, with both the MILF and the AFP accusing each other of instigating the fighting. Matters culminated in 2000 when Manila launched an all-out offensive against the Front, which by July of that year had displaced some 60,000 civilians, at least 250,000 of who remain unwilling or unable to return to their homes. Following the fall of Estrada in early 2001, the incumbent President Macapagal Arroyo launched a new peace initiative, suspending all military operations against MILF and inviting its leaders back to the negotiating table. In addition, she promised a "mini-Marshall Plan" to kick start economic growth in the poverty-stricken Muslim south.

It makes solid sense for Arroyo to try and come to some sort of settlement with MILF. As a new President, she stands to gain both domestically and internationally from projecting a conciliatory image that contrasts with the bellicose and, ultimately, wholly counterproductive stance of her predecessor, Estrada. Success will depend on political acumen and deft management, particularly in terms of her ability to:

· Ensure that any new-MILF agreement will not have a negative impact on the present 1996 Davao Consensus and the political credibility of Misuari.

• Gain the support of the majority Christian population in the southern Philippines who are opposed to devolving more power to the Muslims in Mindanao.

• Marginalize MILF hard-liners who will not compromise on the issue of independence.

• Overcome the deeply-held reservations felt throughout the rest of the Philippines concerning the wisdom of enacting a Shar'iah legal system that is completely at odds with the jurisprudence principles practiced in the rest of the country (something that has already been especially controversial with regard to criminal matters).

• Integrate political reconciliation with a comprehensive program of socio-economic development and infrastructure creation.

Although much smaller in number and far less representative than the MILF, the Abu Sayyaf Group has emerged as perhaps the most visible face of Islamic extremism in the Philippines, due mainly to the large number of Western hostages seized by the group over the past eighteen months. Hostage-taking has been an especially favored finance-generator for the ASG. The practice has been encouraged by the general willingness of victims' families to pay ransoms as well as the fact that no abductee has ever sued in court. The scale of these activities reached new levels in March and April 2000 when a total of seventy-one elementary school teachers, children, and international tourists were seized. Although conditions for the abductees' freedom were originally cast in political terms – notably the release of ASG members jailed in Basilan as well as several Arab terrorists imprisoned in the US – they were soon superceded by stipulations of a purely economic nature. This was most apparent with the foreign hostages, where a ransom of US$1 million each was set. A number of European individuals, acting through Libya, ultimately paid several million dollars for their release. The success of this operation has ensured that kidnapping remains the ASG's favored means of financial procurement. Indeed at the time of writing, the group had abducted a further seventeen foreign tourists (including three Americans), this time from the Dos Palmas beach resort on Palawan Island.

Attracted by the spoils of ransom payments for hostages, the ranks of the ASG have been enlarged by new recruits from impoverished families and villages. Philippine intelligence currently estimates that the ASG has an overall armed membership of 1,104 militants.

Notes

1.   Bgen Ismael Villareal, "Conflict Resolution in Mindanao," *OSS Forum Paper* 2 (1996), 2.
2.   Michael Leifer, *Dictionary of the Modern Politics of Southeast Asia* (London: Routledge, 1995), 174.
3.   See Villareal, "Conflict Resolution in Mindanao," 3; Mark Turner, "Terrorism and Secession in the Southern Philippines: The Rise of the Abu Sayyaf," *Contemporary Southeast Asia* 17/1 (1995): 10; and P.B. Sinha, "Muslim Insurgency in the Philippines," *Strategic Analysis* 18/5 (1995): 637.
4.   Villareal, "Conflict Resolution in Mindanao," 3; Turner, "Terrorism and Secession in the Southern Philippines," 9. In general, it is estimated that some 15,000-20,000 Muslims were killed in Mindanao as a consequence of armed resistance to U.S. colonialism between the years 1903 and 1945. For further details see B.R. Rodil, *The Minoritization of the Indigenous Communities of Mindanao and Sulu* (Quezon City: Alternate Forum for Research in Mindanao, 1994), 49.
5.   See R.J. May, "The Wild West in the South: A Recent Political History," in Mark Turner and R.J. May eds., *Mindanao: Land of Unfulfilled Promise* (Quezon City:

New Day Publishers, 1992), 128; Daniel Lucero, "The SPCPD: A Break-through Towards Peace," *OSS Digest* (July/August 1996), 5; and Dynamic Research and Media Services, *A Study of the New Developments on the MNLF Secession Movement in Relations to AFP Plans* (Quezon City: Office of the Deputy Chief of Staff for Plans, 1989), 2.

6.   Rodil, *The Minoritization of the Indigenous Communities of Mindanao and Sulu,* 43-5; Villareal, "Conflict Resolution in Mindanao," 4; Turner, "Terrorism and Secession in the Southern Philippines," 9-10.

7.   Villareal, "Conflict Resolution in Mindanao," 5-6; May, "The Wild West in the South," 137; Lucero, "The SPCPD: A Break-through Towards Peace," 5.

8.   Derek McDougall, *Studies in International Relations* (Melbourne: Edward Arnold, 1991), 81; Leifer, *A Dictionary of the Politics of Southeast Asia,* 174-75.

9.   Villareal, "Conflict Resolution in Mindanao," 5-6.

10.   Peter Chalk, "The Davao Consensus: A Panacea for the Muslim Insurgency in Mindanao," *Terrorism and Political Violence* NEED FULL DETAILS; Clive Christie, *A Modern History of Southeast Asia: Decolonization, Nationalism and Separatism* (London: Tauris Academic Studies, 1996), 133.

11.   The Sunni, who form the vast majority of the Muslims around the world (80 percent), believe Muhammed to have been the final prophet of Islam and maintain that no specific provisions were made for leadership of the Islamic world after his death. The Sunni argue that, given this situation, the Qur'an and the examples set by Muhammed during his life (seen as providing the model of Islamic behavior) must serve as the twin basis for the future guidance of Islam. Any temporal leader who upholds Islamic law (as set down in the Qur'ran and exemplified by Muhammed) is thus viewed as legitimate, irrespective of whether or not they are also seen to be direct descendants of Muhammed. The Shi'a, on the other hand, maintain that a temporal/earthly leader can be challenged if it does not have divine guidance. They argue that the only true legitimate leaders of Islam are the Imam - direct descendants of Muhammed who constitute an infallible source of spiritual guidance. The Shi'ites accept that the line of Imams ended in the ninth century. Until the expected Imam, the Mahdi, returns, these adherents of the Islamic faith argue that ayatollahs - who are accepted as emanations of God - must serve as the collective caretakers of the Islamic religion. For a good account of the differences between the Sunni and Shi'a traditions of Islam see David Ingersoll and Richard Matthews, *The Philosophical Roots of Modern Ideology* (New York: Prentice Hall Inc., 1991), 273-285; and Mircea Eliade et al., eds., *Encyclopaedia of Religion* (New York: St Martin's Press, 1993), 316-320.

12.   See generally, William Millward, "The Rising Tide of Islamic Fundamentalism I," *Commentary* (Ottawa: Canadian Security Intelligence Service, 1993).

13.   David Rapoport, Fear and Trembling: Terrorism in Three Religious Traditions," *American Political Science Review* 78 (1984): 665.

14.   See Majid Khadduri, *War and Peace in the Land of Islam* (New York: John Hopkins University Press, 1955), 55-82; and Rudolph Peters, *Islam and Colonialism: The Doctrine of Jihad in Modern History* (The Hague: Mouton, 1979), 117-121.

15.   Richard Martin, "Religious Violence in Islam: Towards an Understanding of the Discourse of Jihad in Modern Egypt," in Paul Wilkinson and Alasdair Stewart eds., *Contemporary Research on Terrorism* (Aberdeen: Aberdeen University Press, 1989), 59.

16.   Turner, "Terrorism and Secession in the Southern Philippines, 10; "The Southern Heat Kindles Another Philippine Fire," *Economist,* 27/02/88.

17.   Sinha, "Muslim Insurgency in the Philippines, 638; A. Misra, "Guerrillas in the

Mist," *Pioneer*, 11/07/94; "The Southern Heat Kindles Another Philippine Fire," *Economist*, 27/02/88.

18.   See Lucero, "The SPCPD: A Breakthrough Towards Peace," 4; "Philippines, Muslims Sign End to Civil War," *Weekend Australian*, 31/08/96; "Ramos, Muslims Sign Historic Accord to End 24 Year Civil War," *Australian*, 03/09/96; "The SPCPD Gamble," *Philippine Daily Inquirer*, 15/09/96; and "Peace in His Time," *Far Eastern Economic Review*, 05/09/96.

19.   "To Fight or Not to Fight," *Far Eastern Economic Review*, 09/03/95; Merliza Makinano, "Terrorism as a Threat to National Security," *OSS Working Paper* (1997), 11; Alfredo Filler, "The Abu Sayyaf: A Threat to Law and Order," *Philippine Military Digest* 2/2 (1996): 6; Alfredo Filler, "Muslim Militancy: A New Threat to Security and Stability, a Philippine Viewpoint," unpublished paper prepared for the Armed Forces (AFP), July 1995; Concepcion Clamor, "Terrorism in the Philippines and Its Impact on National and Regional Security," paper delivered before the CSCAP Working Group on Transnational Crime, Manila, May 1998, 4-5.

20.   It should be noted a third rebel Islamic group also exists, the National Islamic Command Council (NICC, otherwise known as the Moro Islamic Liberation organization/MILO). The organization is composed of ex-MNLF generals, reportedly led by Lt. General Melham Alam - Misauri's former Chief of Staff. NICC broke away from the MNLF in 1992, ostensibly in reaction to growing nepotism and favoritism within the parent organization. Although NICC continues to push for greater Islamic autonomy in Mindanao, the group lacks weapons and is currently only of marginal concern vis-à-vis security in the southern Philippines. Personal correspondence between the author and military intelligence, Manila, June 1998.

21.   Specifically, the Tripoli Agreement provided for the creation of an autonomous region in the southern Philippines. This enclave was to consist of the thirteen provinces and nine cities of Mindanao, Sulu, and Palawan, but was to remain under the overall sovereignty of the Republic of the Philippines. Autonomy was to be guaranteed in the administration of justice; the generation of revenues; the protection of ancestral lands; law and order; and education. While the agreement satisfied many of the MNLF's central demands, Misauri ultimately rejected the deal largely because Marcos failed to fully implement its autonomy provisions. Between 1976 and 1996, the main objective of the MNLF was to coerce the Philippine government to fully implement the 1976 Tripoli Agreement - something that was seen to have been achieved (at least in principle) by the signing of the Davao Consensus. For further details see Villareal, "Conflict Resolution in Mindanao," 8-12; and Sukardo Tanggol, *Muslim Autonomy in the Philippines. Rhetoric and Reality* (Marawi City: Mindanao State University 1993).

22.   "The Moro Islamic Liberation Front (MILF) Secessionist Movement," unpublished position paper prepared for the National Intelligence Coordinating Agency (NICA), 5. See also "Anthony Davis, "Islamic Guerrillas Threaten the Fragile Peace on Mindanao," *Jane's Intelligence Review* 10/5 (May 1998): 31; "Crescent Moon Rising: The MILF Puts Its Islamic Credentials Upfront," *Far Eastern Economic Review*, 23/02/95.

23.   Personal correspondence between the author and Professor Aprodicio "Prod" Lacquian, University of British Columbia, Vancouver, July 1998.

24.   Personal correspondence between the author and Armed Forces of the Philippines (AFP) intelligence personnel, Camp Aguinaldo, Manila, June 1998. See also Sheikh Abu Zahir, "The Moro Jihad," *Nida'ul Islam* 23 (April-May 1998): 11; Davis, "Islamic Guerrillas Threaten the Fragile Peace on Mindanao," 32; "Commissar of

the Faith," *Far Eastern Economic Review*, 28/03/96; "Crescent Moon Rising: The MILF Puts Its Islamic Credentials Upfront," *Far Eastern Economic Review*, 23/02/95"; Clamor, "Terrorism in the Philippines and its Impact on National and Regional Security," 7; and "Rebels Without a Pause," *Asiaweek*, 03/04/98.

25.   These areas are seen to be Central Mindanao, parts of the Zamboanga peninsula, Davao, Basilan, Sulu, Tawi-Tawi and Palawan.

26.   Filler, "Muslim Militancy," 20; "The Moro Islamic Liberation Front (MILF) Secessionist Movement," 5-6; Clamor, "Terrorism in the Philippines," 8; Abu Zahir, "The Moro Jihad," 11; "Commissar of the Faith," *Far Eastern Economic Review*, 23/03/96; "Crescent Moon Rising: The MILF Puts Its Islamic Credentials Upfront," *Far Eastern Economic Review*, 23/02/95;"; and "Rebels Without a Pause," *Asiaweek*, 03/04/98.

27.   MILF's leadership has consistently claimed a considerably larger membership than this. In 1995, for instance, Al Haj Murad, MILF's Vice Chairman for Military Affairs, asserted that the organization could, at any time, call upon a standing army of nearly 120,000, including a core of 60,000 well-armed and trained mujahideen. In 1999, the group revised this estimate, placing its strength at roughly 150,000 regular combatants. For further details see Abu Zahir, "The Moro Jihad," 11; "Hidden Strength," *Far Eastern Economic Review*, 23/02/95; "Estrada Moves to Reverse Startling Success of Secessionist Rebels," *South China Morning Post*, 22/12/98; and "AFP: Its War Against MILF," *Manila Times* (Internet edition), 05/01/99.

28.   Personal correspondence between the author and the Philippine National Police (PNP) Directorate for Intelligence, Camp Crame, Manila, June 1998. See also Davis, "Islamic Guerrillas Threaten Fragile Peace on Mindanao," 32-33; "Hidden Strength," *Far Eastern Economic Review*, 23/02/95; "Rebels Without a Pause," *Asiaweek*, 03/04/98; Filler, "Muslim Militancy," 19; Clamor, "Terrorism in the Philippines," 7-8; and "The Moro Islamic Liberation Front (MILF) Secessionist Movement," 5.

29.   "Hidden Strength," *Far Eastern Economic Review*, 23/02/95; Davis, "Islamic Guerrillas Threaten Fragile Peace on Mindanao," 32-34; During interviews conducted in June 1998 at the National Intelligence Coordinating Agency (NICA) headquarters in Quezon City, the author was informed that the MILF currently has an armory of at least 8,200 separate firearms.

30.   "AFP: Its War Against MILF, *Manila Times* (Internet edition), 05/01/99.

31.   According to Philippine military intelligence, a local gunsmith exists within Camp Abubakar which has been operational since 1996; it is believed to have the capacity to produce and convert ammunition, repair firearms and manufacture weapons, including a basic RPG and machine guns.

32.   Personal correspondence between the author and police and military intelligence, Manila, June 1998. Similar views were expressed to the author by Professor Aprodicio "Prod" Laquian, National Campaign Officer for the Estrada Presidential election team, during interviews conducted at the University of British Columbia, Vancouver, July 1998. See also "Worse to Come," *Far Eastern Economic Review* NEED FULL DETAILS; "Hidden Strength" *Far Eastern Economic Review*," 23/02/95; "The Moro Islamic Liberation Front (MILF) Secessionist Movement," 7; Filler, "Muslim Militancy," 20; and Police Superintendent Jose Olaivar, "Proliferation of Firearms and Its Impact on Regional Stability: A Perspective from the Philippines," paper presented before the CSCAP Working Group on Transnational Crime, Manila, May 1998, 10-11. Philippine security forces fully admit they lack the ability to effectively monitor the diverse archipelago in the south.

33. Salamat quoted in "MILF Has a 'Well Oiled' Machinery," *Today*, 29/01-04/02/98.
34. Personal correspondence between the author and police and military intelligence, Manila, June 1998.
35. Personal correspondence between the author and Tom Oldham, the Australian Embassy, June 1998.
36. Clamor, "Terrorism in the Philippines," 8; Filler, "Muslim Militancy," 20.
37. Personal correspondence between the author and then PNP Directorate for Intelligence, Camp Crame, Manila, June 1998.
38. Personal correspondence between the author and representatives from the PNP, NICA and AFP, Manila, June 1998.
39. See, for instance, "Hidden Strength," *Far Eastern Economic Review*, 23/02/95; "Philippines to Tighten Controls on Foreign Students," *Straits Times Weekly Edition*, 25/10/97; and "MILF Has a Well Oiled Machinery," *Today*, 29/01-04/02/98.
40. "Aid from Overseas Admitted by Rebels," The South China Morning Post (Internet edition), 09/01/99.
41. Personal correspondence between the author and the NICA, Quezon City, Manila, June 1998.
42. Personal correspondence between the author and police and military intelligence, Manila, June 1998. See also Miles Clemans, "Asia Watch," *Australia/Israel Review* (12 November – 3 December, 1998): 7; Filler, Muslim Militancy," 21-22; "Southern Discomfort," *Far Eastern Economic Review*, 19/02/98; "Abat, AFP Insist MILF Behind Raid," *Manila Times*, 16/10/97; "Pieces Don't Fit in Army Camp Raid," *Today*, 16/10/97; and "Philippines to Tighten Controls on Foreign Students," *Straits Times Weekly Edition*, 25/10/97.
43. It is also believed that a certain amount of MILF external training takes place in camps located in Sudan and Egypt with MILF cadres, again, traveling overseas on the grounds that they are undertaking theological courses at foreign institutions. Personal correspondence between the author and the PNP Directorate for Intelligence, Manila, June 1998.
44. Personal correspondence between the author and representatives from the AFP and PNP Directorate for Intelligence during interviews conducted in Manila in September 1996 and June 1998. See also "March of the Militants," *Far Eastern Economic Review*, 09/03/95; "The Fire Next Time," *Far Eastern Economic Review*, 28/03/96; "Ex-MNLF Rebs Vow to Fight Nur," *Philippine Daily Inquirer*, 15/09/96; "MILF: Force to Reckon With," *Philippine Daily Inquirer*, 16/09/96; "Filipino Terrorists Using Pakistan as a 'Base of Operations,'" Quezon City GMA-7 Radio Television Arts Network, 16 April 1995; and "Islamic Terrorism Tied to Pakistani University," *New York Times*, 20/03/95.
45. These attacks were in retaliation for Afghanistan's alleged protection of Osama bin Laden, the suspected mastermind behind the August 1998 bombings against the U.S. embassies in Tanzania and Kenya.
46. These attacks were in retaliation for Iraq's continued refusal to cooperate with United Nations officials inspecting Baghdad's suspected nuclear and chemical weapons' sites.
47. See, for instance, "MILF Rebels Declare Holy War on America," *Philippine Daily Inquirer*, 21/12/98; "Muslims, Leftists Hit Bombing of Baghdad," *Philippine Daily Inquirer*, 22/12/98; "RP to Iraq: We're Staying Neutral," *Manila Times* (Internet edition), 19/12/98; and "Philippine Muslim Rebels: Clinton 'Murderer of Islam,'" *Hong Kong Associated Federated Press*, 17/12/98.
48. See, for instance, "The Moro Jihad," 12.

49.   "The Moro Islamic Liberation Front (MILF) Secessionist Movement," 9; "Rebels without a Pause," *Asiaweek*, 03/04/98.

50.   Hashim Salamat and Al-Haj Murad, quoted in "Rebels without a Pause," *Asiaweek*, 03/04/98.

51.   "The Moro Islamic Liberation Front (MILF) Secessionist Movement," 9; "Ceasefire Signed," *Courier Mail*, 28/11/97; "Government, MILF Ready to Sign Truce," *International Herald Tribune*, 29/12/97; and "Peace by Christmas," *Economist*, 27/06/98.

52.   Personal correspondence between the author and Bil Hansen, Manila, June 1998. See also "Rebels Without a Pause," *Asiaweek*, 03/04/98.

53.   Problems in this regard were vividly demonstrated by widespread protests over public executions of two suspected drug traffickers in the MILF-run town of Masiu in October 1997. See "Muslim Leader Justifies Killings," *Bangkok Post*, 09/10/97; and "Manila Agonizes Over Islam's Deadly Justice," *Australian*, 21/10/97. See also, "'Obligation' To Shoot "Killers' Threatens Talks," *South China Morning Post*, 19/03/98.

54.   These thoughts were variously expressed to the author during interviews conducted at the Australian Embassy, NICA, PNP and the National Police Commission, Manila, May-June 1998. See also Davis, "Islamic Guerrillas Threaten Fragile Peace on Mindanao," 35.

55.   See "Rumble in the Jungle," *Australian*, 23/03/99; "Estrada Moves to Reverse Startling Success of Secessionist Rebels," *South China Morning Post*, 22/12/98; "AFP: It's War Against MILF," *Manila Times* (Internet edition), 05/01/99; and "AFP Clarifies 'War' Declaration," *Manila Times* (Internet edition), 06/01/99.

56.   "Peace by Christmas?" *Economist*, 27/06/98.

57.   These individuals had been trained in Libya, Iran and Syria respectively.

58.   Clamor, "Terrorism in the Philippines," 5; Filler, "Muslim Militancy," 16; and "Briefing on Terrorism (Confidential)," unpublished paper prepared by the NICA, January 1996, 6-9. The ASG is also, periodically, referred to as the *Al Harakat Al Islamiyya* (AHAI).

59.   See "Abu Sayyaf to Regroup, Gov't Warns," *Philippine Daily Inquirer*, 22/12/98; and "Kidnappings to Continue in South," *Philippine Daily Inquirer*, 22/12/98.

60.   Clamor, "Terrorism in the Philippines," 5; Filler, "Muslim Militancy," 16; and "Validation of the Existence of the ASG," unpublished paper prepared by the NICA, 14 February 1997.

61.   Personal correspondence between the author and the PNP Directorate for Intelligence, Camp Crame, Manila, June 1998. See also 'Zambo Blast Coverup for Weak ASG,'" *Manila Times* (Internet edition), 05/01/99; and Filler, "Muslim Militancy," 16-17.

62.   'Zambo Blast Coverup for Weak ASG,'" *Manila Times* (Internet edition), 05/01/99.

63.   "Validation of the Existence of the ASG," 2; Filler, "Muslim Militancy," 17.

64.   See "Guerrillas Make a Killing Out of Abductions," *South China Morning Post*, 28/12/98; "'Zambo Blast Coverup for Weak ASG,'" *Manila Times* (Internet edition), 05/01/99; and "HK Hostages Released After 106-Day Philippine Ordeal," *South China Morning Post*, 24/12/98.

65.   Personal correspondence between author and the PNP Directorate for Intelligence, Camp Crame, June 1998. See also "'Zambo Blast Coverup for Weak ASG,'" *Manila Times* (Internet edition), 05/01/99.

66.   Bin Laden is now thought to be one of the main financiers of Islamic extremism around the world. The son of a Saudi construction magnate and a veteran of the

Afghan campaign against the USSR during the 1980s, he has declared a virtual one-man *jihad* against the U.S. Like many in the Middle East, he blames America for Western oppression and corruption of the Islamic world. Western intelligence authorities also believe that bin Laden has been instrumental in bringing together a number of terror groups dedicated to the coordination of a *jihad* against the U.S. and Israel. Known as the World Islamic Front for Jihad Against Jews and Americans, it is believed that the group was established on February 15 after a meeting between bin Laden, other Islamic extremists and senior members of Iran's Revolutionary Guards. See "Saudi Fanatic Plots a Holy War," *Times* (Internet Version), 14/08/98; "Bin Laden: 'Comply with God's Order to Kill the Americans," *CNN Interactive*, 21/08/98; "Prime Suspect," *Sydney Morning Herald*, 15/08/98; "Saudi Millionaire Tops List of Bombing Suspects," *Australian*, 10/08/98; and "Summit of Militants Planned," *Australian*, 25/08/98.

67.   Khalifa was arrested for trying to illegally enter the United States. He was extradited to Jordan to face terrorism charges but was acquitted and has since remained in Saudi Arabia. He has vowed to return to the Philippines to "clear his name." Personal correspondence between the author and the NICA, September 1998.

68.   Personal correspondence between the author and the NICA, Quezon City, Manila, June 1998. See also Peter Chalk, "The Abu Sayyaf Group and Osama Bin Laden: An Unholy Alliance," *Jane's Intelligence Review Pointer* (December 1998); Clamor, "Terrorism in the Philippines," 11; "Briefing on Terrorism," 11; "Validation of the Existence of the ASG," 3; Filler, "Muslim Militancy," 18; "US Enemy No. 1 Sighted in Mindanao," *Philippine Daily Inquirer*, 23/08/98; "RP Tightens Security vs. Extremists," *Manila Times*, 25/08/98; and "Master of Terror," *Courier-Mail*, 29/08/98.

69.   Adam Indikit, "Asia Watch," The Review 24/2 (1999): 7; Clamor, "Terrorism in the Philippines," 6-7; Filler, "Muslim Militancy," 17; "Briefing on Terrorism," 8-9.

70.   "41 Found Dead After Philippine Bombing," *Washington Post*, 27/02/00; "Philippine Ferry Bombing Death Toll Rises to 45," *CNN Interactive World Wide News*, 26/02/00.

71.   Personal correspondence between the author and military, police and intelligence officials, Manila, June 1998.

72.   Personal correspondence between the author and Professor Aprodicio Laquian, University of British Columbia, Vancouver, July 1998.

73.   Personal correspondence between the author and the AFP, Camp Aguinaldo, Manila, September 1996. See also "Briefing on Terrorism," 10; "March of the Militants," *Far Eastern Economic Review*, 09/03/95; and "The Fire Next Time," *Far Eastern Economic Review*, 28/03/96.

74.   Although MILF commanders did participate in the ranks of the IIB, they were generally more concerned with the Islamic struggle that was taking place back in the southern Philippines. Personal correspondence between the author and the PNP Directorate for Intelligence, Camp Crame, Manila, June 1998.

75.   See, for instance, Clamor, "Terrorism in the Philippines," 10; and Peter Chalk, "Political Terrorism in Southeast Asia," *Terrorism and Political Violence* 10/2 (1998): 126-28.

76.   This was well illustrated by the rejection of a proposed anti-terrorism bill in 1996. If passed, legislation would have been enacted allowing arrests without court orders; 30 day detentions without formal charges being laid; the sequestration of bank deposits and assets of suspected terrorists and front organizations; and wire taps. For further details see Susan Berfield and Antonio Lopez, "Bad Medicine," *Asiaweek*, 02/09/96; "Anti-Terrorism Bill Revives Ghost of Marcos," *Australian*, 24/01/96;

and "Legislators Revive Anti-Terrorism Bill," *Manila Times*, 16/10/97.

77. Clamor, "Terrorism in the Philippines," 12-13. Similar rationales for basing international Islamic terrorism out of the Philippines were expressed to the author by Gavin Greenwood, Senior Asian analyst with the highly-respected Control Risks Group (CRG) during interviews conducted in London, January 1997.

78. This is the main militant Islamic group in Egypt.

79. Hong Kong's Kai Tak airport was chosen essentially because planes have to fly low over the densely populated city of Kowloon before making their final approach. It was "hoped" that this would ensure a maximum casualty rate, involving not only the 747 passengers and crew but also those residing in Kowloon.

80. See Clamor, "Terrorism in the Philippines," 10; "The Philippine - Islam Resurgent," in John Laffin, ed., *The World in Conflict: War Annual 7* (London: Brassey's, 1996), 79; Pinkerton's Risk Assessment Services (PRAS), *Risk - Assessment 1995* (Washington: Pinkerton's Information Services Inc., 1996), 40-1; "Islamic Terrorist Attack on APEC Foiled: Report," *The Age*, 20/12/97; "Muslim Militants Threaten Ramos Vision of Summit Glory," *Australian*, 13/01/96; "Manila Steps Up Manhunt for Terrorists," *Australian*, 11/01/96; "Muslim Militants Threaten Ramos Vision of Summit Glory," *Australian*, 13/01/96; "Target for Terror," *Australian*, 19/07/97; "The Man Who Wasn't There," *Time*, 20/02/95; "The "Shadow of Terrorism," *Asiaweek*, 28/04/95; "Islamic Extremism in Asia," *Foreign Report* 2381, 21/12/95; "Islamic Suicide-Bomber Plot to Kill Pope Disclosed," *Vancouver Sun*, 24/03/95; and "Bomb Kills 1, Wounds 6 on Philippines Airliner," *New York Times*, 12/12/94.

81. Of the six, three were Jordanians, namely Isam Mohammad Abdul Hadi, Ashram Yazouri and Hadi Yousef Alghoul, the leader of the group. The three others were Nabil Nasser Al-Riyami (an Omani), Mohammad Kdeab Ismael Abu-Shendi (a Syrian) and Wali Rached El-Kaatib (a Palestinian).

82. Filler, "Muslim Militancy," 22-25.

83. Personal correspondence between author and Office of National Assessments (ONA) officials, Canberra, November 1999. See also "ASIO Briefs Thailand on Olympic Terrorism Fears," *Sydney Morning Herald*, 15/11/99; and ADD RECENT ARTICLE

84. Personal correspondence between the author and PRAS, November 1996. See also "Islamic Terrorist Attack on APEC Foiled: Report," *The Age*, 20/12/97; "APEC Site Gun Arrests," *Australian*, 20/11/96; and "Muslim Militants Threaten Ramos Vision of Summit Glory," *Australian* 13/01/96. In the event the Summit passed without incident

85. Personal correspondence between the author and Dr. Alan Dupont, Australian National University, Canberra, November 1999. Similar comments were made to the author during interviews with representatives from the Australian Office of National Assessments (ONA), Canberra, November 1999.

86. Personal correspondence between the author and the NICA, Quezon City, Manila, June 1998. See also, Clamor, Terrorism in the Philippines," 16-17.

87. Personal correspondence between the author and intelligence personnel from the AFP, Camp Aguinaldo, Manila, June 1998. See also Filler, "Muslim Militancy," 18-19.

88. Much the same argument is used in this regard by the Israeli government in relation to *Hamas* and the Palestinian Authority (PA).

89. Personal correspondence between the author and the NICA, Quezon City, Manila, June 1998.

90. See "Muslim Radicals Hopeful on Peace," *South China Morning Post*, 16/05/98; and "Peace Overture by Abu Sayyaf," *South China Morning Post* (Internet Edition), 08/04/97.

91. Personal correspondence between the author and the PNP Directorate for Intelligence, Camp Crame, Manila, June 1998.

92. Personal correspondence between the author and Tom Oldham, Australian Embassy, Manila, June 1998. See also "Soldiers Shelled our Camp-MILF," *Today*, 11/06/98; "3 Basilan Kidnap Victims Beheaded by Abu Sayyaf," *Philippine Daily Inquirer*, 21/04/98; "Missing Kin Beheaded by Abu Sayyaf," *Manila Times*, 02/06/98; "Villagers Flee as Army Hunts Down Abu Sayyaf," *Manila Times*, 01/06/98; "Sayyaf Recruits Sent on Zambo 'Test Mission,'", *Manila Times*, 26/05/98; "Can Insurgents and Investors Mix?" *International Herald Tribune*, 26/05/98; "Road Bandits Turn Bolder Down South," *Manila Times*, 25/05/98;; and "Vice Mayoral Bet Slain by Abu Sayyaf?" *Manila Times*, 16/05/98.

93. Clamor, "Terrorism in the Philippines," 7; Filler, "Muslim Militancy," 27-29; and "Briefing on Terrorism," 13.

94. See "Kidnappings to Continue in South," *Philippine Daily Inquirer*, 22/12/98; "'Zambo Blast Coverup for Weak ASG," *Manila Times* (Internet edition), 05/01/99; and "Abu Sayyaf to Regroup, Gov't Warns," *Philippine Daily Inquirer*, 22/12/98.

95. Personal correspondence between the author and Tom Oldham, Australian Embassy, Manila, June 1998.

96. It should be noted that even on its own, the ASG - the smallest Muslim group in terms of actual numbers - is still able to call on a hard-core membership of ample size to carry on a sustained campaign of terrorism. Traditionally, most terrorist organizations have operated with less than 100 active members. During the 1980s, for instance, of all the groups that were operating in western Europe, only the Provisional Irish Republican Army (PIRA) and Basque Fatherland, Land and Liberty (ETA) had hard-core memberships of over 100 - with both having less than the 300 cadres that the ASG is currently able to lay claim to. See Alex Jongman, "Trends in International and Domestic Terrorism in Western Europe, 1968-1988," *Terrorism and Political Violence* 4/4 (Winter 1995): 50.

97. See, for instance, "Southern Discomfort," *Far Eastern Economic Review*, 19/02/98.

98. Personal correspondence between the author and Professor Aprodicio Laquian, University of British Columbia, Vancouver, July 1998. Professor Laquian refers to this as "the developmental strategy" for conflict resolution.

99. Mindanao has vast timber, agricultural and mineral deposits at its disposal, not to mention substantial oil reserves.

100. The so-called East-ASEAN Growth Area (EAEG) – an ambitious plan designed to promote trade, agri-business, industrial development and cross-border investment between the large islands of Borneo, Mindanao, Sulawesi, and the Indonesian portion of New Guinea, Irian Jaya.

101. A total of US$52,531,100 has been earmarked for the initial deployment of the UN mission in East Timor (UNAMET). This is a drop in the ocean compared to the amount of money that will be needed to finance infrastructural development on the island. For further information on the planned activities of UNAMET see United Nations, "United Nations Mission in East Timor (UNAMET) Fact Sheet," accessed through http://www.un.org/peace/etimor/Fact_Frame.htm

102. See "Philippines 'Achilles Heel' Threatens its Economic Prosperity," *Australian*, 20/02/96; "Poor Little Dragon," *Foreign Report* 2385, 01/02/96, 5-6; "Campaign To Wipe Out Kidnappers in Philippines," *New Sunday Times*, 13/03/97; "Southern Discomfort," *Far Eastern Economic Review*, 19/02/98; and "When Travelers Are Targets: The Growing Threat of Kidnapping Abroad," *Washington Post*, 12/07/98.

103. Personal correspondence between the author and Bil Hansen, Manila, June 1998.

104. See, for instance, "Govt, Muslims, Rebels See Centennial Rites Differently," *Today*, 11/06/98.

Conclusion

Jason F. Isaacson

Assessment

In Asia today there is a danger that is recognized by many of the region's leaders. That danger is a growing religious extremism with its concomitant volatility and unpredictability. In September 1997, Malaysian Prime Minister Mahathir Mohamed warned of this danger when he said, "if we allow the extremist groups to run wild, we will also become like some countries which are now in turmoil." The Philippine government has recently increased its efforts to crush the secessionists in the south. China is committed to eradicating what it terms "splittism" from Xinjiang, while the Indonesian army has recently made senior appointments in the armed forces which some see as an attempt to dilute radical Islamic influences.

At the same time, Iran's continuing Asia tilt and a major effort by several Middle Eastern countries to build strong commercial and political links with Asia could have the effect of neutralizing government attempts at controlling radicalism. There is no question of the serious consequences if Middle Eastern-style Islamic radicalism were to take root among the laid-back and tolerant Muslims of East Asia.

It is perhaps too soon for a complete analysis of events in Indonesia. To hope that a genuine liberal democracy emerges in Indonesia, despite the recent elections, is still optimistic but at least a real possibility following the emergence of the Wahid presidency. With the Wahid government in office, the fact is that there is a cadre of experienced, well-educated people—especially in the institutionalized civil service—who can contribute to its efficient functioning. Therefore, although it will not be an easy task, this new government has so far undertaken the first confidence building steps in the long delayed process of reform. The economic challenge is enormous. Nevertheless, Indonesia is both sophisticated and developed enough, with a still moderate tradition of Islam, to permit some optimism.

In Malaysia, both from the Mahathir government and the dakwah movement, we have seen a politicization of Islam into a more narrow, illiberal, anti-Western creed. A correspondingly heavy burden has been placed on liberal Muslims to both modernize Malaysian society and the economy. The Anwar affair has dispelled predictions that a future government would smoothly chart a course towards greater liberalization. The 1999 elections highlighted the ruling UMNO party's loss of ground among the dominant Malays to the Islamist PAS. While there are some signs of growing moderation and inclusiveness in PAS, it is an open question whether it can be a force for democratization, as opposed to chauvinism and radicalism The UMNO must inevitably find a new leader, given Dr. Mahathir's increasing age. And, Malaysia's economic health will depend, as it has in the past, on a high degree of communal co-operation when everyone benefited from a rising tide of confidence and growth.

In southern Thailand, the prospect for stability has improved as a result of the serious failures by the radical factions. Their failure has been reflected in a more aggressive counter-terrorism policy by the Thai government, and is tied to the BRN's unpalatable ideology. Nevertheless, the signs continue to cause concern. There is an increasingly radicalized and anti-Western Muslim population in southern Thailand, a new radical Islamic political party, and growing discontent in the underdeveloped provinces of Pattani, Yala, and Narathiwat. There is some cause for hope because of the recent spurt in the economy and in the interest shown by Egypt and a number of other Arab states and Middle Eastern states in investing in the region. There is also a possibility that the Thai and Malaysian governments might co-ordinate their respective counter insurgency efforts. Thailand has provided 1,000 troops to The U.N. Interfet force in East Timor, reflecting a willingness to contribute to regional stability. In addition, Thailand has adopted a new constitution and sought to combat crony capitalism, which augurs well for its future economic recovery. Overall, the country's future prospects for internal harmony and stability appear quite good.

The Philippines' security and stability has been circumscribed since the 1970s by radical Islamist groups, especially in the south. This has forced successive Philippine governments to maintain the armed forces on a virtual war footing. The MILF and ASG now pose more of a long-term threat than had the MNLF. At their core is a radicalized Islam. There is little possibility for an autonomous or independent Muslim region in the south given the political and demographic realities of the Philippines. Economic progress and reform are vital to stabilize the country and extirpate the sources of discontent that make possible the radical fundamentalist Islamist campaign. The potential economic prosperity of the south is one cause for optimism. The favorable prospect of much-needed foreign investment, is another. However, the negative factors—such as civil strife, lawlessness, Iranian involvement—mean there is still cause for concern about the Philippines' future stability.

China, too, confronts ethnic and religious discord in Xinjiang province. Separatist violence was sporadic in 1998, and the bazaar town of Kashi was placed under curfew after eight Chinese police were murdered in their beds. These recent incidents are highlighted against a background of foreign support from separatists in Central Asia, especially Kazakhstan, and from the radical Islamic terrorist camps in Afghanistan under the sponsorship of Osama bin Laden. There are a number of separatist societies including the Uighurstan Society for Freedom with a purported membership of 7,000. As the Chinese government has progressively altered the province's ethnic composition so that the 3 percent Han minority in 1949 has grown to 38 percent and promises to be in the majority by 2010, further tension seems unavoidable. Beijing regards security in the province as of paramount importance. Economic and strategic factors such as the huge oil and natural gas reserves and the province's military installations make Beijing ever more resolute to maintain its mastery in Xinjiang. The conflicting movements of Uighur separatism, abetted by Islamist organizations abroad, and Chinese internal and economic interests, suggest that further and serious conflict may be expected.

The dearth of research into radical Islam in Asia is in itself a cause for concern. One reason for this may be that states affected by separatism such as the Philippines, Thailand, and China prefer not to admit to a problem. This may be cultural. The Asian concept of saving face may be an element of the difficulty. It may, however, be a fear of losing overseas investment if there is an emphasis on factors that suggest future instability. It took Sri Lanka years to disclose that the Tamil Tigers were using Thailand as a training and logistics base. China only admitted recently that it had a separatist problem in Xinjiang.

The outlook in Asia is, therefore, problematic. In addition to a radical Islam there is the danger of the North Korean nuclear threat; the rise in tension between Malaysia and Singapore; the uncertain reaction of both China and Russia to Japan's missile defence program with the U.S.; the Indian and Pakistani nuclear tests; and the recent military coup in Pakistan. Malaysia has temporarily suspended its participation in the Five Power Defence Arrangements that involve Australia, Britain, New Zealand, Singapore, and Malaysia. Australian-Indonesian relations became sensitive following the violence in East Timor and Australia's leadership of the initial U.N. force charged with restoring order to the territory. Add the potential growth of Islamist movements that are predisposed to view all relations with both the West and regional peoples and governments in zero-sum terms, and these problems can only be exacerbated.

Extra-Regional Sources of Radicalization

How receptive are South East Asian countries to Middle Eastern radical Islam? China has resolutely set about fortifying its borders from the influence of external Islamists and entered into a memorandum of co-operation with its Central Asian neighbors. When a ten-man delegation from the Palestinian Hamas organization spent a month in Indonesia in 1994, it was not warmly received. The Indonesian government refused to allow it to spread its teachings or to open a Jakarta branch. What the reaction would have been is speculative, but Indonesia's new president, Abdurrahman Wahid, has a distinct policy of inclusiveness and tolerance coupled with opposition to terrorism and extremism and a view that Islam is the religion of peace. By contrast, Iraq was successful when it sent its parliamentary speaker to meet with President Habibie in December 1998 in order to expand bilateral relations and seek support for the removal of sanctions.

In times of crisis, it seems as if the anti-Israel rhetoric in South East Asia is less intense, priorities obviously being given to curbing anti-government protests. What is evident is a shift in politics to more Islamic parties such as Malaysia's PAS and the ten or so Islamic parties that have emerged in Indonesia since the fall of Soeharto.

This study has detailed the variety of extra-regional links with militant Islamism: financial backing from Saudi Arabia to Muslim separatists in the Philippines; military training and arms provision from Kazakhstan and Kyrgyzstan, Saudi Arabia, and Iran for Muslim rebels in Xinjiang; and the sheltering of Uighur rebels in Afghanistan, despite denials from the Taliban. That efforts can be made against such developments is demonstrated, for example, by the refreshing Thai approach to questions of regional questions and leadership aimed at defusing sectarian tensions, such as Wahid has adopted.

Regional Strategies and Forums

Given the trans-national nature of radical Islam, it is imperative that any strategies initiated by South East Asian states have a multilateral dimension. Regional institutions in South East Asia are fewer and less well established than those in such regions as Europe or the Americas. Nevertheless, a number of important regional developments have been made. For example: Malaysia has agreed to step up its naval patrols to prevent arms shipments from the Middle East passing through Sabah to Islamic extremists on Mindanao.

At least two major international conferences addressing terrorism in the Asia-Pacific have been convened. The first was held in Perth, Australia, in 1992. Its theme was the development of practical measures to counter a shared terrorism problem and covered topics such as the changing nature of terrorism in the Asia-Pacific, barrier controls, aviation security and strategic counter-terrorism planning and training in the Asia-Pacific. The second was held in Baguio, Philippines in 1996. Themes covered included state sponsorship of terrorism; the potential use by terrorists of weapons of mass destruction; how to stop the flow of funds reaching terrorist organizations; and intelligence information exchanges.

Notwithstanding the importance of the above-mentioned initiatives, the response so far has been reactive and ad hoc in nature. Perhaps this is a result of Asian states tending more towards bilateralism and a focus in recent times on economic matters relating to security issues. A further complicating factor is that ASEAN is currently struggling over how far member states may intervene in each other's internal matters. The prevailing principle is one of "non-interference" in the affairs of member states. Thai Foreign Minister

Surin Pitsuwan, with the support of the Philippines, launched a debate more than a year ago over more flexible engagement between member states with the objective of ASEAN having the capacity to tackle internal problems in member countries that pose a threat to regional security.

Indonesia, once the most influential country in regional institutional frameworks such as the Association of South East Asian Nations (ASEAN) and the Asia Pacific Economic Co-operation (APEC), was significantly weakened by economic and political developments in 1998 and 1999. Such a decline has undoubtedly also weakened the effectiveness and stature of APEC and ASEAN. With its vital sea-lanes of communication, the strategic integrity of Indonesia is vital to the U.S., Australia, and all trading nations in general. However, under the leadership of President Wahid it is moving towards a political and economic reformation that bodes well for security concerns.

It is encouraging that multilateral "networks" of various sorts have proliferated in the Asia-Pacific region in recent years. Some of these networks are embodied in formal inter-governmental institutions (the networks of officials associated with ASEAN, APEC, and the ASEAN Regional Forum and others are overlapping "second track" networks) intended to identify issues and develop solutions or means of coping to bring to the attention of the formal governmental processes. There are also networks of more specialized interest groups, especially politically active non-governmental organizations (NGOs).

Formed in 1967, ASEAN helped its foundation members - Indonesia, Singapore, Malaysia, the Philippines, and Thailand - to overcome stormy relations including Indonesia's armed confrontation against the Malaysian Federation. ASEAN is not a regional security organization as such. It has arguably provided the external conditions necessary for the economic growth of its members; and the linchpin of that external framework has been the U.S. role and presence in underwriting the security of the entire region. ASEAN, however is a sub-regional organization that could not play an active role in regional conflict management.

The establishment of the ASEAN Regional Forum (ARF), however, has created a political framework within which leaders can discuss security concerns, and proposals which may give some substance to the concept of co-operative security and confidence measures, and eventually arms control may be considered. The ARF has the potential to emerge as the primary forum for constructive debate on matters such as terrorism, insurgency and illegal migration. It would have been the appropriate structure to discuss Malaysian-Thailand co-operation in respect of insurgency issues in southern Thailand. The Council for Security Co-operation in the Asia Pacific (CSCAP) is a track-two dialogue think tank designed to support the work of ARF. It has endorsed the initial step towards institutionalising more traditional co-operation against conventional, higher intensity issues (such as arms proliferation and intra-regional territorial disputes).

Asia and America should work together in revitalising the institutions that have been somewhat tarnished during the crisis, notably the IMF, ASEAN, and APEC. It is important to move beyond a simple debate between "Asian" and "Western" values in order to reach a balanced assessment of the advantages and shortcomings of all relevant economic, institutional, and value systems.

Some economic determinists point to the economy as being the essential determinant of Islamic radical activity, a compelling argument in light of the Asian crisis. However, the experience in the various case studies under review indicates that there is no single determinant. A complex mix of economic, religious, political factors, together with the external linkages highlighted previously provides fertile ground for radical Islam.

In severely depressed economic regions such as Mindanao and Xinjiang, calls for separatism primarily have their roots in economic strains. In Indonesia and Malaysia, calls for Reformasi were accentuated after the Asian financial collapse. New leaders have emerged, and certainly the Indonesian government has taken on a more Islamic complexion. In Malaysia, while Mahathir's UMNO exhibits a Malay Muslim outlook, it appears moderate in comparison with the Islamic party PAS which won power in the rural state of Kelantan in 1990 and then Terengganu in November 1999. It has been the biggest political winner out of the legal struggle of Anwar Ibrahim, and capitalized on public discontent with the government through a drive for new members and in its gains in the recent national elections.

Whenever a large segment of society begins to find explanations acceptable that proceed from political arguments (whether about the role of Israel, the excessive consumption of the rich, or the extent of foreign influence) to the demonization of whole racial groups, then the outlook of all minorities (and ultimately also majorities) becomes dark. Ethnic violence and religious intolerance directed against Christian and Chinese minorities drive this point home. Hundreds of churches, Buddhist monasteries, and temples in Indonesia have been looted, ransacked, and burned to the ground.

In Mindanao and Xinjiang, Muslims are in the minority, probably as a function of government assimilationist policy. In those countries, separatism is more strident and more violent. In Indonesia and Malaysia, where the majority religions are Muslim, a different struggle exists embodied by Reformasi—a movement in search of democracy, a society rid of corruption, economic recovery, and establishment of human and legal rights. In both countries, political Islam has become entangled in the quest for political reform.

The economic crisis in South East Asia, especially in Indonesia, where political volatility and elements of anti-Western sentiment are evident, has the potential to change the security environment in South East Asia. During boom times, nations tended to turn a blind eye to their own separatist problems, for example, Aceh, Xinjiang, East Timor. Many see a united Indonesian archipelago as essential in providing Australia with a northern bulwark. It is also essential for the maintenance of the vital maritime arteries of communication.

Strategies and Prospects

An influential proponent of the integrity of Indonesia for strategic reasons is Professor Paul Dibb, head of Strategic and Defence Studies at the Australian National University. He is of the view that "Australia is now faced with the prospect of an Indonesia that it hopes may become democratic. But there is a risk of less benign outcomes, which range from an assertive, nationalist/Islamic regime through to the disintegration of the archipelago. These outcomes would not be favourable to our security interests."

By contrast, Gary Klintworth, visiting fellow at the north-east Asia Program at the Australian National University, has a more favorable disposition towards fragmentation: "a smaller, less insecure Indonesia may be a better proposition for Australia than a large, ungainly and insecure state constantly struggling to hold itself together."

Islam in South East Asia has traditionally been a moderating and constructive force. Given the hundreds of millions of Muslims in the region, anything which might convert Islam into a force for the radical and violent revisionism and revanchism it has become in parts of the Middle East clearly has the potential to be dangerous.

It would be pertinent to end on the theme of Anwar Ibrahim who wrote in his book *Asian Renaissance*, "The wave of Islamic revivalism that began with the anti-imperialist struggles of the previous century has gained further momentum in our time among Muslims in South East Asia. The energy potential must be properly directed so as not to deteriorate or be corrupted into blind fanaticism that could precipitate into violent clashes with other cultures. There are indeed signs, however, that these religious energies, aligned with forces of social conservatism, have served to marginalize the Muslims in the rapidly changing world. Thus we need to reassert the universalism of Islam, its values of justice, compassion and tolerance in a world that is yearning for a sense of direction and for genuine peace."

Fortunately, there is genuine cause for optimism about the prospects for constructive and peaceful accommodation between Islam and modernism, best exemplified by the election as president in Indonesia of the pluralistic, inclusive, and moderate Islamic leader, Abdurrahman Wahid. Certainly, each of the countries examined in this study reveal that simple generalizations cannot be made about Islam, the South East Asian region, or any one society within it. Each deserves and repays close examination.

Postscript

In an age of globalization, the inevitable corollary to economic liberalization and the Internet-led communications revolution has been the globalization of extremist ideology and terrorism. This worldwide phenomenon has been no less a factor in the cultivation of Islamic radicalism in Asia.

In Indonesia, Malaysia, the Philippines and Thailand, most radical groups operate a website. Many of these groups now communicate more freely with each other than ever before and draw inspiration from the struggles of their ideological compatriots. Even more significantly, they share their expertise, resources and in some cases their personnel. Thus we have recently seen Malay fundamentalists fighting in Indonesia, southern Thailand and the Philippines; Philippine radicals have found refuge in Malaysia, as have Thai rebels, some of whom have fought in Indonesia, where the assassination of the Philippines Ambassador in 2000 appears linked to Islamic radicals under siege in Mindanao. One common element shared by many of these groups is covert support from Middle Eastern sponsors.

These links are multifaceted and complex, and cannot be laid bare easily. Aside from electronic connections, the arc of states and the thousands of islands that make up South-East Asia allow the transit of people and goods to occur outside official channels with relative ease. Even piracy on the high seas continues into the present day, with the Abu Sayyaf group being but one exponent of this centuries-old form of banditry.

Porous borders and boundaries make the maintenance of security by South East Asian states an undiminishing challenge. ASEAN members are coming to realize that their previous policy of non-interference in their fellow members' affairs will require modification to accommodate the cross-border interlinkages between radical groups, the most potent of which march under the banner of Islam. Unlike the Communist insurgencies that plagued the region in the Cold War era, inspired by an imported European ideology, Islamic rebels in Asia fight passionately for a cause that expresses their core sense of identity.

In October 1999, the rise of Abdurrahman Wahid to the Indonesian presidency gave many hope that he would inspire a renaissance in Islamic thinking in Asia. A voice of Islamic tolerance and humanism at the helm of the most populous Muslim nation promised that a new way could be found for Asian Muslims to embrace both their faith and the challenges of the contemporary era at the same time. Wahid's downfall and the continuing regional economic instability suggest that it would be reckless to predict the decline of radical Islam as an influential force in South East Asian politics.

Index

abangan, 39, 40, 46

ABIM. *See* Angkatan Belia Islam Malaysia

ABRI (Indonesian Armed Forces), 17, 33, 53. *See also* TNI

Abu Sayyaf Group (ASG), 190, 210–12, 225. *See also* Sayyaf, Abu
ASG-GRP negotiation, 208–10
background and objectives, 201–2
foreign linkages, 204–7
linkages with MNLF and MILF, xiii, 207–12
strength, weapons, and financing, 202–3
violent activities, xiii, 197, 203–4

Aceh, 55, 56, 84

Aceh Merdeka (Free Aceh Movement), vii

Acehenese separatism, 52–54

Afghan War, 202, 204

Afghanistan, 202, 225
influence of, xxii
Soviet invasion, xvii

AFP. *See* Philippine Armed Forces

agent provocateurs, 30

Al-Afghani, 198

Al-Arqam, xii

Al-Helmy, Burhanuddin, 117

Al Ikwan, 136

Ali, H. A. Mukti, 19, 20

alim. See ulama

Aliran, 141, 142

Alternative Front. *See* Barisan Alternatif

Ambon, 26

Angkatan Belia Islam Malaysia (ABIM), 103
coalitions, 106
leadership, 112–15, 117, 118, 135
origin and history, xi, 110–16
PAS and, 106, 113–18
UMNO and, 106, 114–16, 118, 121

anti-Semitism, 37, 140. *See also* Jews

in East Timor, 56–59

Arqam. *See* Darul Arqam

Asia Pacific Economic Cooperation (APEC) Summit in 1996, 206, 207, 228

Asian Renaissance (Ibrahim), 231

Asri, 117, 118

Association of Islamic Muslim Intellectuals. *See* Ikatan Cendekiawan Muslimin Indonesia

Association of Southeast Asian Nations (ASEAN), xii, xxi, 211, 227, 228

Association of Southeast Asian Nations (ASEAN) Regional Forum (ARF), 228–29

Australia, 140, 230

Autonomous Region of Muslim Mindanao (ARMM), 193, 199

Awang, Hadji Abdul Hadi, 118

Badawi, 155

Bangkok, 175, 177, 179

Bangsamoro, 192, 194

Bangsamoro Islamic Armed Forces (BIAF), 195

Bank Bali affair, 66

Barisan Alternatif (BA), 149, 152, 154
emergence, 147–48

Barisan Nasional (BN), 123, 143, 151, 153. *See also* National Front
influence of, 94, 103
MCA and, 103, 127, 150–51
media campaign, 148–49
PAS and, 107, 112–14, 117, 125, 137, 143, 144
and 1990s elections, 124–25, 139, 144, 149, 150, 153
UMNO and, 122, 157

Barisan Revolusi Nasionale (BRN), 169–71, 177, 224

Batavia, 53

Berita Harian, 127

Bersatu ("Solidarity"), 175
Bin Laden, Osama, xiv, xviii, 203, 205, 225
"Blackshirts," 189
Bolkiah, Prince Jefri, iv
British colonialism, and Malay State, 99–103, 126
Buddhists and Buddhism, 98, 169, 171, 230
Building of the Faith, 18

Caliph, 201
Catholicism, 26, 54, 55, 187, 190
Central Axis, 65, 71
Central Intelligence Agency (CIA), 173, 206
China
    Beijing, 225
    Xinjiang province, xvii–xviii, 225, 226, 230
Chinese, 3, 14, 148, 151, 230. See also DAP; Malaysian Chinese
Christianization, 38, 49, 187–88
Christians, 23, 25, 188–89, 211. See also Catholicism; Dayak
violence against, 23, 202, 203, 230
Chuan Leekpai, xvi
Clamor, Concepcion, 207
communal politics. See Indonesia, Islam, communal politics
communications technology, v, 144. See also Internet
Communism and Communists, 8
    crackdowns on, 8, 80, 83
    Muhammadiyah and NU's opposition to, 8, 17
Communist emergency, 125–26
Communist Party, Indonesian, 8, 17
Communist Party of Malaya (CPM), 169–70
"consultancy money," 66
Consultative Assembly. See People's Consultative Assembly
Council for Islamic Propagation. See Dewan Dakwah
Crescent and Star Party, viii
Crouch, Harold, 121–23

dakwah (Islamic preaching), 195
dakwah movement(s), 103, 121, 143, 145, 146. See also specific movements
emergence in 1970s, xi, 94

influence of, xi–xii
nature of, xi, 94–95
and the West, 134–37
DAP (Democratic Action Party), 124, 129, 138, 148, 156–58
DAP-PAS alliance/coalition, 138, 143–44
Darul Arqam, 104–10
    fatwah against, 109–10
    PAS and, xiii, 106
daulat (royal authority), 98
Davao Consensus, 192–93, 200, 211, 212
Dayak, 24, 25
democracy, 10, 121, 142, 157. See also Indonesia, liberal, democratic future for
Democratic Action Party (DAP). See DAP
Dewan Dakwah (Council for Islamic Propagation), 18, 28, 37, 50–51, 134
Dibb, Paul, 230
Dompok, Bernard, 155
Dutch, 20, 73, 99, 101
Dwifungsi, ABRI and, 10–11

East Timor, viii, 25, 52, 54–56, 66–67
    anti-Semitism, 56–59
economics and economic justice, 6, 13–14, 153, 229. See also under Indonesia
    and ethnic and racial conflict, xxii–xxiii
egalitarianism, 81
Estrada, Joseph "Erap," 200, 201, 204, 208–9
ethnic and racial conflict, 110
    economics and, xxii–xxiii
ethnic and racial identity, 165, 167, 168. See also national identity
extremism, religious, 71, 106, 191, 212, 223. See also fundamentalism; Indonesia, hard-line extremists; Islamism; specific extremist groups
    Rais's record of, 37–38

Forum Demokrasi, 31
Free Aceh Movement, vii
fundamentalism, ii–iii, 91, 165, 210, 225. See also extremism

globalization, v
Golongan Karya (Golkar), 9–10, 51, 52, 59, 61–64

Government of the Republic of the Philippines (GRP), 190, 199–201, 208–10
GPK-Aceh (National Liberation Front Aceh Sumatra), vii

Habibie, B.J., v, vii, viii, 15, 16, 31, 34, 43, 44, 64, 226
  Accountability speech, 67
  fall of, 66–67
Habibie government, 3, 38, 75
Habibie period, 77
halal, 106
Halim, Abdul, xvi
Hamza, Tunku Razaleigh, 155
Hansen, Bil, 200
Harakah, ix, 154
Harun, Lukman, 48–49
hijra, 165
Hitam, Musa, 123
HMI, 18, 19
Holland. *See* Dutch
holy war. *See jihad*

IAIN. *See* Institut Agama Islam Negeri
Ibrahim, Anwar, 95, 112, 121, 122, 130, 141, 142, 154, 178
Ibrahim, Wan Azizah, 95, 147
ijtihad, 6, 36
Ikatan Cendekiawan Muslimin Indonesia (ICMI), v, 30, 43, 44
Ilagas ("rats"), 189
IMF, 133
India. *See* Malaysian Indian Congress
Indonesia, v–ix. *See also* East Timor; *specific topics*
  economics and economic justice, 22–23, 73, 76
  ethnic clashes, vii
  grounds for hope, 3
  hard-line extremists and regional unrest, 47–49, 52–54
    Dewan Dakwah, KISDI, and new Islamic parties, 49–52
  Islam, communal politics, and civil society
    civil society and culture of public intellectuals, 20–21
    economic crisis and social relief, 22–23
    emergence of Islamic liberalism, 16–19
    generational change and appeal of liberalism, 19–20
    modernist/traditionalist tension, 29
    outbreaks of violence, 23–27
    re-emergence of communal politics, 27–28
    track record of NU and Muhammadiyah, 21–22
  June elections and strength of secularist-nationalist/moderate-Islam alliance, v–vii
    fall of Habibie, 66–67
    modest success of PKB and PAN at June polls, 62–63
    PDI-P drawing away, PKB and PAN drawing closer, 63–64
    PDI-P's success at June polls, 61–62
    rapprochement between traditionalists and modernists, 59–60
    souring of Wahid and Megawati alliance, 60–61
    Wahid joining Central Axis, 64–65
  liberal, democratic future for, 74–76
    bumpy road ahead for new government, 67–68
    civil society, Islam, and democracy, 68–74
  Muhammadiyah, PAN, and Amien Rais
    Amien's journey to the middle, 40–47
    PAN's secular/modernist coalition, 38–40
  Muhammadiyah, PAN, and Rais
    Muhammadiyah's moderate orientation, 35–37
    Rais's record of extremism, 37–38
  NU, PKB and Wahid, 31
    1998 and Reformasi, 29–31
    NU's pursuit of middle path, 31–35
  place of Islam in, 5–9
    central role, 4–5
    recognizing its potential, 4
  regional political autonomy, 73–74
  religious fundamentalism as threat, 2–3
  religious violence in headlines, 1–2
  Wahid government and the future

handling regional unrest and past
    injustices, 71–74
long road to liberal democracy,
    74–76
Wahid and political Islam, 70–71
Indonesian Armed Forces. *See* ABRI
Indonesian Conservative Party (PKI), 17
Indonesian Democratic Party. *See* PDI
Indonesian identity, 54
Institut Agama Islam Negeri (IAIN), 18–
    21, 41, 93, 102, 128, 133
integrationist efforts, 166–67
Internal Security Act (ISA), 117, 119,
    121–22, 125–26, 129
International Islamic Brigade (IIB), 201,
    202
International Islamic University, 93
International Movement for a Just World
    Trust, v
Internet, 144, 149
Ipil massacre, 203–4
Iran, 108
    influence of, xix–xxi
    relations with Thailand, xv–xvi
Iran Libya Sanctions Act of 1996, xx
irredentist efforts, 167
Islam. *See also specific topics*
    types of, 91–93, 95, 98
Islamic Brotherhood. *See* Al Ikwan
Islamic Call Society, vi
Islamic Command Council of MNLF
    (ICC-MNLF), 208
Islamic Development Bank (IDB), xiv
Islamic law. *See* sharia/*shar'iah*
Islamic Medical Centre, xii
Islamic Party of Malaysia. *See* Partai
    Islam Se-Malaysia
Islamic Representative Council (IRC),
    xi, 111, 120
Islamic resurgence in Asia, iv–v
Islamic Saturday Meeting Group
    (ISMG), 206
Islamic Theocratic State in Mindanao
    (MIS), 201
Islamicity, 137, 146
"Islamicity race," 119
Islamism, ii–iv, 71, 76, 207, 225. *See
    also specific topics*
    extraregional links with militant,
    227. *See also specific groups and
    regions*
    reactionary, 35

Islamization, v, vii, xi, 97, 115, 116, 156,
    194
Mahithir era of, 118–20

Jakarta Garrison, 15, 43, 53, 72, 73, 112
Jamaat-e-Islaami, xxi–xxii
Jamaat Tabligh, 104
Jamai-atul Al Islamic Tabligh, 193–94
jamiyah diniyah, 30
Janjalani, Abubakar Abdurajak, xiv, 201,
    208–10
Java, 1, 23–27, 79, 98
Jewish conspiracy theories, xix, 37, 57,
    139
Jews, xix. *See also* anti-Semitism
    Mahathir's crusade against, x
jihad, iii–iv, xiii, 167, 191, 192, 204
    peaceful ways of pursuing, iii–iv,
    191
jihad al-daiwa/jihad al-da'wa, iii, 191,
    195
jihad al-lisan, iii–iv, 191
jihad al-qalam, iii, 191
jihad al-saghir, iv, 191, 199. *See also
    jihad*
Julabbi, Ustadz Shariff, 197–99
Jundullah. *See* Abu Sayyaf Group
Just World Trust, 141–42
Justice Party. *See* Partai Keadilan

Kaban, M.S., 52
Kalimantan, 24, 25
Kazakhstan, xviii
Keadilan, 148, 149, 151–52, 154, 157,
    158. *See also* National Justice Party
Kelantan, x, 107, 117, 172
Khalifa, Mohammad Jamal, 203
Kharrazi, Kamal, xx
Kirgizstan, xviii
KISDI (World Muslim Committee for
    Solidarity), vi, 28, 37, 51, 134
Klintworth, Gary, 230
Krismon (monetary crisis), 14
Kuala Lumpur, 111, 175, 176, 179

Lev, Daniel, 4
liberalism. *See under* Indonesia
Liddle, R. William, 37, 57
Likah Asept Al Islamiyya. *See* Islamic
    Saturday Meeting Group
LIPI, 15

2M leadership, 115
2M team, 123
Madjid, Nurcholish, 18–20, 41
Madurese transmigrants, 24–25
Mahathir, Mohammed, ix, x, 91, 115,
    120–23, 126, 127, 129–30, 132,
    138–41, 143, 144, 158. *See also*
    United Malays National Organiza-
    tion
    confirmed in UMNO, 155
    and election of November 1999,
        146–47, 151
    Malaysian state, the West, and, 138–
        41
    warnings, 223
Mahathir government/regime, 135, 141,
    142, 224
Mahendra, Yusril, 52, 71
Malacca, 97–98
Malay Dilemma, The (Mahathir), x,
    150–51
Malay identity, race and, 102–3, 110
Malay Nationalist Party, 117
Malay Peninsula, 99
Malay State, and British colonialism,
    99–103, 126
Malaysia, ix–xiii. *See also specific top-
    ics*
    Hindu-Buddhist era, 98
    independence, emergency, and politi-
        cal authority, 101–2
    Islamic movements, 103. *See also
        specific movements*
    November 1999 elections, 146–53,
        155
        economy surging after, 153
        opposition figures jailed, 153–54
        and prospects for reform, 155–58
        what was at stake, 149–50
    prospects for change
        political change, 142–45
        social change, 145–46
Malaysia-Indonesia-Thailand Growth
    Triangle (MITGT), 176, 177
Malaysia People's Party. *See* PRM
Malaysian Chinese, 119, 124
Malaysian Chinese Association (MCA),
    94, 103, 127, 150–51, 156
Malaysian Indian Congress (MIC), 94,
    103, 127
Malaysian Islam, 91–93
    coming of, 96–99

and opposition, 93–95
and reformation, 95–96
Malaysian Muslim Youth Movement.
    See Angkatan Belia Islam Malaysia
Malaysian state
    attitudes to the West, 134–41
        civil society and, 141–42
        vs. Indonesian attitudes to West,
            132–34
    Malaysian Islam and, 96–99, 101–3
        political freedom and
        Internal Security Act and emer-
            gency provisions, 125–26
        Islam and political context, 120–
            23
        judiciary, 129–30
        media, 127–29
        money politics, patronage, and
            electoral gerrymanders, 130–
            32
        UMNO split, 123–25
Maluku, 25, 73, 84
Manila, xx, 208–11
Masyumi, 7–9, 18, 19, 28, 36, 50, 117
    and 1955 elections, 102
McKenna, Thomas, xiv
media, 127
    and political freedom in Malaysian
        state, 127–29
media campaign of Barisan Nasional,
    148–49
Media Dakwah, 37, 57
Megawati. *See* Soekarnoputri, Megawati
Middle East, iv, 57, 171, 204, 224
    military training in, 172, 173
Middle Eastern Islam, 54
    links to, xviii–xix
migration, 105
MILF. *See* Moro Islamic Liberation
    Front
Mindanao, xiii
    history, 187–89
Mindanao conflict, xv
    socio-political context of, since
        1971, 189–90
Mindanao Independence Movement
    (MIM). *See* Muslim Independence
    Movement
Mindanao Islamic Republic (MIR), 195
MIS (Islamic Theocratic State in
    Mindanao), 201
Misauri, Nur, 194, 207, 211

MNLF. *See* Moro National Liberation Front
modernism, Muhammadiyah and, 5–7, 12, 35–36
Modernist movement, 134
Modernists, 108
  in Indonesia, 6–9, 17–19, 29, 47, 48, 50
  PAN's secular/modernist coalition, 38–40
  rapprochement between Indonesian traditionalists and, 59–60
modernization, iii, v, 166, 190
Mohamad, Gunawan, 39
Mohammed, Ashaari, xii
Moon and Star Party. *See* Partai Bulan Bintang
Moro Islamic Liberation Front (MILF), v, xiii, 204–5, 210–12, 225
  background and objectives, 194–95, 202
  foreign linkages, 197–99
  strength, weapons, and financing, xiv, 195–97
  violent activities, 197
Moro Islamic Liberation Front (MILF)-Government of the Republic of the Philippines (GRP), 190, 199–201
Moro National Liberation Front (MNLF), xiii, 189, 191–93, 210–12
  ideological basis, 191–92
Moro National Liberation Front Central Committee (MNLF-CC), 194
Moro nationalist movement, xxiii
MPR. *See* People's Consultative Assembly
Muhammadiyah, 4–5, 8, 11, 21–22, 29, 60, 134. *See also under* Indonesia
  cultural and sociopolitical policies, 21–22
  and Islamic modernism, 5–7, 12, 35–36
  membership, 46, 48
  moderate orientation, 35–37
  opposition to communism, 8, 17
  relations with other groups, 71
  "right wing," 47–49
  youth division, 60
Mujahadeen, xxii
Mujahadeen Commando Freedom Fighters (MCFF). *See* Abu Sayyaf Group

muktamar, 120
Muslim Independence Movement (MIM), 189, 191
Muzaffar, Chandra, 141, 142

Nahdlatul Ulama (NU), 4–5, 11, 27, 36, 41, 59, 62. *See also under* Indonesia
  cultural and sociopolitical policies, 12, 22
  and elections of 1955, 102
  and elections of 1971, 9
  formation, 99
  and Islamic traditionalism, 3, 6–7
  leadership, vii, 9, 13, 58, 83. *See also* Wahid
  opposition to communism, 8, 17
  Pancasila and, 13
  primary aim, 22
  pursuit of middle path, 31–35
  relations with other groups, 9, 71
  track record, 21–22
  youth division, 60
Nasution, 18, 19
National Association of Muslim Students, xi
National Awakening Party. *See* Partai Kebangkitan Bangsa
National Fatwa Council, xii
National Front, 147–49, 153, 155, 157. *See also* Barisan Nasional
national identity, 54, 102–3, 110, 165, 169. *See also* ethnic and racial identity
National Intelligence Agency (NIA), 173
National Intelligence Coordinating Agency (NICA), 196, 198, 203
National Justice Party, 143, 148
  new, 143, 147
National Liberation Front Aceh Sumatra (GPK-Aceh), vii
National Mandate Party. *See* Partai Amanat National
nationalism, xxiii, 20, 107, 114, 116, 170. *See also* Indonesia, June elections
Natsir, Mohammed, 18, 19, 50, 51
neo-Modernism, 17, 18
Netherlands. *See* Dutch
New Pattani United Liberation Organization (New PULO), 173–75
  linkages between BRN, PULO, and, 175–77

New Straits Times, 127
ninja, 27
Non-Aligned Movement, 132
"non-interference," principle of, 227
nongovernmental organizations (NGOs), 20–22, 141, 196
Noor, Mohamed Ezam Mohamed, 154
Nouri, Nateq, xx
NU. *See* Nahdlatul Ulama

oil, Iranian, xix–xx
Operation Falling Leaves, 170, 175
Organization of the Islamic Conference (OIC), xiii, 192, 196

Pakistan, influence of, xxi–xxii
PAN-Malaysia Islamic Party. *See* Partai Islam Se-Malaysia
Pancasila, viii
and the secular states, 12–13
Papua, West, 25, 52
Parmusi, 8, 18
Partai Amanat National (PAN), vi, 27, 31, 37, 46, 47, 60, 69
PAN-PKB alliance, 71
Partai Batan Bintang (PBB), viii
Partai Bulan Bintang (PBB), 28, 52, 59, 65
Partai Islam Se-Malaysia (PAS), ix, xii, 93–94, 106–7, 143, 148, 149, 152, 158, 172. *See also* Harakah
ABIM and, 106, 113–18
Barisan Nasional and, 107, 112–14, 117, 125, 137, 143, 144
commitment to Islam, 152–53
DAP-PAS alliance/coalition, 138, 143–44
Darul Arqam and, xiii, 106
Ibrahim and, x
and Mahithir era of Islamization, 118–20
November 1999 elections and, 150–53
origins, 116–18
UMNO and, ix, x, xiii, 106, 113, 114, 116–21, 131, 156, 224
and the West, 137–38
Partai Keadilan (PK), 28
Partai Kebangkitan Bangsa (PKB), vi, viii, 7, 27, 28, 35, 40, 64, 69
emergence, 31
PAN-PKB alliance, 71
Partai Persatuan Pembangunan (PPP), vii, 7, 12–13, 28, 30, 46, 59, 62

PAS. *See* Partai Islam Se-Malaysia
Patani, 165–68
Pattani, 169–73
Pattani United Liberation Army (PULA), 171
Pattani United Liberation Organization (PULO), xv, 170–74
New, 173–77
PDI (Indonesian Democratic Party), 7, 9, 27, 31, 33, 38, 40, 43
PDI-P, 59, 61, 62–65
People's Consultative Assembly (MPR), vi, 61
pesantren, 6, 68, 69, 78, 79, 93, 99, 102, 117
Petronas, xx
Philippine Armed Forces (AFP), 196, 198, 201, 202
Philippine National Police (PNP), 195, 197, 198, 201, 204, 209
Philippine perspective on militant Islamic fundamentalism, 191–94
Philippines (Southern), xiii–xv. *See also specific topics*
funding for religious purposes, xiv
future of, 210–12
historical context of Islamic insurgency in, 187–89
militant Islamic fundamentalism, 190–94
Pitsuwan, Surin, xv–xvi, 227–28
PKB. *See* Partai Kebangkitan Bangsa
PKI (Indonesian Conservative Party), 17
PNP. *See* Philippine National Police
policy horizons, xxii–xxiii
political Islam, i–ii
Wahid and, 70–71
pondoks/pondok system, 102, 117, 169
positivism, 135
PPP. *See* Partai Persatuan Pembangunan
Prabowo, Lietenant-General, 15–16
priyayi, 101
PRM (Malaysia People's Party), 148, 158
protests and riots, viii, 111–12, 154
PULO. *See* Pattani United Liberation Organization

racial conflict. *See* ethnic and racial conflict
radical Islam. *See also* extremism; fundamentalism; Islamism; *specific*

topics
vs. moderate Islam, iii
radicalization, extra-regional sources of, 226–27
Rahman, Kabir Abdul, 171
Rahman, Sheik, 206
Rais, Amien, vi, vii, 31, 34, 48, 63, 65
    Muhammadiyah, PAN, and, 35–47
    record of extremism, 37–38
    Wahid and, 29, 34, 64
Ramadan, 24, 147
Ramos, President, 208, 211
Razaleigh, Tengku, 123–24, 132, 155
reform, Malaysian prospects for, 155–58
Reformasi, viii, 29–31, 95–96, 230
reformation, Malaysian Islam and, 95–96
regional strategies and forums, 227–30
religiosity, 145–46
royal authority, 98
Rupiah, 13, 15

Salamat, Hashim, 194, 195, 207
Sanan, Major General, 174
Santiparb (Peace) Party, 178
santri, 16, 20, 40
Sasono, Adi, vii
Sayyaf, Abu, xiii. *See also* Abu Sayyaf Group
science and scientific thinking, 135
Semangat 46, 124, 125, 144
separatist activity, xxiii, 225, 230
    in Thailand
        prior to 1960s, 165, 167
        since 1960s, 168–77
Shahriarifar, Hossein, 173
"Shanghai Five," xviii, xxii
Sharia/*shar'iah*, ii, xxi, 195, 200
Sharif, Nawaz, xxi, xxii
Shiite Islam, 190
Shiite Islamic culture, 108–9
Singh, Karpal, 154
Situbondo, 23
socialism, 170
Societies Act Amendment Bill, 114
Soeharto, President, v
Soekarnoputri, Megawati, 7, 38, 43, 44, 59, 63–65. *See also* Wahid, alliance with Megawati
    election as Abdurrahman's Vice President, 70

Soros, George, 139, 140
Southern Philippines Council for Peace and Development (SPCPD), 193
"Southern question," 175, 176
Spirit of 46. *See* Semangat 46
"spontaneous migrants," 25
Sri Lanka, xvi
Star, The, 127
State Islamic Institute. *See* Institut Agama Islam Negeri
student protests and riots, viii, 111–12
students. *See dakwah* movement(s); HMI
Sudan, xx
Sufism, 108
Suhaimi, Sheik, 109
Suharto, viii, 8, 9, 30, 34, 38, 43–45, 133
    crisis, chaos, and fall of
        denouement, 14–16
        economic meltdown, 13–14
    New Order regime, 8, 10–13, 17, 18, 22
        managing the threat of Islam, 11–12
        successful developmentalist regime, 9–10
Sukarno, Achmad, 132
    Islam and communal politics under, 7–9
Sukarnoputri, Megawati, vi, vii
Sulong, Zulkifli, 154
Sultanate, 97
Sultanate Islam, 98
Sungei Penchala, 105, 106
Sunni Islam, xvii, 32, 50, 83, 190, 195

Tamil Tigers, xvi
taqlid, 6
technology, impact of, v, 136–37, 144
"telephone culture," 11
terrorism, xvi, 169. *See also* Abu Sayyaf Group; Barisan Revolusi Nasionale; separatist activity; violence
    international conferences addressing, 227
Thailand, xv–xvi, 165–68, 177–79. *See also specific topics*
    history of Islam in, 165–68
    Islamic separatist activity in
        prior to 1960s, 165, 167
        since 1960s, 168–77

Thye, Chea Lim, 154
Tiro, Hasan di, vii
TNI, 56, 64. *See also* ABRI
Treaty of Paris (1898), 188
Trisakti University, 15, 26
Truth and Reconciliation Commission, 72
Tutut, 33

UBANGTAPEKEMA, 171
Uighurs, xvii–xviii, 225
Ulama. *See* Nahdlatul Ulama
ulama, 6, 27, 32, 68, 92, 99, 108, 110, 118
ullama, 197
United Development Party. *See* Partai Persatuan Pembangunan
United Malays National Organization (UMNO), 122, 132, 139, 143, 144, 149, 150, 152–54
    ABIM and, 106, 114–16, 118, 121
    alliances and coalitions, 94, 106, 122, 138
    criticism of, 114, 117, 137
    and the future, 224
    prospects for reform, 155–58
    Ibrahim and, xii, 121
    leadership, xii, 113, 115, 116, 118, 121, 123–24, 144, 155
    Mahathir and Badawi confirmed in, 155
    and the media, 127
    PAS and, ix, x, xiii, 106, 113, 114, 116–21, 131, 156, 224
    political strategies, xi
    split in, 123–24, 126, 129
United States, 57, 173, 206
usroh, 113
Utusan Melayu, 127

violence, 197. *See also* Abu Sayyaf Group; *jihad*; separatist activity; terrorism
    against Christians, 23, 202, 203, 230
    fundamentalist, 165

in Indonesian headlines, 1–2
outbreaks of, in Indonesia, 23–27
"sectarian," 68

Wahid, Abdurrahman, vi–viii, 12, 13, 29–32, 35, 57, 59, 62, 76–78, 226, 231. *See also under* Indonesia
    alliance with Megawati
        reluctance to enter, 44–45
        souring of, 60–61, 63, 65
    election, 231
    idealism, 78–82
    joining Central Axis, 64–65
    opposition, 58, 59
    and political Islam, 70–71
    realism, 82–84
    relations with Amien, 44–45, 60, 71
Wahid government, 75
war, holy. *See jihad*
West, the
    attitudes toward
        Indonesian, 132–34
        Malaysian state, 132–42
        opposition and hostility, x, xvi, 41, 108, 135, 136, 139, 140, 142, 178, 224, 230
    dakwah movements and, 134–37
    Mahathir, Malaysian state, and, 138–41
    PAS and, 137–38
"Western Crusade" campaign, vi
Wiranto, General, 15, 16, 82
World Muslim Committee for Solidarity. *See* KISDI
World Wide Web, 149. *See also* Internet

Yousef, Ramzi Ahmed, xv, xxi, 205, 206
youth organizations, Islamic. *See* Angkatan Belia Islam Malaysia
youths. *See also* student protests and riots
    Malaysian, 107, 110–11
    Muslim, xxii
Yusoff, Marina, 154

About the Contributors*

Greg Barton is Senior Lecturer in Religious Studies in the School of Social Inquiry at Deakin University, Geelong, Victoria, Australia. He is currently completing a biography of former Indonesian President Abdurrahmann Wahid.

Peter Chalk has been a policy analyst with the RAND Corporation in Washington, DC since 1999. He was formerly Lecturer in the Department of Politics at the University of Queensland, St Lucia, Queensland, Australia.

Jason F. Isaacson is Director of the Asia and Pacific Rim Institute of the American Jewish Committee and the AJC's Director of Government and International Affairs.

Colin Rubenstein is Executive Director of the Australia/Israel & Jewish Affairs Council. He was Senior Lecturer in the Department of Politics at Monash University, Clayton, Victoria, Australia until 1998.

* The editors would like to acknowledge the outstanding research contributions of Michael Shannon, Daniel Mandel, and Miles Clemans to this volume.